THE ANATOMY OF CHANGE

THE
ANATOMY
OF
CHANGE

———

BLUEPRINT FOR
A NEW ERA

———

John Banham

Cartoons by Mahood

WEIDENFELD & NICOLSON
London

First published in Great Britain in 1994
by Weidenfeld & Nicolson

The Orion Publishing Group Ltd
Orion House
5 Upper Saint Martin's Lane
London WC2H 9EA

ISBN 0 297 81342 0

British Cataloguing in Publication Data
is available for this title

Typeset by Selwood Systems, Midsomer Norton
Printed in Great Britain by Butler & Tanner Ltd,
Frome and London

For my parents, who showed me the meaning of service to others and taught me that rights and privileges imply duties and obligations

Contents

Foreword

by Lord Hunt of Tanworth

As Britain emerges from recession into a post-GATT world of greater trade liberalisation it becomes even more important to overcome problems of efficiency and competitiveness. New opportunities will certainly be there for us to take: but so will the dangers unless we can regain our competitive position vis-a-vis the United States and the Far East. This requires changes by central and local government as well as by industry and commerce, and the ability of our institutions to cope is being questioned.

Most challengers of the received wisdom suffer however from one or other of two disadvantages. Either they write from a largely academic standpoint with little practical experience of the real world: or that experience is confined to one particular sector or industry from which lessons are drawn which are not generally applicable. No-one could accuse John Banham of living in an ivory tower on the one hand or being too specialised on the other. His interests and his practical experience stretch wide in both public and private sectors. I first met him when I was Secretary of the Cabinet and he led the McKinsey team working on the CPRS's study of the car industry and since then I have admired the way he has brought his analytical, questioning and independent mind to a widely varying set of responsibilities. Often he has not liked what he has seen and has not hesitated to say so: and often he has been proved right.

Given his trenchant criticisms of the Government machine it may seem strange that a former mandarin is writing this Foreword. However interest in modernisation and administrative reform is not found only outside Whitehall, even if insiders may be more constrained by some of the political imperatives; and anyone seriously interested in the problem of initiating and managing change should enjoy this informative and provocative book. John Banham says that he is happy to be described as a iconoclast and certainly he sees the Emperor without any clothes. But his criticism is never just negative. He bubbles with ideas for change inspired by his first-hand observation and experience, and these ideas invariably illuminate the problem and stimulate thought whether or not one happens to agree with all of them. I am therefore very happy to welcome and commend his book as a major contribution to a blueprint for the new era.

Preface

The seeds for this book were sown twenty years ago when I was working in Washington DC, almost in the shadow of the White House.

I had spent two years in the Washington offices of the management consultants, McKinsey & Company at 1700 Pennsylvania Avenue, receiving nightly lessons in American civics as the Watergate drama unfolded. In the spring of 1975 it was time to return to London, to lead an assignment for the Central Policy Review Staff of the Cabinet Office on the future of the British car industry, which was then very much in doubt.

Although aware of the difficult times that had followed the first oil shock, I was not prepared for the talk on the BOAC flight about the possibility of a military coup; vigilantes were said to be drilling on the South Downs. When I arrived at McKinsey's London offices I found candles on the stairwells; this was in the aftermath of the three-day week when manufacturing output was virtually the same as in a supposedly 'normal' working week. As I visited car assembly plants around the country I was regaled with continual stories of labour disputes; one company apparently, was airlifting car windows from Venezuela to avoid production lines coming to a halt.

After a few days back in Britain it was evident that I faced a choice: either return to Washington and join the emigré community sitting it out in relative comfort; or stay and work towards a better future. I stayed, and the situation worsened. Well before the winter of discontent – with cancer patients being denied treatment and stinking piles of refuse lying in the streets – the trade unions appeared to have undue and damaging influence over the national economic and political scene. The so-called 'social contract' devised by Callaghan's Labour government turned out to be neither a contract enforceable at law nor socially responsible.

Ordinary people felt powerless to avert Britain's seemingly inexorable, if relative, economic decline and the deterioration

I

in schools and hospitals. Managements offered a catalogue of complaints about the unions and government. Fear of the future seemed pervasive, economic failure almost to be expected. Success, like good service, came as a surprise. Very few people, other than those who had chosen their parents carefully, enjoyed any measure of financial independence; taxes on personal income made it effectively impossible to build any personal wealth except through speculation in housing. British society, and its politics, remained obsessed with class.

Such was the dire situation that Margaret Thatcher and the new Conservative government inherited in 1979.

To the evident surprise of most of the economic commentators and much informed opinion, by 1990 British business had been transformed by the combination of taming the trade unions, bringing public spending under control, opening up the economy to competition and giving managers both the chance to manage and the incentive to do so. A revolution had swept through Britain's boardrooms, factories, offices and high streets. Long-standing weaknesses in the economy were corrected: industrial relations improved out of all recognition; private investment in skills and innovation reached record levels, as did industrial productivity, manufactured exports and profits. Living standards had never been better for most families.

But in late 1990 it ended in tears. The principal architect of the Thatcher revolution was summarily removed from office. Sterling failed to maintain its position in the Exchange Rate Mechanism of the European Monetary System and had to be devalued amid scenes all too reminiscent of the mid 1970s. Tens of thousands of people lost their life savings in businesses that could well have survived or prospered in Germany, France or even northern Italy; and more than a million home owners found they had mortgages for more than their properties were worth, even though home ownership had been encouraged as an investment certain to hold its value in an uncertain world.

By the end of 1993 Harold Wilson's reputation was enjoying a revival, as the resigned cynicism of the 1960s and 1970s took hold once again. Perhaps we are condemned to see our European neighbours improve their living standards faster, with our best days behind us. The improvements in most people's living standards during the 1980s might have been an illusion, purchased at the expense of investment in the future. Maybe we should expect

2

our governments to be inept – moving from bungle to crisis, as one newspaper Leader put it.

Small wonder that public confidence in those national institutions that the Thatcher revolution left largely untouched is so low, as people ask what went wrong. Parliament, the Civil Service, local government and the National Health Service are all on trial before the court of public opinion. The evidence for the prosecution is strong: a public sector borrowing requirement amounting to some £2,200 for the average household; a House of Commons that is divided over the nation's future in Europe; widespread concern about rising crime and a burgeoning underclass in many deprived inner city areas; an increase in the bureaucracy of the National Health Service, while waiting lists remain long and the latest reforms take their time to produce results.

These problems are all symptoms of a collective failure to recognise that we have entered a new era of low inflation, modest growth and intensified competition. This new era demands change – a new public policy agenda. We are entering unchartered economic and political waters. The familiar landmarks – high inflation and nominal interest rates, regular 'booms' fuelled by speculation in property and followed by equally regular 'busts', a generous social wage and depreciating currency with some degree of protection from the full effects of world competition – are fast disappearing into the haze. Now we must chart a new direction.

This book is my contribution to a blueprint for the new era; in a sense it is the anatomy of change: it deals with ideas for the future, not the politics and personalities of the past. I have written only about problems of which I have first-hand experience, as a management consultant for fourteen years with McKinsey & Company, as the first Controller of the Audit Commission, as Director-General of the Confederation of British Industry, and latterly as the Chairman of the Local Government Commission. This book does not therefore purport to be a comprehensive account of the changes that may be needed, for example, to the Constitution, our defence strategy, national economic policies or the criminal justice system.

The reader will be able to judge whether my experience warrants the attempt to address such large and difficult problems. The views expressed are my own. They do not necessarily reflect those of any of the organisations with which I was, or am now, associated. But

I would like to thank those colleagues and associates of the past thirty years who have put up with someone continually 'tilting at windmills'. A journalist once described me as an iconoclast. He did not intend it as a compliment; but once I discovered the meaning of the word (it is defined in the *Concise Oxford Dictionary* as 'breaker of images') I felt rather flattered. I have never been 'one of us'. Michael Heseltine did not enquire about my political views when he recommended my appointment to the Audit Commission. After four years of making waves in Whitehall, over local government finance and community care in particular, the then Prime Minister questioned the sanity of the President of the CBI when he informed her that I had been invited to succeed Sir Terence Beckett as Director-General in the run-up to the 1987 General Election. Her concern, and that of some of her Cabinet colleagues, was easy to understand. People with views of their own who cannot be silenced can cause considerable embarrassment, with unpredictable consequences especially in pre-election periods – as Sir Campbell Adamson, another former Director-General of the CBI, demonstrated just before the fall of the Heath government.

But the need for a new public policy agenda is too great to be lost in the relief, not to say euphoria, that recovery from the recession should generate. In my view, if we do not change the way we govern ourselves we will suffer further relative economic decline, with all that will entail. Having taken the Queen's shilling I feel I have a duty to give a public account of the lessons that I have learned, in the hope that the mistakes of the past can be avoided. We cannot afford a repetition of the lost opportunity of the past few years.

J.M.M.B.

Blueprint for a New Era

The new era of low inflation, low growth and intensified competition demands a new agenda: better government, a culture of saving and investment in place of one of speculation and spending, and a renewed emphasis on manufacturing.

For a nation that is apparently obsessed with its own history it is all too easy to assume that the future will be like the past. This is a long-standing British tradition. Between the wars, during the period described by Winston Churchill as 'the years that the locusts ate', British generals prepared to fight the last war rather than the next; and Thomas Sopwith had to invest his own money in the production line for the Hawker Hurricane which was to save the nation in the Battle of Britain, then only three years away. Thirty years later the Royal Commission on Local Government based its recommendations for radical change on a set of assumptions about the future that has turned out to be completely wrong.

In both cases those responsible did not appreciate that a new era had dawned. This is not a problem that is confined to the military or public services. Like empires, great businesses wax and wane. Recently around 150 public companies a year have been disappearing. Some combination of market, technical, competitive and managerial problems have driven them into bankruptcy, dismemberment or the arms of a predator regarded by their owners as better able to manage the business. Often the senior managers involved were so preoccupied with day-to-day challenges that they simply failed to realise that the world around them was changing and that a strategy of 'a little bit more, only better' would not suffice.

Such a situation faces Britain today. Just as the corporate state was unable to cope with the oil price shocks of the 1970s, so the Thatcher revolution has not been equal to the challenges of an era of low growth, low inflation and intensified international competition for our manufacturers. These require reforms which go well beyond those that have already been made. A blueprint for the new era must include moves to secure better government, new attitudes to saving and investment in public services, and the restoration of Britain's place as a workshop of the world.

The new era

At this distance it is difficult to appreciate the scale of the problems that Mrs Thatcher inherited; and it is easy, and for some convenient, to discount her remarkable achievements in transforming the economy. Trade union reforms, privatisation of nationalised industries, lower income tax rates, deregulation and increased competition, the sale of council houses, all had a galvanising effect on industry and commerce. It would not be stretching matters too far to say that the Thatcher revolution created, for the first time since 1945, a general sense of confidence that the future could be better than the past.

The economic record of the 1980s is remarkable precisely because the new government recognised that the corporate state was incapable of coping with the inflationary challenges posed by successive oil shocks. The rigidities of a 'tripartite' approach to running the economy were simply not equal to the new challenges. The National Economic Development Council, with its tripartite structure of government, trade unions and business, was simply not able to deliver the revolution that the new era called for. Mrs Thatcher's aversion to the corporate state and all that it stood for was not misplaced. Neither was her confidence in the forces of competition and the market. By 1990 the situation of the supply side of the British economy was vastly different.

Compared with the so-called golden era of UK manufacturing during the 1980s, exports of manufactured goods, an historic weakness in the UK economy, had grown by over half in constant prices; the UK share of world manufactured exports was on a rising trend. Manufacturing productivity had grown faster (averaging 4 per cent a year) during the second half of the 1980s than in any other major developed economy. Manufacturing was relatively more important to the UK economy than it was in France or the United States. Private sector expenditure on innovation was running at record levels, as it was on skills training. Working time lost in industrial disputes was insignificant: in 1990 for the economy as a whole it amounted to less than forty minutes per employee, a sixth of the time lost a decade earlier.

Investment by British companies overseas surged, following relaxation of exchange controls. As a result, by the late 1980s Britain had a larger stock of overseas investment than Japan, Germany or France; the annual appreciation in the value of this portfolio probably outweighed the balance of payments deficit. At the same time significantly more world-class businesses were based in Britain than in West Germany or France. Britain had proved remarkably attractive to international investors: during this period around half of all Japanese investment into Europe came to the United Kingdom.

Meanwhile a revolution had taken place in Britain's high streets as competition between the major retail chains improved services. In the financial services sector, as well as in many former state-owned enterprises, deregulation and privatisation had a galvanising effect. By the autumn of 1993 the combined stock market value of British Telecom, British Gas and the newly-privatised water and electricity companies amounted to almost £80 billion – or some £4,000 for every household in Britain.

A buoyant economy allowed the government to increase public expenditure by some 11 per cent in real terms during the decade, while employment grew by over a million and the unemployment rate fell: in 1981 at 9.8 per cent it was higher than in France, Italy and the Netherlands, as well as Canada and Australia; by 1990 it was 6.8 per cent, lower than in all these countries. The average standard of living increased too. By 1990 real consumption levels, and ownership of most consumer durables, were higher in Britain than in any other country in the EC except Luxembourg.

But, relatively fast, things turned sour as inflationary pressures returned, fuelled by the introduction of the community charge, a hugely unpopular local government tax that replaced the rates, and the privatisation of the water and electricity industries. Real interest rates rose to punitive levels, with the inevitable consequences: cuts in investment, lost jobs and falls in house prices for the first time in most householders' experience. With consumer confidence falling as well, people became reluctant to borrow and spend. Unemployment reached nearly three million. By late 1992

7

the high street banks were providing for close to £10 million of loans every working day.

The abrupt turn-round in the government's fortunes was partly self-induced. The mismanagement of the economy in the period following the so-called stock market crash of October 1987 is now generally acknowledged by those responsible: having let the inflationary genie out of the economic bottle as a result of its own actions – the 'inflationary own-goals' in the argot of the time – the government proceeded to smash the bottle in an attempt to bring it back under control. The recession was longer and deeper than it needed to be because we joined the Exchange Rate Mechanism too late with interest rates too high.

Unfortunately the mismanagement was not confined to the economy. The way that the community charge and the Uniform Business Rate were introduced were case studies in the law of unintended consequences, social and economic as well as political. The overdue reforms of the nation's education system were introduced in the wrong order and failed to address the key requirement of world-class schools – world-class teachers. Even in times of high unemployment there were skills shortages.

Too often important industries were privatised in such a way that they could not be regulated; or how they were regulated made them difficult to sell and less able to compete internationally. Take the electricity and gas industries: it is now generally agreed by informed observers that the way in which the electricity supply industry was privatised was misconceived; the prior warnings about the difficulties that lay ahead were ignored until the consequences for the UK coal industry became apparent in 1992. Similarly government-induced changes to the independent television and brewing industries have not delivered the benefits that the proponents of change had anticipated.

But it was not simply government incompetence that caused the economic difficulties that led to Mrs Thatcher's downfall. The late 1980s saw international developments which had profound implications for the economies of the developed world that were not sufficiently appreciated at the time. The increasing competitive power of the economies of South East Asia, the gradual dismantling of trade barriers within the European Community and the break-up of the Soviet Empire – which was, incidentally, a particularly important market for German industry – together spelt intensified competition for Britain's manufacturers. This new competition could only be met if domestic inflation was kept below 3 per cent and labour costs for every unit of output remained flat – two very demanding targets for an economy that was historically inflation-prone and where the concept of a 'going rate' above that for inflation was well entrenched among national wage bargainers.

These international developments have in effect undermined the price of semi-skilled labour in the economies of the developed world. Heavy investment in education and skills by the governments of the so-called Seven Tigers of South East Asia (Hong Kong, Indonesia, Malaysia, Singapore, South Korea, Taiwan and Thailand) pose a special threat: there are technical colleges in Singapore that are open round the clock, twenty-four hours a day, seven days a week, fifty-two weeks a year; by these standards many British further education colleges are operating only about 20 per cent of the time. It is a similar story in parts of north Africa. It is now possible by facsimile for a department store in Paris to order knitwear from a supplier in Tunisia and to receive the goods the following week. They will have the store's label and will be indistinguishable in every respect from the same goods made in France; but the labour costs will be very much lower.

The scale of the changes that have taken place in the Far East is particularly impressive. Fuelled initially by massive injections of Japanese funds and technology, by 1991 the combined exports of the Seven Tigers were approaching $400 billion. This exceeded Japanese exports worldwide and was more than double the value of UK exports in that year. Annual growth rates of 8–10 per cent in these economies have become commonplace; and it is worth remembering that Japan transformed itself from abject post-war poverty to the status of an economic superpower in only three decades of annual growth of 10 per cent. In Malaysia, for instance, annual car sales more than trebled between 1987 and 1991. By 1992 *Time* magazine was reporting that the country had become the world's leading exporter of computer chips and the third-largest producer after Japan and the United States of semi-conductors. Between 1980 and 1990 the standard of living in Taiwan rose from roughly a quarter of the British level to approaching half.

Meanwhile the two most populous nations on earth, India and China, with a combined population of over two billion and economic growth rates beginning to match those for South East Asia, are emerging from self-imposed isolation. With much of the technology of the developed world, but with labour costs a small fraction of those considered acceptable in the West, inward investment is gathering pace; in 1991 total foreign investment in China probably exceeded $8 billion. A UK manufacturer of yarn investing in mainland China anticipates that labour costs will be under 5 per cent of those in north-west England, where the textile industry finds it difficult to recruit at current wage levels, high local unemployment notwithstanding. The consultants McKinsey & Company have estimated that per capita income in Beijing in 1992 amounted to some $1,400, less than a tenth of the current UK level after adjustments for subsidies and savings (but ignoring 'undisclosed' income). India, with some 200 million consumers enjoying western lifestyles and a large reservoir of technical skills, may not be far behind as the switch from a centrally-planned to a free market economy bears fruit. Computer software is now written in Goa and beamed by satellite to southern California, because Indian software engineers have skills comparable to those found in Silicon Valley but are paid a small fraction of their salaries.

These new challenges cannot sensibly be met by protectionist measures in an increasingly interdependent 'global village'. Apart from social, political and environmental considerations, a trade war can only reduce the scope for Britain to export its way out of our perennial balance of payments deficit. There is no alternative to competing; and the growth of any economy will be constrained by the ability of its manufacturing sector to compete in world markets. And, as West Germany and Japan have shown, meeting the competition in international markets requires low inflation, high investment and an appreciating currency.

It is evident that the days of genius being 'a short memory and a rising market' may now be behind us. We must manage a future that will look very different from the past: spare production capacity all over the European Community will ensure inflation remains low; growth in domestic demand will be no more than half the rate that we have grown accustomed to, at best; and international competition, for savings and investment as well as markets, will intensify as the world economy bears the cost of putting right forty years of mis-government of the former Communist

empire and finances the explosive growth of China and India. This new era demands a blueprint for change.

Blueprint for Change

An era of low inflation and modest growth poses real problems for a society which has learned to live with, and even benefit from, inflation. Most British families adopted a very straightforward strategy over the last two decades: borrow as much money as possible, buy a house and spend to the hilt – secure in the knowledge that most goods would be more expensive next year than they were today. And it worked. There was no need to think about the future or plan for it; in the late 1980s inflation in house prices was a perfectly acceptable substitute for savings. Take 1988: in the spring the talk in pubs and at dinner-tables all over the country was how much local housing values had risen in the past week. During the year as a whole, loans for house purchases peaked at £40 billion while personal savings fell to a low of under £18 billion.

Meanwhile in the City of London takeover fever reached its height in 1989, when 2,700 transactions were completed for almost £60 billion. The 1989 annual of the magazine *Acquisitions Monthly* included an editorial under the headline 'The Battle for Britain'. It was scarcely surprising: during the year overseas investors concluded 225 deals in the United Kingdom for a total of some £16 billion. The introduction to the annual conveys the feeling of the time:

> What a year 1989 proved to be! Hardly a week went by without a mega-bid being announced or increasingly convoluted 'financial engineering' schemes being introduced into takeovers, particularly when high-leveraged bids were being contested. And, as the sector became even more complicated, the Banks had to work harder for their fees; but these reached mega-heights anyway.

For private investors too the 1980s proved to be very profitable. A leading income growth fund investing in major UK quoted companies saw its net dividends per share increase every year between 1983 and 1992, from 2.3p to 10p per share. The underlying asset values grew as well, at least until the setback of 1991, so that £100 invested in September 1982 was worth over £580 ten years later. A similar investment in a building society will have been worth around £250. During this period retail prices increased by under 70 per cent.

The familiar cliché that 'there is no such thing as a free lunch' largely lost its resonance in a society where financial rewards seemed to bear little relationship either to effort or risk. It was all too easy to give way to the delights of ballistic thinking, assuming, in effect, that the bubble will go on expanding indefinitely.

The new era will demand a different approach. Instead of spending on our personal enjoyment with an enthusiasm greater than anywhere else in Europe, we will need to invest much more. However, increasing investment will only be possible with more saving and less waste by government, as well as by businesses and individuals. And only government can create the climate necessary for manufacturing to flourish. So the blueprint for the new era will need to reflect three objectives: better government; more saving and investment in the future; and a world-class manufacturing base so that Britain is once again a workshop for the world.

Better government

In an era of sound-bite politics it is perhaps understandable that the reaction of the media to the difficulties of the last few years has been to think in terms of personalities and parties. The search for scapegoats is a natural human tendency: 'throw the rascals out' appears a neat and quick solution to a painful problem. So the Prime Minister who was largely responsible for the Conservative victory in the 1992 General Election was being written off barely a year later, buffeted by economic difficulties, schisms over Europe and differences over public spending and taxation.

But the reality is that John Major and his Cabinet colleagues are not to blame. A gale of change needs to blow through the corridors of Westminster, Whitehall, local government and the National Health Service, just as it has through British business.

The machinery of government is itself cumbersome and overly complex. In the current management jargon it needs to be completely re-engineered, so that ministers and the Prime Minister are able to discharge their difficult responsibilities effectively. The power of the Treasury must be curbed and central strategic direction of the government machine strengthened.

Parliament, which enacts some thirteen pages of law and eighteen Statutory Instruments *every day* while it is sitting, needs to be more effective in preventing legislation reaching the statute book that has to be repealed or substantially redrawn within a very short time. The checks and balances that are supposed to prevent such mistakes as the community charge must be in place. The way Whitehall works is in itself part of the problem. The culture, style of management and shared values of the Civil Service as well as the way work is done within a bureaucracy were suited admirably to a different era. But all will need to change if the pressures and tensions as Britain adjusts to the new realities are to be managed successfully. Nowhere is a change more urgently needed than in relations between central and local government. Tackling the problems of juvenile crime and truancy, homelessness, poor educational standards and, in particular, the fear that prevents many elderly people from leaving their homes at night will only be possible with an effective partnership between Whitehall and Westminster and local authorities. At present, far from partnership, there is mutual suspicion and even contempt.

The National Health Service (NHS) presents special problems as one of the icons of the welfare state. But the most recent reforms of the NHS cannot remove the basic underlying dilemma that has confronted successive governments. Taxpayers are not willing to see their taxes rise to pay for the world-class health care they consider to be their right. As a result Britain has one of the most economic health care delivery systems in the western world. But it is far from being the most effective; and the cracks are beginning to show. They cannot be papered over by management reforms, however necessary these might be.

It is tempting to believe that change of the magnitude described in Part I is impossible. But the private sector, and many previously nationalised industries especially, proved during the 1980s that it *is* possible for large and complex organisations to transform themselves. In the public sector a number of local authorities (as well as the people of New Zealand, where a reform programme has been under way in the public service) have shown

**that beneficial change is possible. To secure the neces-
sary political commitment from those who are beneficiaries of the present way of doing things is not easy.
Moreover the new era requires more than re-inventing
government, or even making government work. We
must again become a nation of savers and investors in
our collective and individual futures.**

A nation of investors

One of the most popular BBC Radio 4 programmes is *Gardeners'
Question Time*. The panelists on the 2,000th edition were invited
to say whether they would rather be gardeners in the past, the
present or the future. Predictably, none of the four wished to be
gardeners in the future; all dreaded it, for one reason or another.
Such attitudes are by no means confined to gardening. Indeed the
disappointments of the past may have led to a general lack of
confidence that translates all too easily into a fear of the future.

Again, it is easy to see why. Apart from a brief and spectacular
period of growth between 1981 and 1989, the British economy has
been relatively in economic decline since the latter part of the
nineteenth century. From a position at the top of the international
league table of GDP per capita in 1890, and third in 1945, by 1990
the United Kingdom stood at fifteenth, slightly behind Italy and
only just ahead of Australia.

Reasons abound for this poor relative performance. Indeed what
seems like an industry has grown up identifying the underlying
causes of Britain's decline and fall into the second division of
world economic powers. Some believe that the problem lies in the
education system and in a bias against mathematics, science and
'doing and making'. Others point to the well-entrenched social
class structure and the national disdain for engineering and manufacturing, in contrast to the public esteem for engineers and industry in relatively more successful economies. Still others blame
history: if the United Kingdom had had a revolution or had lost a
world war, we might be less self-satisfied and more willing to
consider the need for new ways of doing things.

The industry seeking to explain Britain's relative decline is
prolific in almost every sense except one: it is notably short on
solutions. A good example is Peter Hennessy's well-regarded treat-

ise of well over seven hundred pages on Whitehall; this devoted just eleven pages to describing a system for the twenty-first century – underlining, incidentally, the importance of reforms to Parliament.

Yet the underlying causes of our national economic weakness are not difficult to identify. Until Mrs Thatcher came to office few politicians were prepared to confront the difficult problems facing the economy. Trade unions sought to protect their members' jobs at the expense of consumers and taxpayers. Borrowing and spending were preferable, both for individuals and the public sector, to sorting out the kind of restrictive practices that made the British economy an international byword for waste and inefficiency, removing incompetent managers or raising taxes. The result has been a long-term propensity to inflation and a currency whose international value has eroded steadily (if erratically) ever since the end of the Second World War. In 1950 the pound sterling was worth DM 11.75; it had declined to DM 2.88 forty years later.

To compete with our continental rivals, never mind the Seven Tigers of South East Asia, we will have to spend less on our personal comforts and invest more in our collective longer-term future. This will entail, among other things, investing more and wasting less in our public services, particularly in the NHS, local government and the massive social security budgets. We are still wasting some £10 billion of taxpayers' money every year by fudging the reform of the social benefits system, teaching empty desks, and failing to discharge patients from hospital as soon as they are ready to go home. Up to a third of the acute beds in the NHS would be redundant if every health district reduced patients' length of stay to that of the lowest quarter – according to a recent Audit Commission report entitled, appropriately, *Lying in Wait*.

This waste should be channelled into investment. The most important investment that could be made in our collective future is in world-class education at all levels, from nursery school to university. This is widely accepted as the key to the success of Japan. Yet the seemingly continuous changes to the nation's education system over the last quarter of a century have not resulted in the generality of our young people emerging from school with the knowledge, skills and attitudes they will need to sustain the quality of life they have come to expect. In almost any international league table our school-leavers lag behind their Japanese, French and German counterparts, in science and mathematics particularly; and the young people in the Seven Tigers are rapidly catching up.

But education must not be regarded as stopping at the school gate. In a world where people expect to have half a dozen different jobs in their working lives, continuous (or lifetime) learning will be a characteristic of the new era. And even if the education reforms bear fruit, employers will have to continue to play a major part in developing the skills needed to compete with the world's best. As a nation we will need to invest considerable sums to avoid a recurrence of the skills shortages that have spurred inflationary wage rises in every past economic recovery.

Greater investment in the built environment is also urgently required. The shambles of the rail connections to the Channel Tunnel are simply a symptom of a much wider and deeper problem. At present our motorway and rail networks point in the wrong direction, at our economic past rather than the future. Congestion on our inter-urban motorways is costing some £15 billion a year; and *still* there is no clear national strategy covering road, rail, air and sea transport for equipping the economy with the world-class transport infrastructure that will be essential if the UK is to compete successfully from the edge of Europe.

Finally we must take action to prevent the growth of a disaffected urban underclass with no stake in the future of our society. As long ago as January 1987 the Audit Commission warned that the Southside of Chicago, and Harlem and the Bronx in New York provided a foretaste of the future that is in store unless action is taken to address the underlying problems facing the deprived boroughs of inner London: high welfare dependency; a majority of children born into single parent families, often with very young mothers; youth unemployment of 70 per cent or more; extremely high crime rates, often drug-related; and uneasy relations between the police and local young people. Seven years later the situation remains one of the most difficult challenges facing the public and private sectors. It is a challenge that is still not being met successfully.

Part II describes just how each of these requirements for our transformation to a nation of investors can be achieved. Unless and until it happens there will be no possibility of Britain's manufacturers being in a

position to compete with the best in the world. But unless they are, the resources will not be available to meet our collective aspirations to ever-higher living standards.

A workshop for the world

High relative inflation and a depreciating currency are particularly damaging for manufacturers who have to import components and raw materials. As a result, for generations it has been easier for 'the brightest and best' to earn their living in the City, the property market or the professions – where senior figures regularly (and quietly) earn salaries that are headline news for industrialists carrying far greater responsibilities. At a less rarefied level householders have come to regard home ownership as a safe alternative to saving: 'safe as houses' is a phrase reflecting a fear of inflation and suggesting an implied strategy for managing the risks involved.

Above all, inflation and a depreciating currency discourage both saving and investment. Saving makes little sense to the individual if its value is eroded by inflation and it means forgoing purchases that will be more expensive later. A green field investment makes no sense to industrialists who will earn better returns for their shareholders buying up others' under-performing or under-valued businesses. Indeed for much of the post-war period investors would have been better off with their money deposited with a building society than in UK manufacturing, while for successive governments it has been easier to cut investment in future capital projects rather than current spending. The constituency for the future at Westminster is notably thin when it comes to the division lobbies.

The new era of low inflation and modest growth will, however, produce a very different situation. Inflation in house prices will not do householders' saving for them. Takeovers will become increasingly and prohibitively expensive, since the market will by then have found out the incompetents. Manufacturing will become the best (if not the only) way for the UK to participate in the future growth of the Pacific Rim and eastern Europe. It is also critical to the service sector. It is no accident that twelve of the world's top twenty-five banks are Japanese; nor that the resurgence of the UK economy during the 1980s coincided with the transformation of Britain's manufacturing sector, very much for the better.

However, the great British public took a long time to notice the change. If one of the most damaging prejudices in British society is the disdain for making things, it is a disdain that is of long standing and runs, like a fault line, through the British economy: 'we over-value doing', as Dr Arnold, Headmaster of Rugby School, put it in the second half of the last century, just as our relative economic fortunes began to decline. More recently a former Chairman of Ford UK overheard a teacher telling her class on a visit to the Dagenham assembly plant that 'if you don't work harder, this is where you will end up'.

The most talented people are still urged by their parents to acquire a professional qualification and take up jobs in financial services, the City, the professions or public service. Surveys show that only seven out of every hundred undergraduates even consider manufacturing as a career, compared with one in five considering finance and one in three targeting careers in the media; and whereas in Japan there are nearly five applicants for every place to study engineering at university, in the UK there is on average only one qualified applicant for every place. And many UK graduates in engineering and technology find employment outside the manufacturing sector.

This disdain was compounded in the early 1980s by a widespread belief within industry that Mrs Thatcher's government neither understood nor particularly cared about the nation's manufacturing base. And the more the Opposition called for an industrial strategy – without defining what this might mean – the greater the efforts to discredit those arguing that government policy should promote the long-run international competitiveness of British business: they were either closet socialists or 'whingers'.

By 1990 matters had reached the point where it was necessary for the Confederation of British Industry to set up a Manufacturing Advisory Group comprising leading industrialists to determine what should be done to make manufacturing matter more. Its report, *Competing with the World's Best*, was published in late 1991. It makes interesting reading in the aftermath of the devaluation of sterling, which happened in large measure because the international financial markets were disturbed by a large continuing balance of payments deficit in the trough of a severe recession. The markets concluded, understandably but wrongly, that the

British economy was fundamentally in worse shape than that of France or Germany.

Success in manufacturing is central to the continuing prosperity of the people of the United Kingdom. Future living standards, the quality of life and career prospects depend on our ability, as a nation, to generate wealth and pay our way in the world. Some five million people are employed in UK manufacturing, with another five million jobs dependent upon it. The strength of manufacturing industry in the UK – some 80 per cent of which is UK-owned – is therefore a matter of critical national concern.

To assert the importance of manufacturing is not to undermine the contribution of other activities: agriculture, energy, construction and services. But we cannot expect to see a relative weakness in manufacturing made good by our strengths in services or by North Sea oil revenues. Though services account for about a quarter of our overseas receipts, their contribution to UK exports has declined relatively to goods over the past twenty years. If we continue to run a balance of payments deficit it will be financed by a reduction in our overseas holdings abroad; so the contribution of investment income to the balance of payments will fall further. Over the past decade oil revenues have also declined in real terms and the healthy invisibles surplus, built up in the mid 1980s, halved between 1986 and 1990 to just £4 billion, or less than 1 per cent of GDP.

Moreover the activities which make up manufacturing create markets for service and other industries, as well as supplying them. This interdependence, and the intense international competition in the markets for manufactured goods, creates a direct correlation between success in manufacturing and national prosperity. It is no coincidence, therefore, that the world's most successful post-war economies, Germany and Japan, also have the strongest manufacturing industries.

If Britain is to rebuild its manufacturing base and remain in the front rank of world economic powers, some important changes will need to take place – in addition to creating an environment of low inflation, steady but sustainable growth in domestic demand and a tax burden in line with that carried by our international competitors. For a start the pervasive mythology that 'Britain does not make anything any more' will need to be debunked, while the underlying realities of our present situation must be more widely understood. Few commentators appear to understand the extent of the transformation that has taken place in British industry since 1979. As a result it is much more difficult than it needs to be to build that general confidence in our economic future which is essential in a turbulent world.

The balance between the risks that investors run and the rewards they expect will also need to change. Throughout the 1980s individual investors, and financial institutions like pension funds, were presented with a range of apparently low-risk opportunities that held the prospect of attractive returns: property, and the sale of nationalised companies, are but two examples. In order to compete for savings, industrial companies were forced to pay out more in dividends than was wise. This is a recipe for longer-term industrial decline. Companies must recognise a wider group of stakeholders, beyond employees and shareholders; suppliers, customers and the local community all have an important stake in the future of any business. Corporate greed – evident in unjustified and unjustifiable increases in top management pay – must be reined in. Good corporate citizenship must become the norm; and boards of directors must ensure their management delivers against the highest ethical standards.

Finally government needs to play a more constructive role in promoting manufacturing. After all, central government and the National Health Service purchase over £60 billion a year of goods and services; and government sets the regulatory and economic environment in which manufacturers have to operate. It has to negotiate the reduction or elimination of barriers to international trade. It also provides direct support to exporters in the form of export credits and export credit insurance particularly. Regulators must themselves be regulated lest serious damage results to the global prospects for some of the most important industries in our economy. The regulatory process needs to be more exposed to public scrutiny; and regulators need to be accountable for their decisions.

The scale of the challenge is immense. UK manufacturing productivity is still some 30 per cent lower than in West Germany overall, 35 per cent below Japan and around 45 per cent below the United States. Closing the productivity gap with West Germany alone by the end of the twentieth century will require annual productivity growth of at least 5 per cent. So there can be no question of a collective sigh of relief at the ending of the recession, in the confident expectation that we will be floated up the economic beach as the tide comes in. Sustained and substantial annual improvements in every aspect of every business must become routine. Best world practice must become common practice. Meanwhile the national addiction to inflation must be removed and the excessive volatility of domestic demand dampened: a world-class manufacturing base cannot evolve in boom and bust conditions.

The extensive nature of this blueprint for the new era underlines the uncomfortable reality that there are no quick remedies available for our present condition, notwithstanding the sirens of the media and the manifestos of politicians. There is no realistic alternative to taking the long view. We do not need to re-invent government but to make the machinery we have work properly. We need to look beyond consuming and to save and invest for our futures. And we must build on the progress of the past decade to create a strong and internationally competitive manufacturing base. Of these requirements the most difficult to secure will be better government, to which we now turn.

PART I

BETTER GOVERNMENT

It is a paradox of the past fifteen years that the Thatcher revolution swept through the boardrooms, factories, shops and offices of Britain's businesses but left largely intact many of those institutions for which the government itself was, and is, directly responsible.

As a result serious mistakes were made which have adversely affected not just our standard of living but the quality of our national life. These mistakes have occurred despite the widely acknowledged strengths of our present system of government: a competent, hard-working and conscientious team of ministers; an independent and incorruptible Civil Service which has for decades attracted some of the most able people in our society and is widely thought to be world-class; a Parliament apparently able to call the government of the day to account, and with a mind of its own; local authorities and a National Health Service which have successfully absorbed a series of radical changes that could well have overwhelmed less robust institutions.

The conclusion seems inescapable. It is not the people working in these institutions that are to blame for the mistakes of the past, and for the resulting failure of the British economy to perform to its full potential. Rather, it is the system within which they are all required to work that needs to be reformed if public confidence in our institutions is to be restored. Indeed the general public is well ahead of the political establishment in appreciating the need for a new agenda in Whitehall and at Westminster. Nearly two decades ago opinion was fairly evenly divided between those who thought well of our system of government and those who thought that it needed to be improved. By the early 1990s there was a two-to-one majority supporting the need for change. Probably a majority now considers that the British system of government is out of date; the figure was 45 per cent in 1990.

Here, in Part I, I therefore describe how the existing system can be improved. We need administrative machinery that works. But since no government can expect to have a monopoly of wisdom or good ideas, there must be effective checks and balances to the power of the executive. The Civil Service should focus on policy-making; the trend of separating mandarins from management should accelerate. The fractured relations between central and local government need urgent repair. While the fundamental dilemma facing the nation's health services should be addressed squarely: taxpayers are simply not willing to meet the bills for world-class health care. Each of these themes is explored further in the chapters that follow.

Advising leading public and private sector organisations in the UK, on the Continent and in the United States, has provided me with a basis for assessing what does and does not work in management terms. This experience included work on policy issues for the Central Policy Review Staff of the Cabinet Office, the Department of Trade and Industry, the Department of Employment, the Department of Health and the Welsh and Northern Ireland Offices. I also worked with the Scottish Development Agency and the National Economic Development Office.

Since leaving McKinsey in early 1983, I have had high-level exposure to Parliament, ministers and senior Civil Servants – at the Audit Commission, CBI and latterly at the Local Government Commission.

1
Machinery that Works

Government by committee is a long-standing British tradition to be seen in action every night of the week in local authorities. And its most fervent admirers do not suggest that it is a notably effective method of working.

The British Cabinet is much more than a committee of senior ministers. It is the government, collectively responsible for ensuring that the manifesto put to the electorate is implemented and for all major government decisions. The quality of its performance is especially important when general government expenditure amounts to over 45 per cent of our Gross Domestic Product and government decisions affect virtually every aspect of society as well as the nation's economy.

The tradition of collective responsibility is not confined to central government. Unlike the situation in many other countries, where there are directly elected mayors, in Britain local authorities also operate a system of management by committee. Many ministers began their political careers in local government. It must have been an interesting experience, to put it mildly. Writing in January 1987 of the situation facing local government in inner London, the Audit Commission observed that:

A practice of management by members has evolved, whereby members seek to do officers' work for them. Most authorities have at least ten standing committees and many more sub-committees. There will be several committee meetings most days, each requiring papers as well as officers in attendance. The result is predictably cumbersome and expensive, not just in members and officers' time and central overhead costs, but also in delays. Auditors' reports refer all too frequently to the long time it takes to secure action [on problems such as rent arrears] where, two and half years after the problem first surfaced, the Council's committee structure is still talking about what to do.

> The problems of management by members are compounded by the high turnover among members ... Less than 20 per cent of the members now in office has more than four years' experience. There is therefore a dearth of experienced Councillors. And many members are more concerned to protect the present jobs of Council employees than they are to improve services or reduce waste and inefficiency.

Thus the risks of government by committee. Meanwhile the pressures mount on Prime Ministers who are expected to lead the government with very limited staff support. Confronted by a similar situation in the United States, a Presidential Commission concluded in 1945 that 'the President needs help' and recommended a substantial strengthening of the White House staff and the creation of the Office of Management and Budget which is now located in the Executive Office Building next to the White House.

There is a similar need in Britain. At present the British government is run rather like a holding company with no head office, which is forced to promote its directors from a limited pool of internal candidates. The Prime Minister needs help in three particular ways: a streamlined Cabinet, access to a wider pool of executive talent and more central staff support.

A streamlined Cabinet

Just as the strategic health of any company depends in large part on the effectiveness of its board of directors, so the success of the UK government depends on the Cabinet working well as a decision-making body. Yet it fails many of the tests that would be applied to corporate boards by potential investors. Looked at from a business point of view it is too large for effective decision-making, comprising twenty-three people including the Chief Whip. Ironically British government has become more complex as Britain's influence in the world has reduced: whereas in 1945 there were thirty-two junior ministers excluding the whips, in 1992 there were sixty-five. Almost all Cabinet members are 'executive' in the sense that they are answerable for their decisions to the House of Commons – only two Cabinet members, the Lord Chancellor and the Leader of the House of Lords, are not members of the House of Commons. There is an uneasy balance between geographic and functional responsibilities, and the Cabinet has often lacked cohesion.

A board of directors with these characteristics would expect to be under consistent pressure from its major institutional share-holders to reform itself, or risk seeing their company taken over. Reducing the size of the Cabinet to perhaps fifteen members should make it easier to reach collective decisions on difficult issues and to reduce the risk of damaging splits or cliques under-mining the cohesion of the government as a whole. This reduction could, to a large extent, be achieved by the elimination of separate departments for employment and agriculture and relieving the Secretaries of State for Scotland, Wales and Northern Ireland of their Cabinet responsibilities. Moreover there seem no good grounds for having two Cabinet members from the Treasury, which is quite powerful enough already; no board of directors would expect to see the Finance Director and the Chief Account-ant on the board simultaneously. In any event there are good grounds for these changes, as we shall see, apart from the principal need to reduce the size of the Cabinet for decision-making pur-poses.

The Department of Employment is the successor of the old Ministry of Labour and was established in 1916. It had, according to Peter Hennessy, a tradition that was 'a mixture of improving the conditions of the work-force and mediating in disputes between capital and labour'. Over the years it has become the sponsoring ministry within Whitehall for the trade union movement and the training 'industry'. Neither function is as relevant today as it was a decade ago: the conciliation function is now the responsibility of a separate body, the Advisory, Conciliation and Arbitration Service (ACAS); less than one in four members of the private sector work-force even belongs to a trade union, while employers rather than government are responsible for over 90 per cent of all expenditure on vocational training – with the nationwide network of private sector-led Training and Enterprise Councils playing an ever larger role. In such circumstances there is a strong case for transferring the department's training and industrial relations responsibilities to a revitalised Department for Commerce, as described in Chapter 16. After all, world-class skills are vital to the long-run international competitiveness of British commerce.

Similarly the Ministry of Agriculture, Fisheries and Food, founded in 1889 as the Board of Agriculture, is a product of a bygone era of importation of cheap food from the Empire, rationing and a drive for self-sufficiency. The department has a larger staff than the Department of Trade and Industry and twice as large a budget, even though agricultural output accounts for under 2 per cent of GDP compared with 21 per cent for manufacturing.

But the past is less relevant than the future. Whitehall departments already have regional outposts, and their local activities are gradually being better co-ordinated with the appointment of a senior Civil Servant taking charge of all central government initiatives in each region. There is an obvious case for this work to be supervised by ministers. The economic importance of London and its problems of urban deprivation rank alongside those of Scotland or Wales; but it is not receiving comparable levels of public support. Similarly, although the south-west (along with Greater London, the south-east, the West Midlands and the north of England) had higher unemployment than Scotland in July 1993, public spending in the region was around £1,000 a year lower than in Scotland for every resident.

In these circumstances there must be a case for appointing ministers to oversee government programmes in every region; and they should all be outside the Cabinet, to assure those involved that public expenditure will be allocated even-handedly, on the basis of local need. This would clarify the structure of government and reduce the size of the Cabinet at the same time.

A wider pool of talent

Streamlining membership of the Cabinet alone will not be sufficient to overcome the existing weaknesses in the machinery of government. If corporate experience is any guide it will be desirable to have greater continuity in key Cabinet posts. Apart from other considerations, it is simply unrealistic to expect any minister to master a complex brief and make a discernible impact on a department of state in under three years (usually the minimum period of any top management contract). Yet instant expertise appears to be the trademark of British Cabinet ministers; on average Cabinet members can expect to hold a portfolio for little more than two years.

As a result, inevitably, power lies in the hands of the permanent Civil Servants who are not publicly accountable for their advice on policy issues. Furthermore it seems perverse to confine the selection of the top management team within the national government to people who, almost by definition, have little if any experience in managing large undertakings. The present conventions evolved in an entirely different era when it made sense to think in terms of a separation of policy and its implementation because the focus of parliamentary time was on international affairs and defence matters, rather than the minutiae of domestic administration. This was an era before most Members of Parliament devoted almost all their time to politics, when parliamentary terms were much shorter and the legislative load lighter, and before aggressive radio and television commentaries on parliamentary affairs.

As the House of Commons becomes more of a legislative factory, membership has become a full-time occupation. It is a career whose objective appears to be preferment and office under the Crown. So members are, generally, younger today than they were fifty years ago and are more likely to come from middle-class backgrounds. The average age of the 140 members of the newly-elected class of 1992 was forty-two, and more than seven out of ten were graduates. Of the sixty-nine new Labour members twenty-five had held positions in trade unions either as elected officials or employees; but only four were manual workers. A high proportion of the new intake were already professional politicians: nineteen were former members of the House of Commons or serving members of the European Parliament; twelve were on the fringes of politics, in think tanks and consultancies or researchers or advisers; no less than sixty-four had direct experience as members of local authorities. Very few of the new members had significant industrial management experience.

This is the 'pool' from which the Cabinet members of the future will be selected. It is one of the last vestiges in British society of the cult of the gifted amateur – the notion that management is not a science but an art which anyone can practise with sufficient intelligence, ambition and commitment.

In Peter Hennessy's chilling words for those concerned with the good government of the United Kingdom:

A modern government has just under 100 posts on offer, four-fifths of them filled from the House of Commons. Those 80–85 Ministers or Whips are drawn from the 326 + MPs in the majority Party. If you remove the elderly, the undeniably incapable, the unambitious and the irrefutably callow, the pool is pretty tiny. A majority of MPs elected three or more times sooner or later receive office.

It seems unarguable that the pool from which the government is drawn is too narrow. Obviously all the best management talent in the United Kingdom does not sit in the House of Commons; few successful managers could afford to take the reduction in pay that membership would entail. So the nation is denied access to the best available people to provide strategic direction to the public services, spending between them the equivalent of some £12,000 a year (or nearly £230 a week) for every household in the land. This does not need to be the case; there is no legal requirement that ministers should be members of one of the Houses of Parliament – indeed the present Solicitor-General for Scotland, Thomas Dawson, is not an MP.

One possible answer might be for each Cabinet to include four or five people selected on the basis of their knowledge of the issues with which they would be dealing, their management experience and track record. Their appointment might be subject to confirmation by the relevant Select Committee of the House of Commons on a free vote. They might be members of the House of Lords; if they were particularly successful they might be invited to continue to serve under a succeeding administration.

The notion of a Ministry of all the Talents seems peculiarly naïve in an era of conviction politics and career politicians. But a number of precedents exist for such an arrangement. In Churchill's first post-war Cabinet there were six members of the House of Lords; and Harold Macmillan's 1957 Cabinet had five. Even in the recent past Lords Carrington, Mackay of Clashfern and Young of Graffham have all made major contributions to the Cabinets in which they served. Outsiders have not always been successful in the Whitehall jungle. Frank Cousins, who made his name as a trade union leader, and Sir John Davis, who had been Director-General of the Confederation of British Industry, are two who are often viewed as not transferring very happily. But in both instances they were expected to become parliamentarians and were surrounded on both sides by people who must have had a strong vested interest in their failure and been envious of their preferment.

Widening the choice available to Prime Ministers in selecting their Cabinet would have a number of advantages. The Cabinet would have direct access to a range of experience and members with a 'feel' for the world outside Westminster and of the problems facing the government on the ground. That could prevent serious mistakes. It is difficult to imagine the initial mishandling of the pit closure programme happening if the Cabinet had included people with recent experience of the industrial scene. The Cabinet, and indeed the Prime Minister, would benefit from the inclusion of people who can afford to be independent and are not interested in further advancement. People with top-level management experience in the private sector would be well placed to accelerate the development of junior ministers, who would continue to be drawn predominantly from the government's supporters in Parliament.

On corporate boards non-executives are often referred to as 'independent directors'. Most chairmen and chief executives welcome access to advice from people of wide experience, justified confidence in their own judgement and with no personal axes to grind. People with little to lose except their reputations can afford to take the long view and to express their opinions without 'fear or favour'.

Central staff support

In some respects a smaller Cabinet drawn from a wider pool of talent will place even greater pressure on the Prime Minister. For many years there has been a debate about the desirability of creating a more logical structure in the form of a Prime Minister's Department to strengthen the central management capability at the heart of Whitehall. One of the most serious failures of central strategic direction within British government in recent years has been the sudden ballooning of public debt. Having declined continuously as a proportion of GDP from over 70 per cent in 1971 to under 35 per cent twenty years later, the trend has been reversed abruptly. Total national debt could well reach 50 per cent of GDP by the end of the century since the annual public sector borrowing requirement grew from zero in 1990–1 to an estimated £50 billion in 1993–4. This serious lack of control over the debt burden reflects either a failure to predict the financial impact of the recession on the public finances or a failure to control spending. Both charges must be laid at the Treasury door.

On managerial grounds alone there is a strong case for hiving off the Treasury's responsibility for monetary policy to an independent Bank of England, and merging the parts of the Treasury responsible for control and overall allocation of public expenditure into the Cabinet Office. The Chancellor of the Exchequer would become the Deputy Prime Minister. All but the most senior staff would be recruited from other government departments or the private sector, on short-term contracts (with a significant performance element in their total payment package).

Such a radical approach would entail the abolition of a department of state that has existed for over seven centuries. But it is evident that half measures will simply be ineffective. Any attempt within Whitehall to build an alternative power base to the Treasury is almost bound to fail eventually – as the experience of the Department of Economic Affairs in the mid 1960s and (more recently) attempts to build up the Department of Trade and Industry into an effective department to promote the supply side of the economy clearly demonstrate. While a prolonged period of bureaucratic fighting over turf can only be extraordinarily disruptive.

Unfortunately the style, ethos and indeed folk memory of the Treasury has become part of the problem rather than a solution to the failures of national economic policy-making. Treasury officials seem to have little idea how they are perceived by business or within government or with what resentment their track record is viewed. The Chancellor's waiting-room is almost a caricature of the institution itself: dimly lit and uncomfortable, with a massive but musty portrait of some ancient and fearsome-looking mandarin glowering down at those foolish enough to question the current economic orthodoxy – whatever it might be. In 1987 Lord Beloff described the Treasury as a bunch of bank clerks who think they are mandarins. The typical reaction of business people emerging from Great George Street in more recent times is little different.

A Cabinet Office expanded into a Prime Minister's Department and incorporating the public expenditure responsibilities of the Treasury in a slimmed-down form would mark a new start after the débâcle of the last few years. It would bring substantial advantages as well.

It would reinforce the capability for strategic and policy analysis at the heart of government and would be available to the Cabinet as a whole. Many observers believe that the Central Policy Review

Staff established by the Heath government, and abolished by Mrs Thatcher in 1983 for thinking (and worse, leaking) the unthinkable about future affordability of the nation's social security system, filled a gap in Whitehall. It enabled the Cabinet to consider issues that crossed departmental boundaries in more depth than is currently possible. A number of such issues need careful examination including the needs of the inner cities and London (in particular); the role of local government; energy policy and the future of nuclear power; management of the peace dividend; and Britain's future role in Europe. At present neither the Cabinet Office nor the Prime Minister's Policy Unit has the resources and time to explore the issues involved in the depth that the problems warrant. An expanded Prime Minister's Department would be well placed to meet this need.

Moreover a smaller Treasury within a Prime Minister's department will have no choice but to focus on the major problems and opportunities facing government in terms of controlling and allocating public spending, delegating much more responsibility and authority to ministers and their departments. At present Treasury officials become involved in the minutiae of public administration and inevitably drag the Chancellor of the Exchequer and Chief Secretary into what can only be distractions for hard-pressed people grappling with important, and often intractable, problems. For instance, with public spending running at over £280 billion a year, it is difficult to believe that senior Treasury officials should seek to second-guess well-regarded ministers in the department concerned over the decision to spend no more than £250 thousand (out of a departmental budget of well over £1.5 billion) on measures to promote a key part of the government's agenda. Or that they should be required to agree the details of the performance-related pay scheme for the twenty-five employees of the Local Government Commission, which would cost at most £50 thousand a year and would be met from an annual operating budget which had already been agreed by the Treasury and the Department of the Environment. Such matters should be left to those who will be accountable if the organisation in question is less than the success it needs to be. If the Local Government Commission fails through lack of resources, the one certain thing is that those Treasury officials responsible for the situation will not be called to account in any meaningful sense.

At a moment when public spending needs to be brought back

under control such a concern with minutiae is dangerous: it clogs up the bureaucratic machinery with trivia, delays and decisions and blurs the focus on important questions. A perpetual concern for the pennies will not allow the pounds to look after themselves. They have already been doing so to an uncomfortable extent for far too long. It is the kind of attitude which resulted in unit fines being set at levels which called into question some of the basic principles underlying the 1992 Criminal Justice Act. It is also the reason why the M25 was built with three rather than four lanes in each direction (although this also avoided planning difficulties).

Finally a more effective Cabinet Office will provide the Prime Minister with much needed support in discharging responsibilities that would tax the energy of any single individual at the best of times. And the past few years have been far from the best of times for British governments. As anyone who has been even on the fringes of public life will readily confirm, the physical strain of constantly chairing meetings, frequent international travel, regular late nights and early mornings continually in the public eye, is intense. Exhausted people cannot be expected to make sound decisions. As Chris Patten once put it, 'It is extraordinary that in our system of government we both have more Ministers than others and, in my experience, more tired and put-upon Ministers than others.'

Inevitably the strain is greatest on the Prime Minister, who bears the ultimate responsibility, often surrounded by colleagues who are either rivals or see themselves as potential successors, and who is rarely, if ever, presented with simple problems. Coping successfully with serious domestic economic and political crises is only likely to be possible if there is relevant expertise in the Cabinet as well as effective staff support for the Prime Minister at the heart of government. We cannot afford to leave our leader without strong support and a deputy able to absorb some of the workload. This is particularly the case in a parliamentary democracy where, in the cockpit of the House of Commons, there is a premium on form over substance and conflict over constructive discussion and debate.

No government is likely to have a monopoly of wisdom; mistakes are inevitable, especially when difficult questions are addressed in secret and well away from expert and independent opinion. This characteristic of the British public service makes it all the more important that Parliament and local authorities provide an effective check and balance to an 'overmighty' executive. Unfortunately neither is well placed to fulfil this role at present.

I have viewed Parliament from many angles. As a (temporary) Civil Servant I was drafting answers to Parliamentary Questions in the early 1960s. In Washington in the 1970s I found myself giving evidence to the Veterans' Affairs Committee of the House of Representatives – a particularly intimidating experience for a 'Limey'. I have given public evidence on three different occasions at the House of Commons Public Accounts Committee. I have had prime responsibility for implementing two pieces of legislation: Section 2 of the Local Government Finance Act 1982 which set up the Audit Commission; and Part 2 of the Local Government Act 1992 which established the Local Government Commission and the review of the structure of local government in shire England.

As a lobbyist at the CBI, I sought to persuade Members of Parliament to take account of the views of business on the issues before them. During that time I served on the Hansard Society Commission on Women at the Top. More recently, as Chairman of Westcountry Television and as a Director of National Power, I have seen how damaging ill-thought-out legislation can be.

2

Checks and Balances

Parliament produces on average thirteen pages of new law and eighteen Statutory Instruments every day that it is sitting.

British governments are usually elected with the support of only a minority of the electorate – Mrs Thatcher's third administration with its massive overall majority in the House of Commons was formed with the support of under a third of those eligible to vote. So it is particularly important that the Mother of Parliaments is effective in exerting a check on the power of the executive to tax and otherwise impose on individual citizens.

Unfortunately closer acquaintanceship with the workings of Parliament leads observers to disillusion and concern rather than the enchantment sometimes claimed by admirers of our system of government. Few observers of the process associated with the passage through Parliament of the Maastricht Treaty can have come away with their confidence in the efficiency and effectiveness of our form of Parliamentary democracy enhanced. This was not an isolated example. Many debates are formalities conducted in a near-empty chamber. Members often vote in divisions at the conclusion of debates which they have not heard. Few have knowledge of the issues under discussion because the staff support available to members is minimal and their working conditions can best be described as archaic. A recent independent study by the Institute of Public Policy Research summarises the situation in the following terms:

The central role of the Commons is to scrutinise Government policy, holding Ministers to account. However, several factors combine to impede this. MPs have to work with inadequate office facilities, and lack of systems for obtaining, analysing and using information. Even if these handicaps are overcome, procedural rules often blunt the

39

impact of Backbenchers' intervention. Finally, MPs' career patterns provide little incentive to develop the knowledge-in-depth usually needed for effective scrutiny.

All this is in considerable contrast to the situation in Washington, where, in addition to a written Constitution, the Founding Fathers of the United States handed down a system of governance that separates responsibility for legislating from that of the executive branch headed by the President. Thus Congress, the Supreme Court, an independent Federal Reserve Bank, States that guard their rights jealously, and a Fourth Estate with full access to official information are all capable of blocking presidential initiatives. Without a general consensus in favour of change, little can be achieved.

Not only does the US Congress play a different constitutional role to that of the House of Commons, the scale of the staff support available to members is massive by contrast. The Congressional Budget Office provides expert and independent analysis of the President's proposals. The General Accounting Office provides the information needed by Congress to manage spending budgets, thus holding the executive to account at the policy level. The Office of Technology Assessment harnesses non-governmental academic, technical and scientific knowledge to give Congress supposedly impartial analysis of longer-term technical issues. The Congressional Research Service employs nearly a thousand research and information specialists who are at the disposal of members, committees and staff.

Meanwhile the research division of the (overloaded) House of Commons Library only has some thirty researchers. The Parliamentary Office of Science and Technology, set up only as recently as 1989, has a permanent staff of four. Very few British MPs have more than one research assistant – often young graduates, with limited experience and expertise.

The scale of staff support for legislators is not the only contrast between London and Washington. Their salaries in 1993 were very different as well. A US congressman would be paid a salary of $150 thousand and all reasonable office and travel expenses. This is not far out of line with the compensation of senior executives in a medium-size company, and close to the salary paid to a member of the Federal Cabinet. By contrast a British MP's salary is considerably less than a Cabinet minister's and well below the earnings of the average senior executive in industry; and his or her allowance for secretarial and research support is only £40 thousand a year.

There are those who argue that the system of checks and balances inherent in the American Constitution poses its own dangers to the Republic. In recent years, with the erosion of Party discipline in the Congress, Presidents have become even more constrained to the point where the national interest appears to be threatened by Washington's inability to respond to the challenges of the times. But it would be wise to pause before concluding that all the problems lie in Washington. Too much ill-considered legislation has reached the statute book at Westminster that would never have survived the public scrutiny of congressional hearings in Washington. It is safe to assume that the 1988 tax-cutting budget measures, the M25 and channel rail link and unit fines fiascos would not have happened if the various propositions and plans had been exposed to the grilling that awaits all legislation on Capitol Hill. Or, put more brutally, despite all the legislative effort the British economy might well be in substantially better shape today if Parliament had been in permanent recess from October 1987 onwards. Reform has been too slow and too limited.

'Reform in this house proceeds exceeding slow'

The British Parliament has four ways of preventing the arrogance of office resulting in the kind of serious mistakes that have proved so damaging in recent years. Sufficient numbers of MPs who normally support the government can defy their whips and vote down a measure. Parliamentary Questions can so expose the weaknesses in a proposal that the government is forced, out of embarrassment, to withdraw it. Detailed scrutiny of the legislation at the committee stage can result in amendments, or even defeats, for the government on substantive issues. Select Committees and the Public Accounts Committee can issue reports so damning that legislative proposals have to be withdrawn or substantially amended.

Demonstrably, none of these techniques has been effective. It is easy to see why. With limited staff support, to expect Members of the House of Commons to exercise independent judgement on most of the issues before them is plainly unrealistic. MPs who are safely retired will readily confess that only perhaps fifteen or twenty of their back-bench colleagues will have an in-depth understanding of a complex issue such as local government finance, the future of the Exchange Rate Mechanism, the details of road traffic forecasting or even the Treaty of Maastricht. Even if an MP did have an opinion that differed from that of his or her Party, it would be asking a great deal of anyone to put their future ministerial prospects in jeopardy. And making a habit of defying the whips is a short passport to status as a permanent back-bencher – a status sought by very few MPs in current circumstances. By contrast, most members of the United States Congress are not career seekers in the sense that they seek posts in the administration; they wish to remain legislators. Neither are they in awe of the Party whip. The US congressman explaining to a home-town audience how he voted down a measure that is popular locally because the Party whips told him to do so could anticipate a short further career in the House. A comparable British audience will not even trouble to ask their Conservative MP why he or she voted for a particular piece of legislation.

In any case parliamentary business is largely controlled by the government, with the Opposition having about thirty-six days (out of about 160 in a typical session) when it can choose the subject for debate. MPs have little advance notice of even major debates and often have to react very quickly to major and complex initiatives by the government.

Parliamentary Questions, similarly, have a poor track record in doing more than provide raw material for parliamentary sketch writers and sound-bites for the nightly television news. There are around fifty thousand oral and written questions a year. But rarely do they lead to any change in ministerial direction. As the research study cited earlier concludes, 'Procedure and practice often frustrate any depth of scrutiny ... Each Ministerial team is [only] quizzed at four-weekly intervals ... The cards are stacked against any attempt to elicit information from an unwilling Minister.'

Again for very obvious reasons. Hostile questions tend to come from the Opposition, which, usually, lacks the detailed information necessary to pose the 'killer' question that will expose the flaws in ministers' arguments or proposals. The art of drafting answers to Parliamentary Questions that protect ministers and reveal little of substance is well developed in Whitehall as viewers of *Yes, Minister* will understand. Ministers rapidly become practised at not answering supplementary questions in other than generalities. And if all these defences fail, members are able to put only one supplementary question, while a minister can usually rely on some help from the benches behind him. Small wonder that many viewers on television now regard Question Time in the House of Commons as a quaint anachronism at best, and a poor substitute for the real thing on BBC Television every Thursday evening. At worst it degenerates into an unseemly shouting match.

Apologists argue that most of the 'real work' of the Commons does not take place on the floor of the House but in the committees which consider legislation line by line and clause by clause. However membership of committees is determined by the whips, who appear to nominate more on the basis of Party loyalty than on expert knowledge. As a result committees are not specialised in the sense of including only members who have taken a particular interest in any given policy area. Nor does committee procedure encourage detailed enquiry. MPs have little expectation of changing the substance of a bill and it is as rare for a minister's amendments to be rejected as it is for the Opposition's to be accepted. In addition the committee stage of most controversial legislation is often guillotined well before detailed committee discussion is complete. And, in any event, many of the misjudgements catalogued earlier did not involve primary legislation at all; what was needed was effective pressure on ministers to take action in time to *prevent* problems arising. It always seems easier for parliamentarians to look at the road from the rear-view mirror than through the windscreen.

In short, the House of Commons' means of calling ministers to account seem not to be effective in present circumstances. Hugo Young of the *Guardian* may have used intemperate language, but it is difficult to disagree with his message:

> Accountability is a word most people understand. It means explaining or justifying one's actions and inviting a verdict upon them. In most worlds it is not theoretical, merely a word. In politics it has degenerated into an abstraction and become part of the debauchery of language and Government characteristic of our time.

Against such a background it is easy to see why there were such high hopes of the Select Committees introduced by the new Conservative government in June 1979. Introducing the reforms, the then Leader of the House of Commons acknowledged that:

It has been increasingly felt that the 20th Century Parliament is not effectively supervising the Executive. While the power and effectiveness of Whitehall has grown, that of Westminster has diminished. The proposals that the Government are placing before the House are intended to redress the balance of power to enable the House of Commons to do effectively the job it has been elected to do.

Select Committees certainly have important advantages. When questioning a minister, members can ask as many supplementaries as they wish. The members themselves often become expert in the subject matter before the committee, and have the advantage of being able to listen to arguments and discussions that continue for days or weeks before having to come to a conclusion.

However, many of the hopes of those concerned with the future of Parliament have been disappointed. This may be partly because Select Committees shadow departments and tend to spring into action only *after* mistakes have been made. It is not just in the health care field that prevention is better than cure. For example, the Energy Committee had been disbanded before the furore over pit closures blew up – because there was no longer an independent Department of Energy. Even though the privatisation of electricity was having some unintended consequences in the form of an unregulated 'dash for gas' and non-competitive electricity prices for intensive users; and an imminent review of the future of nuclear power had major implications for the UK nuclear power engineering industry.

Even the so-called queen of the Select Committees, the Public Accounts Committee (PAC), has failed to prevent a catalogue of waste and executive incompetence. Partly this reflects the convention that the PAC examines matters after the event; it is difficult to audit accounts of a company that is not yet trading. Moreover the PAC is explicitly not concerned with policy; and it is often misguided policies that lie at the root of a problem. Further, the committee does not usually question ministers, focusing instead on memoranda and reports from the Comptroller and Auditor-General, and examination of the accounting officers – even if the events under investigation took place before the individuals concerned took up their appointments.

Even if the committee comes upon a rich vein of official incompetence, the members can fail to press their enquiries home to the point where someone is called to account, either for lack of expert knowledge and staff support or because of the politics of the situation. One of the worst such cases in recent years was the De Lorean affair, examined by the Public Accounts Committee during the 1983–4 session. Its report was published in July 1984, more than two years after the company was placed in receivership after it had in effect lost more than £75 million in assistance from public funds in the form of grants, loans and bank guarantees. The PAC report did not offer an opinion on whether the (Labour) government should have supported the project in the first place, even though ministers had available to them a study from the management consultants McKinsey & Company (led by the author), which stated that the government was being asked to fund 'an extraordinarily risky venture'.

Neither did the committee comment on whether the government was right to place the company in receivership when it did, before the car had the chance to prove itself in the workplace and demonstrate that Northern Ireland could indeed 'make it'. In McKinsey's view at the time, withdrawal was premature, with the British taxpayer 'getting the worst of all worlds: almost all the investment, with very few of the potential returns'. Moreover although the principal blame for the taxpayers' loss was ascribed to Mr De Lorean personally he was never examined by the committee, which thus had no opportunity to hear his account of events, which might have been illuminating. And notwithstanding the committee's conclusion that: 'Hardly any of those who dealt with him [De Lorean] on behalf of the British taxpayer at a high level can have escaped substantial blame or criticism for their failure to prevent a major public waste of money', no minister resigned. Fully ten years later attempts (financed by UK taxpayers) were still under way in the United States courts to recover some of the losses.

Even when ministers appear before Select Committees – and they can only be compelled to do so by a vote of the full House of Commons – they and their Civil Servants have an inevitable advantage in terms of the briefing available to them. And if they feel remotely threatened the twenty pages of rules under which Civil Servants give evidence will put their minds at rest. As a result very few committee reports are actually debated on the floor of the House; and these reports are often published too late to affect policies or actions.

The present situation is thus profoundly unsatisfactory. Surveys suggest that popular confidence in our legislature is lower than in most other western European countries. Parliament's role with respect to European legislation is marginal. A sitting Labour MP writes in terms with which many observers agree:

> The number of bills (all of them important and contentious) on which discussion has been cut short by the Government has risen from 6 in the years 1950–1960 to 43 between 1979 and 1990 ... Any institution which can be forced in short order to enact the Community Charge Bill, the Football Spectators Bill, the Dangerous Dogs Bill, the Security Service Bill and, in the last decade, 48 Local Government bills when all rational observers could see that to do so would be ridiculous, must have something seriously wrong with it. [John Garrett MP, *Westminster: Does Parliament Work?*, 1992]

Parliament is simply not able to protect the electorate from the consequences of the arrogance of office. It seems to be respected by ministers and their officials only in the sense that actors respect their audiences; the customers pay and a poor performance can damage careers – permanently in extreme cases. If Peter Hennessy is right that 'the moment the appointed public servant ceases to walk in fear of the elected Member of Parliament, the system and constitution really will be in a state of disequilibrium', then reform is long overdue.

A Reformer's Charter

There may be widespread agreement that the present situation is unsatisfactory, but few proposals for change have been put forward. Perhaps there is a general recognition that Parliament is simply not willing or able to reform itself. Perhaps, too, MPs have come to believe in the publicity about the international reverence for the Mother of Parliaments. But in an era of charters, the voters may eventually insist on a 'Reformer's Charter' to build on the Select Committee structure, and strengthen the accountability of individual MPs so they can reasonably be called upon to explain their actions to their electors.

The legislative overload needs to be reduced as the first priority for reform. There is inadequate preparation or prior consultation on individual measures. Yet MPs' hours are excessive – over sixty a week for a typical MP; and there are many late-night sittings. In industrial parlance Parliament is analogous to a factory producing too wide a product range to inferior quality standards. It is, evidently, failing to 'get it right first time'. The sheer scale of the production process is awesome. In 1991 sixty-nine Acts of Parliament took over 2,200 pages of legislation, and 2,945 Statutory Instruments were approved. Returning to the industrial analogy this means throughput of thirteen pages of law and eighteen Statutory Instruments *every working day*. In 1951, when the welfare state was in its infancy, there were 675 pages of legislation and 2,335 Statutory Instruments. According to the Law Society, there are now over three thousand Acts in force in the United Kingdom. The Society points out that the whole statute book of Sweden is shorter (by several hundred pages) than the official index to our statute book!

The legislative process itself needs to be redesigned, as a recent Hansard Society report makes clear. The most obvious initial step would be to reduce the number of measures brought forward, so that those that are introduced can receive the necessary scrutiny in detail by expert committees. At minimum, bills should be passed to the relevant Select Committee before their second reading; and the time available to discuss each clause should be agreed automatically, in advance – so that every clause is at least discussed in detail by the most expert members available. In the words of the Select Committee on Procedure:

> It should be the aim of Departments to ensure that the Select Committees are furnished with any important information which appears relevant to their enquiries, not waiting to be asked for it specifically . . . It is difficult to see why Committees cannot be told what options are under consideration, as well as their cost implications.

This would both require governments to bring forward only the most essential legislation and reduce the chances of ill-considered measures reaching the statute book. The European Community is not the only place where legislative indigestion poses a serious danger to good governance.

At the same time the influence of the whips could be reduced, so that there are more occasions when individual MPs are free, and are seen to be free, to vote as their own views and conscience dictate, without the government's future being in the balance on every occasion. After all, only a small minority of bills introduced in each session – about one in seven – are partisan in the sense that they contain solely provisions that are contested between the parties. Four in ten bills can be classified as minor.

For example, the committee stage of the Dangerous Dogs Act 1990 was taken on the floor of the House of Commons. Five new clauses and thirty amendments were tabled; of these, twenty-one were not even discussed because, under the guillotine, the debate did not extend past Clause 1. In the House of Lords a total of a hundred amendments was tabled during the committee and report stages and at third reading. Of these, fifty-four were called and twenty-eight agreed – all but one of which was put forward by the government. Five Statutory Instruments have been promulgated since the Royal Assent, including SI 1991/2636 which modified the time scale for having exempted dogs tattooed. There seems no reason why the whips should have been concerned about such matters – which in any sensible system would have been dealt with by local government in any case.

Whipping could be confined to votes of confidence; with all other votes, on the floor of the House and in committee, MPs would be free to vote as their conscience and commitments to their electors dictated. Had such an arrangement been in place, it seems inconceivable that the community charge legislation would ever have reached the statute book, or that the electricity supply industry would have been privatised and regulated in its present form. And individual MPs could reasonably be called to account for their actions by the local media and those who elected them. No longer would it be acceptable for members to be 'intellectually absent by command of the whips' when controversial or difficult measures were being discussed.

Of course, freedom to form their own opinions and vote accordingly will only make sense if MPs have access to independent and expert advice on the issues involved. At present half of Select Committee members do not consider that committees are scrutinising departments adequately. Every committee of the House should have expert staff of perhaps as many as ten or a dozen people who would be the servant of Parliament as a whole, and available to answer individual MPs' queries on issues of concern to that particular committee. In the US House of Representatives a congressman might have a staff of ten people to help handle constituency and legislative matters; and every committee would have perhaps a dozen professional staff serving it as a whole.

In addition Select Committees could be set up at the beginning of every parliamentary session to focus attention on *prospective* problems crossing departmental boundaries, where expert advice independent of the Civil Service might be needed. A number of problems immediately suggest themselves as worthy of parliamentary scrutiny, including the following:

–   Has the UK manufacturing base eroded to the point where lack of internationally competitive manufacturing capacity is a constraint on economic growth and employment prospects? And, if so, what can and should the government be doing about the situation?

–   Is an urban underclass emerging on any significant scale in Britain? And, if so, what action can be taken to prevent developments such as those that have ravaged parts of many US cities?

–   What are the implications (if any) for the state pensions system arising from the massive increase projected in intergenerational bequests over the next decade? These are expected to increase in real terms by over £10 billion a year by 2005, compared with the situation in 1990.

–   Will failure to proceed with a nuclear power station building programme result in higher electricity costs for British electricity consumers or an unacceptable damage either to the environment or to the prospects of the UK nuclear engineering industry?

–   Is local government being effective in taking over responsibility for care in the community from the National Health Service? Is the necessary top management and funding in place with appropriate plans for implementing the complex changes?

In each case the issue crosses departmental boundaries in Whitehall. They are all thus particularly likely to fall between the bureaucratic cracks, as ministers and their officials naturally concentrate their attention on those problems and opportunities that are plainly their particular responsibility. Each committee's report should be the subject of a substantive motion and debated on the floor of the House. Only seven out of over six hundred reports since 1979 have in fact received such treatment.

Each committee should have a budget of, say, £2 million per session, to enable members to secure the necessary independent and expert advice. As Professor Philip Norton puts it: '[Parliament] has to strengthen the resources at its disposal. That requires political will. Without that willpower, Parliament is in danger of being overloaded with work and unable to meet the demands made of it' [*Does Parliament Matter?* 1993].

Expensive mistakes will also be less likely if the legislative process is more open to outside opinion. Those who have given evidence both on Capitol Hill and to committees at Westminster are likely to confirm that the latter is fairly tame by comparison. Public hearings that challenge, or at least explore, the key policy assumptions would have a therapeutic effect, not just on ministers and their officials but also on would-be challengers and their advisers. They have certainly enlivened, positively, the work of the Local Government Commission for England, whose draft recommendations for the organisation of local authorities in each area under review receive very direct public and effective local scrutiny by those with an interest in the issues involved.

To start the process, every department could publish an annual report along the lines of that now produced by the Department of the Environment in respect of action taken to implement the pledges set out in the White Paper, *This Common Inheritance*. Select Committee hearings on these reports would provide ministers with an opportunity to summarise what they are seeking to achieve, to record progress and identify future problems and opportunities. The Citizen's Charter mandates such an approach. But open government does not come naturally to Whitehall. It is over twenty years since the author first suggested that the Department of Health should issue annual reports on the health of the nation. After two decades of organisational change within the National Health Service, and incessant political debate about the scale of investment in the service fuelled by the rhetoric of cuts and market mechanisms, attention is finally turning to the needs of patients and people. And not before time. This tradition needs to change in the interests both of better national governance and improved national economic performance. Freedom of information legislation – such as was introduced in Australia, Canada and New Zealand a decade ago – would be an important step in redressing the imbalance of power as between government and those seeking to call ministers to account.

Finally MPs will need to be better paid if experienced people are to be able to abandon their present employment to stand for election to Parliament without undue financial sacrifice. There is a strong case for paying all MPs the same salary as a middle-ranking minister. The cost would be modest, around £12 million a year. If it resulted in a more effective check on the £280 billion of public spending that Parliament approves every year, the nation's taxpayers would be getting an excellent deal. This would particularly be the case if more people were content to remain legislators rather than enter the scramble for the fruits of office; the decline of independently-minded 'good House of Commons men and women' needs to be halted.

But restructuring in Whitehall and a revolution at Westminster will achieve less than might be hoped unless there are further changes in the way that the Civil Service operates.

I am proud to have started my career as a Civil Servant as a Temporary Assistant Principal in the Foreign Office. As a management consultant I carried out a wide range of assignments for government departments; and in 1983 I returned to the public service as the first Controller of the Audit Commission – one of the initial examples of privatising one of the functions of central government. The next four years brought me into contact with ministers and senior officials in almost every home department, since they all had at least an indirect interest in the 'economy, efficiency and effectiveness' with which local government services are provided.

I was privileged to give the 1988 Redcliffe-Maud Memorial Lecture on which this chapter is based. At the time I had not the slightest idea that I was to find myself following in Lord Redcliffe-Maud's footsteps in Avon, Cleveland and Humberside...

3

Mandarins and Management

'The Civil Service has embarked on a process of change, while those driving it have lost their nerve.' [Sir Peter Kemp, former Permanent Secretary at the Office of Public Service and Science, 1993]

Britain has one of the most centralised systems of public administration in the developed world. Decisions that would be taken by *Länder* in Germany, states in the United States, provinces in Canada or departments and regions in France are taken by ministers in London. The subsidiarity concept, it seems, is not to be applied too close to home. Indeed the way in which the police, education or health services are managed in Britain would be instantly recognisable to refugees from the former central planning regimes of central and eastern Europe.

The reasons are straightforward enough. Britain is a relatively small country and does not have the problems associated with the administration of vast areas (the Canadian province of Ontario is about the same size as western Europe). Ministers are accountable to Parliament for the way in which, for example, public funds are spent; and their Civil Servants must be in a position to protect them from the potential incompetence of local management. Moreover what happens in Parliament reverberates around the country, with its powerful national media and highly-concentrated economy.

But the consequences of the centralisation of decision-making are far from straightforward. Any mistakes tend to be big ones. Progress in tackling problems is often slower than might be hoped for, or than circumstances warrant, simply because mobilising and co-ordinating action in Whitehall is a time-consuming business. Experimentation is discouraged: what is right for one part of the country must surely be right everywhere – this is essentially the reasoning that delivered the community charge to England and

53

Wales a year after its flaws were evident in Scotland. And ministers are deluged with paperwork, making it difficult for them to concentrate on the most important issues.

All this might have been an acceptable price to pay for sound administration and competent management. Unfortunately the evidence suggests that government and management do not mix well. The problems inherent in the present situation are best illustrated by a case example, community care, from which some general lessons can be drawn.

The case of community care

By the middle of the 1980s some £6 billion a year was spent from public funds providing long-term care for elderly, mentally ill, mentally or physically handicapped people, excluding the cost of acute hospital care and GP services. About one and a half million adults in England and Wales received some form of care, ranging from an hour or two of home help each week to a full range of long-term care twenty-four hours a day. Of these a million were aged over sixty-five; and half a million were younger people who were either mentally or physically handicapped or required long-term support following mental illness.

For two decades the policy of successive governments has been to promote community-based services, allowing the reduction of long-stay hospital provision. This is generally considered better for the patients in most situations. It is also more economical in many cases: in 1987 a frail elderly person living in his or her own home with day and domiciliary support would typically cost public funds some £135 per week; the same person would cost about £295 per week in a National Health Service geriatric ward.

But fifteen years after community care was first adopted as public policy it was far from a reality in many places. Progress with the build-up of community-based services had generally been slow, and in some places was not keeping pace with the run-down of long-stay institutions in the NHS. Progress had been slowest for mentally ill people. In 1991 there were thirty thousand fewer NHS hospital beds for the mentally ill in England than ten years earlier; but community facilities had not kept pace, with only an additional nine thousand day-care places, for example. No one knew what had happened to many people after they were discharged. In effect the NHS had simply lost thousands of former patients.

As if that were not bad enough, a very uneven pattern of local authority services had developed, with the care that people received as much dependent on where they lived as what they needed. In well over half of local authorities expenditure on services for the mentally ill was less than £1 per head of the population, even though one in ten people each year consult their general practitioner about a mental health problem, and one in a hundred is referred to the specialist psychiatric services. Yet for years there has been general recognition of the significance of the social and environmental aspects of mental illness.

Meanwhile over 300,000 people still lived in residential care. The reduction in NHS facilities had been offset by the growth in private residential homes where some residents were entitled to receive help with their fees from supplementary benefits. In 1984 some forty thousand residents were receiving such help at a cost of some £200 million; but the Audit Commission estimated that by 1987 the cost was £500 million a year, and growing rapidly. At best there seemed to have been a shift from one pattern of residential care based on hospitals, to an alternative, supported in many cases by supplementary benefit payments – missing out more flexible and cost-effective forms of community care altogether. At worst the shortfall in services grew, with many vulnerable and disabled people left without care and at serious personal risk.

While the government's policies required a shift from hospital-based (health) services to locally-based (local authority and health) services, the mechanisms for achieving a parallel shift in funds were inadequate. In fact expenditure on NHS mental illness and mental handicap in-patient services had increased. But responsibility for introducing and operating community-based services was fragmented between health authorities, local authority social services and housing departments and the social security system. Each organisation had different priorities, styles, structures and budgets. For community care to become a reality these agencies had to work together. But there were many reasons why they did not, including the lack of positive incentives, bureaucratic barriers, perceived threats to jobs and professional standing, and the time required for interminable meetings (joint planning alone could easily be occupying the equivalent of thirty professional staff full-time in a large county).

In such circumstances it was not surprising that by the mid 1980s joint planning and community care policies were in some disarray. The result was poor value for money. Too many people were cared for in settings costing over £200 a week, when they would have received more appropriate care in the community at a total cost to public funds of £100–£130 a week. Conversely, people in the community may not have had the support they needed.

The Audit Commission's summary of the situation in 1986 concluded:

> The one option that is not tenable is to do nothing about present financial, organisational and staffing arrangements. Redeployment of the assets released by the rundown of long-stay hospitals, combined with the projected increase of 37 per cent in the number of very elderly people over the next ten years presents a 'window' of opportunity to establish an effective community-based service to provide the care needed for frail elderly, mentally ill and mentally handicapped people. If this opportunity is not taken, a new pattern of care will emerge, based on residential homes rather than a more flexible mix of services which includes residential care where appropriate. The result will be a continued waste of scarce resources and, worse still, care and support that is either lacking entirely, or inappropriate to the needs of some of the most disadvantaged members of society and the relatives who seek to care for them.

Yet, seen from the point of view of those needing community care, nothing is precisely what seems to have happened for over six years. After the Audit Commission's report was published – against the strenuous objections of the Department of Health at the time (1986) – reports by the National Audit Office (1987) and Sir Roy Griffiths (1988) confirmed its original diagnosis.

Prolonged debate followed in Whitehall, again behind closed doors, about the costs and risks associated with transferring responsibility for community care, together with the necessary resources, to local authorities. By the time this question was resolved, in favour of local government, two years had passed. Legislation was then required, which did not reach the statute book until 1990. Meanwhile there remained widespread concern that local authorities lacked the commitment, resources and management skills to make a reality of community care more than two decades after the policy was first introduced.

The start of the transfer of social security funds to local government and the introduction of new assessment procedures did not take place until April 1993. And as late as February 1992 the Audit Commission was warning that there were:

> inevitably some who question whether the finance will be sufficient to match the considerable new responsibilities that go with it ... the fundamental changes to organisation structure have still to work their way through. Big changes in policy and practice at all levels are still needed if the Government's objectives of a user-driven and cost-effective system of community health and care services are to be realised and it is likely to take many years for this process to reach completion.

In the event, the many forecasts of disaster proved unfounded. The Audit Commission reported in December 1993 that 'so far implementation has proceeded smoothly'. Nonetheless incidents of mentally ill people committing violent crimes brought ministers under pressure from local communities and the media to reverse aspects of a policy that had been gestating for at least eight years and in operation for less than six months.

What went wrong?

All of this took place during a decade which has seen the most radical changes in the Civil Service since 1870 when Gladstone implemented the recommendations of the Northcote-Trevelyan Report, which laid the foundations of the Civil Service we know today. In addition to the Citizen's Charter, designed to strengthen the role of the consumer of public services and to deliver 'citizen empowerment', these have included: devolution of functions via the 'Next Steps' programme to agencies outside the Whitehall sphere of influence, such as the benefits and defence agencies; the market testing and contracting-out of public services from the Civil Service; the sale to the private sector of some Civil Service functions, such as the Property Services Agency; and a shift away from a standardised and centralised system of Civil Service pay and conditions, including legislation enabling independent departmental and agency recruitment practices and the use of short-term contracts for Civil Servants.

But it would be wise to recognise that most administrative reform fails to meet the expectations of the would-be reformer. Community care is not an isolated instance. Successive reorganisations of the National Health Service since 1974 achieved little other than increased administrative costs and complexities. The prior expectations of reform generally fail to be realised for one or more of the following reasons:

- failure to distinguish between the symptoms and the underlying causes of a problem. Where there is popular pressure for change it is generally in response to symptoms – e.g. shortage of goods in the shops, waiting lists for operations – rather than the underlying causes that give rise to them. The underlying causes may be very difficult to treat with the time and resources available. In the case of community care these included the difficulties of health, social security and housing authorities working together
- lack of agreement on the nature of the problem, or even on whether it is a problem. Administrative solutions to problems that do not exist, or which can be tackled without wholesale reform are not uncommon, as anyone familiar with local government in the United Kingdom will know. The complaints about the council tax reminded those involved of nothing so much as the rating system. In the case of community care the Treasury refused to countenance arrangements that would free capital resources in long-stay psychiatric hospitals before the unit was closed and in time to provide facilities in the community. The idea of some form of 'sale and leaseback' arrangement was unacceptable
- an incomplete approach. Typically, administrative reforms do not consider the problem in the round. Function, funding and organisation issues are often considered separately rather than together, as is generally essential. Again, the situation of local government over the past few years illustrates the dangers involved in looking at elements of a wider problem in isolation
- failure to appreciate the complexities of managing change. Very few administrative reforms cover in a consistent or coherent way all the elements that must be managed if change is to be successfully introduced: strategy, management systems, skills, style and staffing levels. For some

no doubt cultural reason the British public service seems to be almost obsessed with the structure of organisations to the near exclusion of other important determinants of any organisation's effectiveness. Plainly the general public were not well prepared for the advent of community care

- lack of appropriate benchmarks. Success is rarely defined in terms which the general public can understand and can assess for themselves. The problem is compounded by the fact that we tend only to value that which can be measured; so the focus is on inputs rather than outputs, and on cost rather than quality. For the general public, the success of the community care programme will remain in doubt as long as there are so many obviously disturbed people sleeping rough, and the media carry stories of random personal attacks by former in-patients

- uncertain leadership. Particularly where ministers are concerned, rapid turnover and varied leadership qualities mean that, too often, 'the trumpet gives forth an uncertain note', while the dictates of parliamentary accountability mean that risks have to be avoided and 'fairness' assured for the staff concerned. These requirements may be incompatible with successful reform

- conflicting political and personal priorities so that the necessary resources are often not available, or the necessary priority focus within government is unacceptable. Cabinets cannot be single-minded, by definition, when every member has his or her own political and personal ambitions and agenda. It is all too frequent for local government, in particular, to be overloaded with change – as different central departments simultaneously push their own priorities for reform of education, the police, community care and social housing, while the threat of structural change hangs over the councillors and officers who will have to implement the reforms.

As a result administrative reform is invariably more expensive, takes longer and produces fewer benefits than proponents expect. The public is generally, and justifiably, sceptical. So it is all the more difficult to secure the bi-partisan support and general commitment necessary to launching any successful enterprise. As Disraeli is said to have put it, 'Britain is a very difficult country to move ... one in which there is more disappointment to be looked for than success.'

Another way

The preceding argument must have seemed to the reader like a counsel of despair: administrative reform is bound to disappoint. But it is important to recognise that it is not the people who are at fault but the system and culture within which they work. The record of the former nationalised industries once they have been privatised demonstrates that there was nothing wrong with the management capability of the Civil Servants who were running the businesses. In many cases the same managers led the industries into the private sector with conspicuous success. But this very success – in terms of productivity, profitability and international competitiveness – also highlights the debilitating effects of the Whitehall machine. This invariably holds up decisions, pares capital expenditure programmes and imposes constraints on the ability of management to manage.

A negative culture within Whitehall, of preventing spending and mistakes rather than encouraging and facilitating change, is inevitable. Public spending needs to be controlled while all the political pressures are in the opposite direction – to spend more and resist any cuts. Parliament has been unable, or unwilling, to fulfil this role. In the words of an anonymous Treasury official, quoted by Peter Hennessy, 'Parliament is incapable of exercising its financial responsibilities. We must do it for them.' So it is scarcely surprising that Treasury officials see themselves as the custodians of the public finances, standing guard against the waste and profligacy induced by governments' periodic need to seek re-election. The humiliation of the intervention of the International Monetary Fund in British economic policy in 1976 must rankle every bit as much in the collective folk memory of Great George Street as does the failure to keep Saltley Colliery open during the miners' strike that helped bring down the Heath government in the mess of the Police Staff College at Bramshill. This sense of public duty, combined with an obsessive concern with secrecy and constant importuning from special interests, has produced an institution which is at once feared, envied and isolated from its potential allies in the private sector.

Indeed the divide between the public and private sectors represents a serious, self-imposed, national handicap. Too often a mutual incomprehension, not to say contempt, seems to prevent effective communication between business people and politicians and public servants. On both sides the implicit assumption appears to be that nothing sensible is likely to emerge from discussions from the other side. 'After all, if they were really competent, they would be over on this side, wouldn't they?'

The Redcliffe-Maud Memorial Lecture of April 1988 addressed the general theme of the relationship between the public and private sectors in Britain. Real growth in general government expenditure over the previous decade, excluding privatisation proceeds, had averaged 2 per cent a year, not significantly different from the average growth through the 1970s. Moreover the increase would have been even greater had pay, which makes up two-thirds of total public spending, kept pace with the private sector. And productivity gains – then running at 5 per cent a year or more in manufacturing – seemed conspicuous for their absence: local authorities, Civil Service and the NHS had only $1\frac{1}{2}$ per cent fewer staff than ten years earlier. And from the official statistics it was not clear how much of the reduction was due to transfers to another payroll, usually in the private sector. Privatising the local authority audit function in 1983, for example, did not result in any reduction in the staff levels of the (excellent) District Audit Service; but the entire complement was removed from the published manpower figures for the Department of the Environment.

To this former management consultant, accustomed to seeing overheads reduce by 20 per cent and gains in operating productivity of 5 per cent every year, the collective management performance of Whitehall was less than impressive. Indeed it looked suspiciously like an organisation on auto-pilot; one that was being administered rather than managed.

No one should be surprised that managing in the public service is particularly difficult. The lack of clear accountability, rapid changes in leadership (and thus priorities), centralised pay bargaining and control over conditions of service, no balance sheet and no distinction between revenue and capital – not to mention the goldfish bowl of political and media scrutiny – add up to a formidable list of competitive handicaps for public sector managers to overcome.

There is more. The management style and traditions of the

public service are simply not compatible with the demands of a competitive marketplace. The hallmarks of the public service include concerns for fairness rather than results, process rather than outcome, language rather than analysis, economy rather than value for money, avoidance of risk and mistakes rather than reward, appearance rather than reality, consensus rather than conflict. Add to this management mix a superabundance of armchair critics in the media, Parliament and sundry Ombudsmen – not to mention the Public Accounts Committee, the Audit Commission and the courts – and it is possible to see why the skills of the private sector do not always transfer easily to Whitehall, or indeed to town halls.

By contrast, senior managers in the private sector are often aggressive, opinionated and difficult. They are used to taking risks and deciding difficult questions on the basis of incomplete and inadequate information. Not surprisingly the record of businessmen in government is mixed because very different values are involved: in the words of a senior manager from Procter and Gamble, among the world leaders in the packaged goods industry:

> To manage is to see, crossing functional barriers to grasp units, markets and cultures.
>
> To manage is to act, taking initiative in pursuit of performance, standing accountable for the results.
>
> To manage is to risk, putting the brand, the business and your job on the line.
>
> To manage is to lead, encouraging, communicating and building on the future.

The different values explain why attempts to turn mandarins into managers hold only a slim prospect of success. Rather than seeking to reform a system that is in some respects allergic to management, it would be better to recognise the realities and find alternative solutions: completing the privatisation programme; contracting out as much as is possible; decentralising operations, with maximum authority delegated to local managers; hiving off activities into independent organisations; increasing the number of people recruited from outside, and the interchange of staff between the public and private sectors.

These are not wild experiments, but well-tried approaches. A well-managed company will decide where it adds most value; and functions which do not fall within this core are considered for contracting out, such as catering, cleaning, security, vehicle and building maintenance, energy management, data processing, recruitment and training. The culture of the public service needs to shift from a direct provider of services to 'enabling' services to be provided by purchasing them from independent suppliers. This approach has brought many benefits in the private sector:

- concentrated resources. Firms have learned to 'stick to their knitting', concentrating on activities they know best and in which they add most value. Why use scarce management resources on non-critical functions which others can perform better?
- more specialisation and innovation. As specialists, contractors are able to develop expertise across a wide range of contracts. They can thus supply tested solutions to an individual client's problem and use their purchasing muscle to secure favourable prices for equipment and materials
- improved flexibility. As the recession has shown, demand fluctuates from year to year, both for a company's products and for specialist functions which it buys, such as architecture and legal services. For more routine functions, like building maintenance, it often fluctuates seasonally as well. Contracting out avoids the overheads and risks of having people and machines lying idle: many firms now set themselves up to have their production capacity fully used throughout the year. They buy in additional capacity in times of peak demand; it is usually easier to change contractors than to lay people off
- greater discipline. Putting contracts out to tender causes a firm to ask exactly what level of service it wants and why. It is a good antidote to the inertia of 'we do it this way because that is the way we have always done it'; and it can be a spur to improved quality control as well – since the contractor's performance will need to be monitored
- less unnecessary capital spending. Contractors are able to spread their capital costs over the whole range of their contracts. This means that their customers do not need to use their scarce capital on projects which are not central to their competitive position and do not add distinctive value to their customers.

63

But ministers have needed to be both vigilant and determined to ensure that inertia does not stifle initiatives to contract-out public services to the private sector at birth. Few people welcome change. Opposition to contracting-out public services runs deep within the trade unions and among many councillors; and well-publicised failures can easily undermine the process. This is despite the obvious advantages: if private sector experience is a reliable guide, putting contracts out to competitive tender should yield savings of around 20 per cent in annual running costs. For Whitehall as a whole, this would be worth not far short of £4 billion a year. (A report for the Downing Street efficiency unit in 1991 suggested that a 25 per cent cut in the size of the Civil Service was possible.)

Yet how many NHS hospitals have contracted-out their catering? Why is the figure so much higher in the private hospital sector? Many awkward questions remain to be answered. Are we continuing to provide services simply because the special interests concerned will make such a fuss if the status quo is challenged? The case of free public libraries in an era of mass media, video-tape recorders and paperbacks is less compelling than when it might have taken an agricultural worker two weeks' pay to buy *Tess of the d'Urbervilles* in hardback.

Indeed it seemed in the spring of 1988 as though most of the inflationary pressures in the economy came from the public sector – the rises in local authority and water rates and electricity prices had added a full point to the Retail Price Index.

The Redcliffe-Maud lecture concluded:

What if we go on as before? The cost of failure will be very great... A failure to reduce the tax burden on business to make room for needed investment, non-competitive energy prices for intensive users of electricity, an expensive shambles in the field of local government finance, and British industry priced out of world markets unnecessarily by a combination of currency speculators and self-fulfilling prophecies about the resurgence of inflation, leading to interest rates higher than necessary would reflect a colossal wasted opportunity. Instead of maintaining the momentum of the short-lived economic recovery, we will be hard pressed to stand still.

Now the nation seems to have awakened, slowly, with a painful hangover. It has indeed been *The Morning After*, as a former US Secretary of Commerce entitled his perspectives on the excesses of the American economy during the past decade or so. And there is a general recognition that things cannot be allowed to go on as they are. But progress has been painfully slow, as Sir Peter Kemp, the senior Civil Servant responsible for the Whitehall revolution, stated in *The Times* Essay in November 1993: 'The Civil Service is in crisis ... market testing has yielded only a quarter of what was expected and led 240,000 people to strike, and an efficiency unit recommendation that senior positions should be advertised has been torpedoed.' His vision for the future was 'a much smaller core Civil Service, back nearer 50,000; ministers advised by independent advisers recruited openly and on contract; production engineers to translate policy into action; and services provided by independent agencies...'

Nowhere is the need for change greater than in the relationship between central and local government.

A vibrant, self-confident and independent local government is essential both as a counterweight to Whitehall and Westminster and to the delivery of improvements in local services. It can also help to reinforce that sense of community which is vital to efforts to tackle the problems of crime and social disintegration.

Yet the legacy of the so-called 'Loony Left' casts a long shadow. So has the treatment of Alderman Roberts at the hands of Grantham Town Council over forty years ago.

As the first Controller of the Audit Commission from 1983 to 1987, and most recently as the Chairman of the Local Government Commission for England, I have seen more of local government over a longer period than most if not all of the commentators and ministers who have influenced its direction. Much of it is worthy of praise. The antics in Liverpool and Lambeth as well as at the GLC and elsewhere in inner London were the exception.

There now exists the opportunity to re-engineer (or at least renew) local government. This chapter reflects the views I formed (and published) while at the Audit Commission and CBI.

4

Politics and Local Government

Reviews of local government have rarely, if ever, considered function, finance, structure and management together. Yet, all too often, changes in one sphere make life more difficult in another.

'Whom God would destroy He first sends mad,' wrote James Duport in 1660 plagiarising Euripides. He could have been describing the legacy of the 'Loony Left' of British politics which seriously weakened public confidence in, and support for, local government. Conspiracy theorists may believe that these antics were deliberately designed to provoke the Conservative government into over-reaction that would rebound to their electoral disadvantage. Deliberate or not, the strategy almost worked; Mrs Thatcher's fall was hastened, if not caused, by the ham-fisted way in which the community charge was introduced.

But the behaviour of the leadership of the Greater London, Lambeth and Liverpool councils has left a more enduring and damaging legacy: deep-rooted contempt among many on the Conservative benches in Parliament for local government generally. Indeed in recent times criticism of local government has been one of the very few ways that can be guaranteed to secure vocal backbench support for hard-pressed ministers. The demonology of Militant remains as potent as ever. The excellent management record of many local councils, under all types of political control, is masked by the continuing incompetence of a few, while the memories endure of the bonuses paid for putting the head-collars on the horses that were deemed to be dragging the refuse collection carts round the City of Liverpool.

The result has been a steady erosion of the powers of local government, and the resources available to spend at local discretion; and an ever-greater central control over local initiatives.

By 1991 government grants accounted for 75 per cent of total local authority current expenditure, and the proceeds of the community charge for less than 13 per cent. A decade earlier government grants accounted for under half of all local authority expenditure, and the rates contributed over a third. The situation has now reached the point where many people are tempted to write off local government entirely and to replace it with local administration funded from national tax revenues.

However, what is seen (even in France) as a highly centralised system has failed to achieve the economy that successive governments have sought. Elaborate schemes designed to control increases in local government current (day-to-day) expenditure have failed to deliver the goods. Official statistics illustrate the failure of the attempts over the last decade to bring the party bemoaned by Anthony Crosland to a halt. The figures for current and capital spending, in 1991 prices, tell their own story:

	Current £bn	Capital £bn
1981	53.3	5.3
1983	57.7	4.2
1985	57.4	3.8
1987	60.9	4.9
1989	60.2	4.6
1991	63.4	4.8

Thus, despite seemingly continuous changes to the system of financing local government, penalties for over-spending, rate and charge capping and the removal of the power to determine business rates, and the abolition of the metropolitan counties – not to mention an incessant drumbeat of ministerial criticism – annual local government current expenditure was around £435 a household higher in real terms at the end of the decade than at the beginning.

Failure to control costs is not the only cause for concern about the future of local government. As its power and public standing reduced, local councils became politicised to an extent that would have been unimaginable before the 1974 reorganisation that created the present two-tier system of councils in rural England. In many authorities elected members are attempting to use committee structures developed for a very different era to do their Chief Officers' jobs for them, often with the benefit of no prior managerial experience at all. It takes endless hours in committee rooms and party meetings. Small wonder that it is increasingly difficult to persuade qualified people to stand for election to the local council, or that few ordinary citizens know who their local councillors are, or what they can reasonably be held responsible and accountable for. (Opinion surveys suggest that a sizeable minority of people believe that the National Health Service is run by local government.) Small wonder too that in May 1993 voter turnout in the county council elections was disturbingly low, in line with that for the election to the European Parliament of 36 per cent – in 1989 turnout in the UK for the EC elections was markedly lower than in any other community member (the average was 59 per cent).

Clearly any public institution that the electorate does not understand, is unwilling to pay for, and unlikely to vote for must be heading for the history books. However, the demise of local government and its replacement by local administration would be deeply regrettable. In any western society power needs to be diffused; an over-powerful central government is always at risk from its own incompetence. Moreover many of the most difficult domestic problems facing the nation – juvenile crime, the need for education reform, homelessness, introduction of new community care policies, inner city regeneration – require local action and co-ordination that central government would find it very difficult to provide.

So the present mutual resentment between Westminster and Whitehall on the one hand and town halls on the other is potentially very damaging, and must be exorcised from the body politic. This will only be possible if local government is firmly rooted in local communities; if the role of local government in providing public services is clarified; if the present unwieldy structure is streamlined; and if there is a closer link between the structure and financing of local authorities.

Community government

One of the problems facing ministers and councillors alike is that the role of local government in the United Kingdom has been constantly evolving for a thousand years. Of course the need to keep the map of English local government in good repair has been recognised since the late 1880s, when the first modern local authorities were introduced. At first reliance was placed on local initiation of boundary changes and private bill procedures. Such changes were always difficult, a tradition going back to Saxon times: 'The division of the Western Midlands into Shires which completely disregarded the boundaries of ancient peoples could only have been carried out by a King strong enough to ignore local resentment and quite indifferent to local traditions' [Edward the Elder, AD 899–924].

Between the end of the Second World War and the 1973 reorganisation of local government, boundaries were reviewed roughly every decade. But these reviews rarely considered function, finance, structure and management together. All too often changes in one sphere make life more difficult in another. Successive 'reforms' of the way local government is financed appear to ignore the major changes that have taken place in local government's functions over the past twenty years. These have seen explosive growth in personal social services which now cost over £6 billion a year, a reduction in local authorities' role in providing social housing, the transfer of community health services to the National Health Service and recently of community care to local government, increased spending on leisure and recreation, which has risen to over £2.4 billion a year, and reduced powers to subsidise public transport.

The scale of the increases in expenditure on different services between 1981 and 1991 is quite striking, even after allowing for inflation.

Personal social services	£1.59bn
Police	1.52
Education	0.78
Recreation	0.43 ·
Fire Services	0.28

Only transport showed a reduction, of £850 million, due to the elimination of subsidies and bus deregulation.

But these changes have not taken place against any blueprint of the desirable future role for local government. They have simply resulted from a series of ministerial judgements, which have not taken any account of whether local government finances, structure and management can take the strain. This is only in part ministers' fault. They have not received advice that has stood the test of time particularly well. The political landscape is littered with the bleached bones of those rash enough to think ahead. In a chapter of their 1969 report entitled *The Need for Change*, the Redcliffe-Maud Commission defined its view of the challenge of the future. In the light of the experience of the past twenty-five years it bears re-examination. The report spoke of:

- England having a population of sixty million by the end of the century.
  In the event latest projections suggest it will be under fifty million
- an increase in the 'basic school population' – meaning five-to fifteen-year-olds – of 50 per cent by 1997.
  In fact between 1980 and the early 1990s the number of secondary pupils declined by 27 per cent in England and Wales. Only a slight recovery is expected by the turn of the century
- an increase in the number of old people (that is, men over sixty-five and women over sixty).
  But it did not even refer to the problems of the very old – those over eighty-five. Between 1984 and 1990 there were virtually no increases in the number of people aged sixty-five to seventy-four; but there will be a rise of around 35 per cent in those aged eighty-five or over
- under fifteen million cars on the English roads by the mid 1980s.
  In fact in 1985 there were over eighteen million private and light goods vehicles on our roads.

The report also assumed that:

- local authorities, who were then building nearly half of all new homes, 'must be responsible, in concert with central government, for deciding where the necessary houses are to be built and for seeing that they are built'.
  In 1992 local authorities accounted for just 2½ per cent of all new

homes built in England; and the massive (£20 billion) backlog of maintenance and improvement expenditure on public housing continued to rise

- 'the Authorities must plan where and when land is to be developed, to provide both for the existing population and for the 30 per cent increase expected in little over thirty years.' The commission looked to local authorities to resolve (or at least manage) the conflicts 'between town and country, between what people want and what they can have'.

  Too often conflicts are managed by planning enquiries and the courts in present circumstances

- urban renewal was one of the most formidable of all the challenges. 'Most of the older towns need a vast amount of rebuilding, and at the same time to be reshaped.'

  The challenge remained largely unmet until the mid 1980s

- reorganisation was expected to provide a pattern of local government competent to tackle the huge associated problems of planning and transportation, otherwise 'Central Government may feel driven to take a part of the responsibility out of Local Government, wholly unsatisfactory though that is bound to be'

- there was 'plainly a case for thinking that the medical and related services (of the NHS) would be best provided by local government, in association with the personal social services, if the structure and the finance were such as to make that possible'.

  It wasn't. And the 1974 reorganisation of the NHS saw community health services transferred from local government to the NHS, while care in the community is only now becoming a reality a quarter of a century after the policy was first articulated in Alexander Fleming House

- water supply, sewerage and sewerage disposal were seen as 'basic to a great deal of the work of local authorities: to planning, housing and general development . . . These ought to be local government services, provided as part of the comprehensive responsibility for the health and wellbeing of the people'

- local authorities would be increasingly the main – and for the more elaborate facilities the only – providers of recreation and leisure facilities.

  It seems quite inconceivable today that anyone could have envis-

aged that most golf courses, bowling alleys, amusement arcades, holiday camps or discos would be run by local authorities. But they did.

On this evidence there was no case for the upheaval of 1974. Those that follow need to ask how the great and good of a quarter of a century ago came to such misjudgements.

To begin with, they misread the politics, assuming (like all ballistic thinkers) that the future would be like the past and that the 'nanny state' was a permanent feature of the British political landscape. They also misread the economics, along with virtually everyone else. They were writing, of course, before the first oil crisis and the realities of international competition had really dawned on the British public and its politicians. This was an era when the world still effectively owed us a living.

And they misread the managerial problems. Indeed they failed, largely, to address them. Yet we now understand that organisation structure cannot sensibly be considered separately from considerations of finance and function. And that *all* of the elements that determine any organisation's effectiveness must be considered together: strategy, systems, skills, management style, staffing and, of course, the shared values that knit any organisation together. As was stated earlier most of these elements are generally ignored by would-be reformers of our public services.

Finally the 1969 Royal Commission and its advisers were just plain unlucky. They could not have been expected to anticipate the turmoil of the 1970s, which in turn changed the demographic outlook so fundamentally.

But the most important reason for the continuing problems facing local government in many areas is that the structure is not firmly rooted in the reality of local communities, nor in history. In 1974 the then government was, rightly, not prepared to eliminate institutions (counties) which had existed one way and another for a thousand years and had served England well. On the other hand it recognised that in many rural areas the county town was seen as remote from local communities. So the current two-tier system was born. It has created exactly the kind of problems that can be expected to arise from any bureaucratic compromise. It is expensive in terms of administrative costs. It is difficult for ordinary citizens to understand who does what; the financial arrangements are very difficult to disentangle as between the various tiers of local government. And many of the resulting authorities are administrative creations, in many cases too large to be local and too small to act strategically.

What is needed is a truly local local government, based on the reality of local communities and with a much clearer role than is at present the case.

A clearer role

Local government does not, of course, play the same role in respect of each of the services for which councillors are expected to be held to account by their local electors. Sometimes local government is merely an agent of Parliament, as with primary and secondary education or community care. In other cases local government has been the agent of a Whitehall department, paying housing benefit which might otherwise have been carried out by the Department of Social Security through its benefit offices. Local authorities can be regulators, of environmental health and trading standards, for instance. They provide services to the local community, such as refuse collection, street lighting, road sweeping and library services. Finally local councils compete with the private sector in the housing, leisure and recreation markets.

Each of these different roles is, no doubt, legitimate in its own right. But it would be foolish to pretend that the situation in each case is accepted by local councillors or understood by local people.

The arrangements for paying for local government services make an unclear situation worse. In 1992 nearly £39 billion of the £53 billion of current grants made from central to local government were not allocated to specific services, but rather formed a so-called block grant which is distributed to over 400 local authorities to spend as they wish. This system has serious disadvantages. The grant is, in effect, core funding; but local people are still invited to hold their councillors to account for the adequacy of local services, while central government has the invidious task of allocating this massive sum of money to over 400 individual local authorities, and determines the extent to which local residents are required to contribute via the council tax. The vagaries in the grant distribution arrangements are notorious, and to a large degree account for the variation in community charges levied by similar authorities with similar spending patterns.

74

Ideally the funding arrangements for individual services should reflect local government's role in their provision. For example, where the local authority is an agent of Parliament there could be a grant adequate to fund the services at standards that Parliament has determined; only then can ministers sensibly be called to account for any shortcomings. Arguably, the officials in these services should be Civil Servants, and all Chief Officer appointments should be approved by the minister responsible, as is now the case for Chief Constables.

By contrast, all local community services could be paid for locally via the council tax, which could also be used to 'top up' government grants, where local people wished to supplement the resources made available for the local provision of national services. There would not need to be any capping of the council tax, nor penalties for over-spending. Providing the local people agree and are able to meet the costs involved, local spending on community services need be no concern of Parliament or government. When set against annual public expenditure of some £280 billion, the total sums involved (less than £10 billion a year) are not so great as to imperil the public finances. In any event, recent history shows that governments would do better to rely on the reluctance of British householders to see their councils spending their money, than on complex attempts at central planning and control. Reforms to the financing of local government should be complemented by streamlining its structure, and making individual councillors more accountable. This is now in prospect.

Streamlining the structure

The review of the structure of local government in non-metropolitan areas in England now being carried out by the Local Government Commission could present a considerable opportunity: to bring the Citizen's Charter to life in the areas in question; to make it easier to introduce further reforms in education, social services, community care and the police services; and to establish much clearer local accountability for local services.

The commission is entering a political minefield as all concerned recognise. Public opinion, which is not generally interested in local government, is easily outraged if ancient boroughs or local identities are seen to disappear or not be reflected in organisation structures (a petition of twenty thousand signatures has called for the restoration of the Ridings of Yorkshire). While Party interests are at stake locally and to some extent nationally, individual MPs are intensely interested in the proposals for 'their' areas. Powerful and well-financed organisations exist to represent the interests of elected members and staff both of counties and districts. To make matters worse the commission is looking for a final solution to a long-standing problem which can probably never finally be solved – because the nature of the relationship between central and local government will continue to change, as the reforms of education, community care and the police take hold. Meanwhile, local authority members and officers defined the commission's task in simple, even simplistic terms: in each area the commission was expected to choose between adopting the county or the existing districts (or some combination of them) as the new unitary authorities.

There are managerial issues to be addressed as well. The sheer scale of local government in England requires, at least for some important services such as education and personal social services as well as land use planning, an element of strategic management and the high-quality managers necessary to carry it out. But at the same time local government must be able to 'deliver' to small local communities; and local people will want to know who is in charge; accountability is a personal matter – it is difficult to hold a committee or a council accountable for the quality of local services.

Removal of a tier of local government and the restoration of some ancient boundaries and rights would certainly constitute an improvement on the present arrangements. But this should not be the end of the matter. Local authorities could remain relatively remote from most people, with the separate identities and interests of different boroughs effectively submerged; while the tier of local government nearest to him or her (the town or parish council) could remain relatively impotent. Accountability of members and officers could continue to be diffused in the bureaucracy and committee structures. It would still not be clear who should be taken to task if specific local services provided by the council fall short or costs are excessive.

Perhaps most importantly, local authorities would remain dominated by the interests of those providing services, rather than focused on meeting the needs of individual families or the communities in which they live.

The traditional structure of largely self-contained services under a Chief Officer who in turn reports to a committee of councillors will not be flexible enough to meet the challenge of community care, or to tackle the problems of juvenile crime. The latter cannot be managed unless police, teachers and social services work effectively together. Caring for people in the community must involve social workers and people with an understanding of the local housing market, as well as doctors and nurses. This co-ordinated action will not happen spontaneously. It will require devolving considerable management authority and responsibility to the community level, so that decisions can be taken without constant reference to a remote authority. It will also require local general management and locally elected representatives to monitor what is going on on behalf of the electorate. It will involve investment in information technology to make every town hall the nerve centre for all local services – a 'one-stop shop' where citizens can access their local government and their elected representatives.

Moreover, looking ahead, local government in twenty years' time is likely to be as different from the present as today's authorities are from those they replaced in 1974.

A Europe of rural regions is likely to have evolved, as the price for reform of the Common Agricultural Policy and of (freer) trade with the predominantly agricultural countries of central Europe, and as the EC seeks to reduce the disparity of wealth within the Community.

As power and influence shifts to Brussels, MPs at Westminster will want to take a more direct interest in local programmes. So the days of the block grant are probably numbered, and local government could be increasingly replaced by local administration. At the same time health and local authorities will probably be growing closer together as governments seek to avoid the political fall-out of the imbalance between limited resources for health care and virtually limitless demand driven by technological change and unfavourable demographics, and as they recognise the importance both of the prevention of illness and of health education.

Pressure on local government's resources will be even more constrained than at present, reflecting continued pressure on public finances in an era of low inflation and low growth, as well as intensified international competition, unfavourable demographics and rising concern for inner cities. So administrative overheads must be kept to a minimum.

As far as local authorities themselves are concerned, as their operations are contracted-out, sold or devolved to independent organisations (for example, boards of governors or trusts), they will need to take on a more strategic role, combined with a concern for quality and results. They will be catalysts, enablers, and facilitators rather than providers or financiers of local development. As the transport infrastructure and telecommunications improve, distance will seem much less important and relevant, particularly if management can be devolved to the community level. Most people wishing to contact their council can do so by telephone; the number of telephones in use has risen from under fourteen million in 1970 to over thirty-five million today. Electronic town meetings could become a reality, bringing up to date the Saxon institution of the hundred court, in which the local electors met every four weeks at a fixed meeting-place to decide any matters of general concern.

In such circumstances there is a strong case for larger rather than smaller unitary authorities with devolved management responsibility to the community level and linked with local parish and town councils. Thus, within each unitary authority in England:

- management responsibility for all local services would be devolved to local, neighbourhood watch size, communities under the overall direction of a local general manager. He or she would be accountable to the members (up to three) elected to represent the interests of each community on the new council. There would be a single service information centre in each community, perhaps based in the local public library
- the council would in turn delegate to these local councillors responsibility for the oversight of those services financed by the local council tax – for example, refuse collection, environmental health, social housing, street lighting and sweeping, parks maintenance and libraries; the relevant services would be structured to reflect community boundaries
- each councillor could be personally responsible for particular local services; the council's local officers would therefore be directly responsible to elected members, although they would also have a professional 'line' to the council's Chief Officer for each service
- local parish and community councils would have the right

78

to meet with 'their' local councillors once a quarter, say; and they would provide the support ordinary citizens might need to obtain redress for any of the local authorities' short-comings.

The new councils would remain statutorily responsible for all the services Parliament authorised them to secure or deliver. Committees of councillors, supported by professional officers, would oversee the delivery of those services funded by Exchequer grant – for example, education, community care, social services, services for children in care, fire, land use planning and refuse disposal. The council as a whole (or its Policy and Resources Committee) would determine development priorities and the major capital programme for the authority. Every local MP not holding government office could become a local alderman, thus cementing the links between Parliament and local government.

From the point of view of the average citizen, the proposed approach would bring their local council much closer to their day-to-day lives and would reflect 'real' local communities more accurately than the present arrangements. It would be clear who was responsible for what – since there would be only one or two councillors responsible for the quality of the service in a given community, and no committees for them to hide behind or be impeded by. It should be reasonable to expect the council to tackle the problems of juvenile crime, homelessness or the ill-treatment of elderly people. Councillors would be so busy that there would be little time to play at national politics; and if they were paid a non-executive director's fee of, say, £10 thousand a year, there would be less incentive to hold interminable meetings. More people would want to serve as local councillors as they would have clear authority and accountability and would not be required to spend frustrating hours in committee meetings. And the present frustration of many of the seventeen thousand parish and town councillors would be channelled into a constructive representational role.

These benefits should flow from the review of the structure of local government in shire England. They would be much easier to realise if the financing arrangements could be brought into line with the structure of local government.

Finance

Local government finance has been likened to the Schleswig-Holstein question of which it was once said that only three people have ever understood it; one was mad, the second was dead and the third had forgotten. Unfortunately for the successive Controllers of the Audit Commission they are required to join this select band. As long ago as 1985, in a review of the system for distributing government grants to local authorities in England and Wales (the figure in 1992 was over £50 billion), the Audit Commission concluded that the government's approach was itself causing substantial waste and inefficiency within local government. The summary stated that:

> The uncertainties associated with the present arrangements for distributing Block Grant to Local Authorities are now leading to higher rates than are necessary. Over the past two to three years, General Rate Fund Balances have increased in total and the use of special funds has become more marked, as Local Authorities have sought to manage the significant annual uncertainties in the present system for distributing grants. For ratepayers, this means that rate bills in the last three years have probably been on average some £400 million or more a year higher than would have been necessary had there been fewer external uncertainties outside Authorities' control.

Moreover, while encouragement of efficiency and effectiveness was among the main stated objectives of the system, it had some unintended by-products: incentives were inappropriate; accountability for local services was blurred; pressure for improvements in value for money was weaker than it would need to be if painful decisions to redeploy resources were to be taken; there was an insufficient delegation of authority and responsibility at the local level.

Alarmed by this and other reports, the government put forward its own ideas for reform in January 1986 in a discussion paper, *Paying for Local Government*. At no stage were the authors of the Audit Commission reports consulted on the appropriate response. None the less, ministers set out what seemed a very sensible approach in the foreword to *Paying for Local Government*:

> Effective local accountability must be the cornerstone of successful Local Government. All too often, this accountability is blurred and weakened by the complexities of the national grant system and by the

fact that differences arise among those who vote for, those who pay for
and those who receive Local Government services ... in almost every
respect, the existing Local Government finance system makes it almost
impossible for local electors to relate what they pay to the services
provided. We must put this right. If people can understand the costs
of the different services provided to them, and if the costs are fairly
distributed, they can make sensible choices, not only about the balance
between local priorities, but also about the overall level of spending.

However closer examination by the Confederation of British
Industry, whose members were, by then, contributing around
£10 billion a year towards the cost of local government through
business rates, revealed serious problems, not so much with the
policy but with the proposals for putting it into effect. Specifically,
from the business point of view, there would remain a large element
of cross-subsidy by business of local residents; business and other
non-domestic ratepayers would be paying some £2 billion a year
for services from which they derived little or no benefit. To set this
sum in some relevant context, *total* manufacturing investment in
1992 was just over £10 billion (in 1985 prices).

Because the Uniform Business Rate (UBR) detached local authorities from business financially, they had no incentive to provide
services to business or to take business interests into account in
planning decisions; nor would they be able to attract new businesses to their areas on the basis of careful spending policies.
Moreover the proposal to set the UBR at the then average current
rate poundage consolidated the existing waste and inefficiency
within local government. It assumed that there was no slack in
local authority expenditure patterns; and would not place pressure
on local authorities to implement the value improvement opportunities that were known to exist.

It was clear that there would be large rate rises for businesses
outside inner London and the north of England. After the proposed introduction of the UBR at the level then envisaged, and
after the essential revaluation, average rate bills were predicted to
increase by 20–30 per cent in the south-west and West Midlands,
for instance. In the Thames Valley increases of up to 90 per
cent were projected after revaluation; the Confederation of British
Industry stated that such rises of this magnitude would put many
small and medium-size manufacturing concerns and shops out of
business. This was particularly galling as the list of authorities

where business rates were set to increase most read like a roll of honour of well-managed local authorities. Penalising success is rarely a sound strategy, as a stroll down high streets from Newbury to Penzance in the depths of the recession demonstrated.

While accountability for local services seemed bound to remain confused and particularly so during the transition period, overall the government's proposals resulted in some three-quarters of local authority budgets being outside local control. At the same time ministers accountable to Parliament would still lack the power to see that local authorities did not divert Exchequer funds intended for 'their' services to other local (and still lawful) purposes. At least where local authority services were concerned, the annual round of public expenditure planning would remain something of a charade – notwithstanding the detailed inter-departmental negotiations that resulted in the government's spending plans in the first place.

In any case the proposals seemed inconsistent with the government's plans for inner cities. The poll tax would bear most heavily and be most difficult to collect in precisely those inner city areas where the previous arrangements were unsatisfactory. This was not surprising because the Green Paper was prepared during 1985, well before these initiatives were under consideration. Administrative costs also seemed certain to increase as would the cost of evasion and non-payment, because the community charge bore on individuals rather than families or households.

In short, by the beginning of Mrs Thatcher's third term it was evident that the flagship of her legislative programme was seriously flawed, even though its objectives were sound. Suggestions that all was not well were dismissed with the familiar refrain that 'there is no alternative'.

As it happened, an alternative approach *was* available, and presented to the then Secretary of State for the Environment in the autumn of 1987, before the community charge legislation was even published. The CBI proposed that different types of local service should be financed differently, to reflect the desired pattern of accountability and responsibility and the reality of who was paying for what. The services provided by local authorities would be divided into four categories, each funded differently:

- the Exchequer would make specific grants to the relevant authorities to cover the cost of national services such as

polytechnics and further education colleges, secondary schools, school meals and milk (part of the welfare state, in effect) and all child care services. The block grant to local authorities would be reduced, pound for pound, to compensate
- local businesses would contribute, via local business rates, towards the local cost of those services (only) from which they benefited directly. These included non-advanced further education, police, fire, road maintenance, street lighting, refuse collection and disposal, museums and libraries. Non-domestic ratepayers might meet 75 per cent of the costs of these services; and local business representatives would be co-opted on to the relevant local committees
- council housing and leisure services – for which there is a local market – would be expected to be self-financing; there would be no cross-subsidy for tenants or users, other than that provided by the social security system. This would mean that pricing 'signals' would be realistic. In particular, council tenants would understand the cost of keeping their homes in decent repair – and would be able to take this into account when deciding whether or not to exercise their 'right to buy'
- community services including primary and nursery education, as well as care for the elderly and services for local households would be financed by the community charge. The cost incurred by each authority (that is, county and district) would be separately identified. The collection and other costs would be considerably lower if the charge were levied on a per-household, rather than per-adult, basis – possibly with reduction for pensioners living alone.

Exchequer grants would compensate those authorities which had particularly heavy needs for community or property services (for example, because there was a high local crime rate, the risk of fire was unusually high, or there was a high proportion of primary schoolchildren or elderly people within the community).

The benefits of the CBI's proposals appeared substantial. The government's stated objectives and manifesto commitments would have been met. The criticism levelled at the Uniform Business Rate and the prospective administrative costs of the community charge would have been avoided, to a great extent. Market forces would have operated where local markets existed. Accountability for local services would be much clearer, both nationally and at the local level. There would be every incentive for local people (including the business community) to press for implementation of the value improvements already agreed to be available – a matter to which we shall return in Part II. Major problems on revaluation of domestic houses would be avoided; and the new scheme could have been implemented without an extended transition period.

So there was an alternative. But it was too late. Notwithstanding the opposition of the Treasury to the community charge, the government's collective mind was made up. The then Secretary of State for the Environment simply reminded those supporters seeking to help the government avoid the crevasse that obviously lay ahead that his party had just won a General Election.

In the event, the community charge and other reforms cost the Prime Minister her job and nearly cost the government the 1992 election. Whether the replacement council tax is ultimately any more acceptable to the electorate remains to be seen. What is clear is that the criticisms of the Uniform Business Rate remain valid. And the new tax does nothing for accountability: there will be only the most tenuous link between the level of the council tax and the cost and efficiency of local services for householders. It will remain almost impossible for local electors 'to relate what they pay to the services provided'.

*   *   *

There is a need for a renewal of local government and a re-engineering of the way it works. Local authorities should be community-based; and local (as opposed to national) services should be locally financed and under local control. They should be smaller and leaner than the bureaucracies now in place, enabling services to be delivered rather than providing them directly. They should think strategically (and in regional terms when necessary), but deliver locally in towns and villages. In other words they would be flexible organisations fit for the next century rather than the 'big is beautiful' bureaucracies of the 1970s. They should also be well placed to play a greater role in health care.

I have strong family connections with the National Health Service. My father was a consultant surgeon from 1946 until his retirement in 1976; and my mother is a State Registered Nurse who played a leading role in establishing the social services in Cornwall. She has held senior appointments within the NHS.

While at McKinsey in the early 1970s I was involved in the review of the Department of Health and in the 1974 reorganisation of the NHS in England and Wales, working among others with Robert Maxwell CBE, now the director of the King's Fund. I then spent two years in Washington, working on health care issues confronting the US federal government. On my return I prepared a critique of the 1974 reorganisation, for the then Opposition spokesman on health care, Sir Geoffrey (now Lord) Howe, and for the Royal Commission on the National Health Service. This reflected my US experience.

I was determined that the Audit Commission should eventually become involved with health care. Making a Reality of Community Care *was one of the more influential publications of my time at Vincent Square. This owed much to the Chairman (Sir David Cooksey) and the then Director of Special Studies at the commission, Dr Ross Tristem.*

5

The Health Care Dilemma

The NHS has a low pay, low motivation, low performance culture. [Eric Caines, former Director of NHS Personnel, 1993]

Following the revelation in late 1993 by the Chairman of the Audit Commission, Sir David Cooksey, that in one hospital it took six people to change a light bulb, including seventeen work steps and twenty minutes of overhead time, the London *Evening Standard* leader writer went to town under the headline: 'The Scandal of Our NHS':

> In the past, news like that would have been greeted by shrill triumphalism from the Right, as evidence that the NHS is a Welfare State dinosaur that needs to be reformed. But now it has been reformed – and the changes have only increased the bureaucratic nightmare ... There is one light bulb that should have been changed a long time ago. It is the one that appeared over [Health Secretary] Virginia Bottomley's head when she thought it was a good idea to wreck our NHS in the name of competition. [30 September 1993]

Never mind that the reforms were initiated before Virginia Bottomley entered the Cabinet. As it happens, the light bulb saga was only one of a catalogue of shortcomings within the management of the NHS that had been identified by the Audit Commission. Sickness absence for administrative and clerical staff was running at ten to twelve days a year on average, two and a half times the level to be expected in comparable private sector jobs. For nursing staff the average was eighteen days, three and a half working weeks. Strict demarcation between groups of staff and levels produced exactly the kind of absurdities that crippled many industries in the 1960s; thus it took 127 minutes and ten people to take and read an X-ray, but only twenty-three minutes actually to shoot, develop and read it. The rest of the time was spent pushing paper and patients around. Only 5 per cent of total NHS spending had been put out to competitive tender; and there was little evidence that trusts or managers were seeking to go beyond the legal requirements to explore market testing.

These were not isolated examples of mismanagement. Successive Audit Commission reports of nursing management, day surgery and arrangements for discharging patients had shown startling variations between outwardly similar hospitals: in some cases sickness absence is ten times higher than in other hospitals; in two-thirds of hospitals in one study at least sixty acute beds were blocked by patients clinically fit to be cared for in the community. Savings worth over £200 million a year had been identified from better management of energy, water, sterile supplies and nursing services.

All this comes after more than forty years of a National Health Service which the public (who are both patients and taxpayers, though often not at the same time) expect to produce common and excellent standards of management and care across the system as a whole. With costs spiralling to over £35 billion a year – a real increase of £9 billion (or £380 a household) in the past decade – and public spending under increasing pressure, it is plain that something more must be done in addition to pressing on with the management reforms.

The dilemma

That 'something' will entail confronting a basic dilemma that has existed ever since the NHS was founded to ensure that everyone has access to medical care when they need it, regardless of their ability to pay for it. Lord Beveridge assumed that national expenditure on health care would eventually fall, as the backlog of neglect among people unable to afford doctors' bills in the past was made good. The reality has been otherwise. The resources available to the NHS have always been limited by what the Exchequer can afford. But costs have risen steadily in real terms, fuelled by a combination of increases in demand for treatment, an ageing population and the advances of medical science and technology. So doctors and nurses and the NHS bureaucracy have been left to manage a situation in which voters consider that they have a right to world-class treatment when they need it; but they are reluctant to see their taxes increased to meet the bills.

Any question of rationing health care, by charging for treatment or imposing delays in admissions to hospitals, raises very difficult ethical problems as well as the political temperature. Few have wished to risk debunking the many myths surrounding the NHS. So it is not generally realised that the share of total domestic expenditure in Britain spent on health care is lower (6.6 per cent in 1991) than in any other OECD area countries except Greece, Portugal or Spain, and almost exactly half that of the United States. On key indicators of health, such as infant mortality, death rates from lung cancer and coronary heart disease, the British public suffers by comparison with the best in the world. The OECD figures for years of potential life lost as a result of 'preventable' deaths (excluding suicides) show that the rate for women was higher in Britain than in any other major developed country except the United States; it was 50 per cent higher than in Japan. It was the same story for men: for example, years of life lost in 1989 due to ischaemic heart disease were higher in Britain than in any other major developed country, and over twice the rate for the other six countries of the G7 Group of leading industrialised nations.

Meanwhile the public is invited by politicians to believe that any shortcomings in the service can be corrected by a combination of better management and less bureaucracy, and a new injection of taxpayers' money. One of the rites of the autumn round of public spending decisions is for the British Medical Association and opposition parties in Parliament, whoever they happen to be, to proclaim that the NHS is seriously under-funded and that without an injection of £x billion the service and the morale of doctors and nurses will be undermined and expensive wards will close before the financial year is out.

Squaring the circle – of the virtually limitless demand (and need) for care to be met from limited public resources – has seemingly been left to the mysteries of management and market forces, even though managers in the health service do not manage doctors or nurses in a way that Florence Nightingale would recognise. And market forces are expected to operate in an environment where there is often no market, limited competition and few reliable, understandable or relevant price signals for the ultimate customers – doctors and their patients. As if these were not handicaps enough, the directors of the new NHS Trusts are beginning to realise that the more efficient a hospital becomes the higher the costs per case are likely to be, because the most expensive (and intensive) part of the treatment takes place soon after patients are admitted. So hospitals interested in saving money would be well advised to treat fewer patients and keep them in hospital for longer. A classic example of a perverse incentive, and in marked contrast to the trends of recent years.

Astonishing as it may seem, for the first twenty-five years of its existence the basic dilemma unresolved by the founders of the NHS was largely ignored – lost in political disputes over prescription charges, the role of private medicine and the pay levels of the staff. By 1970 the NHS was known as the largest civilian organisation in the western world, and prey to all the difficulties that centralised bureaucracies are heir to. Twenty years later, little fundamentally seems to have changed in the management of the NHS even though the technology and possibilities for health care have developed enormously.

There are still no means of identifying in any systematic way what the health needs of the population in any particular area are, let alone deciding what needs to be done about them and what resources are required. For instance, basic indicators of mortality or morbidity are simply not available on a local basis. By contrast, twenty years ago the US Center for Health Statistics and Statistics Canada provided detailed demographic and mortality statistics for every county. Counties in the United States are often much smaller than in the United Kingdom, many having populations of five thousand or less. In fact NHS resources have been allocated largely on the basis of what was spent in the previous year, with little attempt to determine whether last year's budget made sense. As a result there can be no real confidence that variations in funding between areas accurately reflect the health care needs of the population involved.

In addition, the NHS still concentrates on providing increasingly sophisticated and expensive treatment and not enough on improving health. However, the greatest potential for improving health – as opposed to health care – is not to be found in increasing the number of doctors, nurses or hospital beds, but rather in what people can be taught and motivated to do for themselves. Thus a study of seven thousand residents of Alameda County, California showed that at age forty-five men and women who followed six of the following health practices had an average life expectancy seven to eleven years longer, respectively, than those individuals who followed fewer than four of them: eating regularly and not between meals, eating breakfast, sleeping seven to eight hours each night, keeping a normal weight, refraining from smoking, drinking moderately and exercising regularly. Failure to observe such a daily regimen apparently had a greater bearing on morbidity and mortality than all the influences of medicine. Yet the impact of the NHS on personal behaviour of this type is very limited.

The problems have been compounded by the fact that practising doctors do not regard themselves as in any way part of the management of the service – although their actions effectively determine the resources that are needed; and without their support no change can be introduced successfully in the way patients are treated or resources deployed. The situation is further complicated by the generally low esteem in which doctors hold administrators (or managers) and administrators hold themselves.

As a result money is often wasted. Concentration on hospital treatment rather than keeping people well, unnecessary admissions and excessive lengths of stay once patients are admitted to hospital, failure to make the best use of doctors' training and skills, and poor management of nursing and hotel services (which account for almost 40 per cent of the cost of running a hospital) all mean that scarce resources are not being used to the best advantage. The NHS budgeting system makes matters worse. There is no positive incentive for people to conserve resources: indeed 'underspending', as it was known, is penalised and most of the planning effort concentrates on the distribution of the additional funds available.

Intense professional jealousies have not helped. In the 1960s the stream of government-sponsored reports on individual professions in health and social services – for example, nursing, scientific and technical staff, social services, pharmacy, building and engineering, medical administrators – only served to increase professional loyalties at the expense of loyalty to patients and to the service. Every report looked at the problem largely through the eyes of the profession involved and was particularly concerned with considerations of organisation and career structure. In almost every case the diagnosis of what was wrong with the present arrangements and how patients were suffering as a result was either sketchy or non-existent, as was the attempt to define the benefits for patients (as opposed to staff) that would result from the changes proposed. To describe the NHS as a service in the accepted sense of the term is a misnomer; it remains a sometimes uneasy coalition of thirty or more proudly independent and mutually suspicious professions.

The fundamental nature of the basic dilemma facing government is evident: the very same problems that afflict the NHS today were precisely those that were apparent twenty years ago, before the 1974 reorganisation.

Lessons from 1974

Successive structural changes of the last two decades have failed to achieve their objectives. Just two years after the 1974 changes there were obvious symptoms of some basic problems in the reorganised health service. Members (or non-executive directors) of Area and Regional Health Authorities, Family Practitioner Committees and Community Health Councils were still searching for a useful role. Community Health Councils risked turning into complaints bureaux; and the quality of their secretariat varied widely. Family Practitioner Committees were largely confined to handling disciplinary cases, and appeared to have only a limited policy-making role.

Then, as now, labour problems in what is one of the last bastions of trade union power in Britain, the dispirited air of senior administrators and preoccupation with internal organisational questions were persuasive indicators of poor morale; while the 1974 reorganisation spawned an elaborate network of advisory committees, statutory authorities and management levels. The result was a massive bureaucratic problem.

The complex medical committee structure meant that in some areas as many as one doctor in three was a member of some committee or team, taking up a substantial amount of their time, while advisory committees and working parties proliferated – for example, no fewer than forty-one different official groups were involved to some extent in manpower planning within the NHS. There was widespread cynicism about the value of health and social services authorities sharing the same boundaries, and a fairly general feeling that the quality of local authority members of health authorities was not particularly impressive: apart from other considerations, their attendance record was often poor.

Just as these symptoms tended to reinforce each other, so also their underlying causes were interrelated. Six main ones stood out in a review carried out by the author for submission to the Royal Commission enquiring into the future of the NHS in the mid 1970s. Most important, there were insufficient funds to meet the open-ended demands placed on the service: per capita expenditure on health care in the United Kingdom was then running at less than a third of the United States level. One result was that the NHS had fewer doctors and nurses, paid them less than other countries where British doctors and nurses could practise, and relied heavily on overseas doctors for junior hospital staff.

In addition the statutory framework on which the 1974 management arrangements was based represented, perhaps inevitably, a compromise between those who wanted health and social services under local government and those who wanted to see part, at least, of the social services (residential care, home helps, meals on wheels) incorporated into the NHS. The existence of areas and districts introduced immense complications and added costs. There was excessive concentration on the organisation structure and a failure to introduce complementary planning, budgeting and information systems. A planning and control system had been developed, tested and refined in four different areas and the necessary manuals written. Further development was certainly needed – comprehensive health planning had nowhere been done successfully; but physicians were enthusiastic about the approach. Yet nothing happened in nearly three years, other than the production of a series of drafts for consultation, each more complex than the last.

In other words the planning systems that were vital to the functioning of the new organisation were not in place. So delegation was impossible, without in effect abdication of responsibility for the way public funds were spent.

There was no positive incentive among managers in the health service to save money; yet the dramatic improvement in productivity during the three-day week and national strikes (for example, of laundry workers) demonstrated that there was ample scope for reducing costs. On the other hand, removing – or even transferring – senior staff who had failed to perform adequately was notoriously difficult, if not impossible.

There continued to be excessive concern for special interests at the expense of the NHS as a whole. Fewer than one job in a hundred in the NHS was directly affected by reorganisation, in that the day-to-day nature of the job or its organisation relationship changed. Yet the reorganisation of the NHS was often handled as if the objective was to keep all the different professions, trade unions and pressure groups involved happy (or at least quiet) rather than improve care for patients. Thus, the forty-strong NHS Reorganisation Steering Committee contained only eight who did not have a professional axe to grind. And since ministers wanted all the conflicting interests kept on board, it was hardly surprising that the result smacked of the lowest common denominator. The NHS Staff Commission insisted on holding national competitions for senior posts in the new structure to give everyone a chance – rather than asking the authorities to select from the staff already available locally within the service. This decision caused considerable delay and brought few real benefits:

- competent people had to apply for their own jobs, causing immense anxiety and disruption at a time when all energies should have been concentrated on making the new organisation work
- delay was inevitable while the national competitions were organised, jobs advertised, shortlists prepared, selection committees held, etc.
- in the event, most posts were filled by the local people anyway, prompting observers to suggest that the whole elaborate process was a charade – if not a farce. And little new blood came into the management of the service from industry as might have been hoped. But reorganisation resulted in massive increases in salary for existing staff, almost regardless of their technical competence to do the job
- district boundaries were often drawn to ensure the maximum number of districts (and thus senior jobs), rather than the effective management of the service – not surprisingly, since those involved in proposing district boundaries expected to be filling the posts involved.

Finally there was an absence of effective leadership. Apart from the rapid turnover among senior ministers, the outgoing Conservative government did little to 'sell' the 1974 reorganisation, either to the general public or, more important, to the staff and professions involved. And the incoming Labour government made no secret of their lack of enthusiasm for the statutory framework or the management arrangements. Worse, the absence of effective leadership meant that there was no coherent view at the national level of where the NHS was going, or how the service was going to obtain the funds needed to keep pace with escalating demand and pressure to improve the pay of non-medical and nursing staff. This failure was widely recognised in the service itself and undermined the confidence of those working in it.

The reader will recognise many of these twenty-year-old problems in the NHS of today. There are signs that the general public is no longer as satisfied as it once was with an institution that was widely thought to be the envy of our competitors. By 1990 only Americans, Italians and Spaniards were less satisfied with their existing health care system than Britons. Fewer than one in three people in the UK were satisfied, according to the OECD, compared with over half in Canada – but only around one in ten in the United States. Clearly we must learn from the mistakes of the past.

A better prospect

Two decades and three reorganisations after the author wrote *Realising the Promise of a National Health Service*, the underlying contradictions within the NHS remain: world-class health care free at the point of consumption costs more than the British taxpayer is apparently prepared to afford. And a centrally planned and managed health care delivery system cannot make up the difference; if anything, its waste and inefficiency make matters worse. While the government's health targets imply substantial scope for improvements in the nation's health by the turn of the century by preventive measures: for example, halving the rate of conception among young women; a 40 per cent reduction in the death rate of people under sixty-five from coronary heart disease and strokes; a third reduction in the death rate from domestic accidents among children and those over sixty-five; a 25 per cent fall in the death rate from breast cancer among those invited for screening and a reduction of 20 per cent in the incidence of invasive cervical cancer.

It would be wrong to imply that there has been no progress in addressing some elements of the fundamental health care dilemma

facing Britain. Many more people recognise that they must contribute towards maintaining their own health and the cost of
treatment should they fall ill. Some 11 per cent of the population
is now covered by private health insurance, compared with 4 per
cent twenty years ago. There has been a significant expansion in
the provision of private health care as well. Today there are around
135 thousand acute hospital beds and places in private nursing
homes, compared with twenty-five thousand in 1971. Efforts are
under way to break down the highly-centralised and bureaucratic
management of the NHS. The new organisational distinction
between purchasers (health authorities) and providers of health
care (trusts and GPs) has begun to clarify their respective roles
and creates at least the possibility of an internal market for health
care. This, eventually, will lead to a more rational distribution of
specialist facilities and less waste: under the old regime it was
difficult, especially in London, to prevent duplication of under-
utilised specialist resources and services (such as renal transplant
surgery).

But the underlying tensions, and many of the old problems,
remain. Eric Caines, former Director of NHS Personnel, has
stated that 'the NHS has a low-pay, low-motivation, low-per-
formance culture', where the present job could be done with 20
per cent fewer resources. There is *still* very little expenditure on
prevention of illness: total annual expenditure on health promotion
clinics amounts to less than £3 for every member of the population;
and there remain very wide variations in almost all aspects of
expenditure. For instance, the cost of prescribed drugs varies from
£60 a person in one authority to little more than £30 – a fairly
typical range in authority performance. There seems to be little
match between patterns of need for primary care and the way in
which family doctors and nurses are deployed.

There are major systems weaknesses as well. As the Audit Commission puts it in a recent (1993) report: 'With the health of the
population as its primary objective, information on health status,
treatment outcome and effectiveness has become fundamental.
Yet information in these areas has traditionally been poorly
developed in the NHS.' In other words, annual expenditure of
some £1,500 a household is being administered – rather than
managed in the legitimate expectation that it is being spent economically, efficiently and effectively. Assessing the quality of health
care and the outcome of treatment is not the only problem when

it comes to the application of market forces. Hospitals' prices vary widely; but costing systems are still relatively crude, and the figures quoted seem to qualified observers unlikely to be a true reflection of providers' costs in many cases. The commission commented that: 'Purchasers have so far judged that prices are not a good basis on which to consider switching between providers. Many purchasers have little real choice of providers, information on what is or could be provided is poor, and the process of contracting is both complex and unfamiliar.'

If price, cost, quality and outcome signals are all unreliable it is very difficult to see how a market can operate efficiently. Small wonder, then, that the Institute of Health Service Administration and the Royal College of Nursing reported (also in 1993) that the NHS spending decisions are 'complex, crude, poorly understood outside a small group of practitioners, interpreted by public relations experts to defend Government sensitivities and inadequately debated'.

In short, market forces may not be equal to the task of diffusing the basic tensions that need to be managed within the NHS. So it may be necessary for Parliament to consider steps to generate additional funds for health care, limit unnecessary demand for services and further streamline the management structure.

Raising money

The political consequences of leaving it to the management of the NHS to bridge the gap between public expectations and what can be afforded are likely to be increasingly unattractive. It seems clear that there must be a significant increase in funds available to the NHS if the service is to be able to continue to meet international standards – even if expenditure on the NHS rose by a third, spending per capita would not be excessive by the standards of other western European countries. But it seems equally clear that raising additional funds through direct taxation is going to be impossible – public expenditure is already too high and there are no volunteers for the significant cuts that would be needed to accommodate £10 billion of extra NHS spending.

In such circumstances ministers may wish to syndicate their political risks with local government. Particularly if local authorities were to undertake responsibility for purchasing primary and continuing health care for the frail elderly, it should be possible to supplement the available NHS resources from the proceeds of the local council tax. So each responsible authority would continue to receive an allowance for every resident based on the total available NHS funds and adjusted for demographic and socio-economic differences – another twenty-year-old idea whose time has finally come. It would then be up to the local community to decide whether, and if so to what extent, they wanted to supplement the allowance from Parliament from their own local resources. Provided, of course, that charge capping was removed.

In addition, some health services could be financed out of individuals' health insurance premiums. For instance, central government might fund standard primary, preventive, emergency and longer-term care directly out of taxation, while insurance premiums could meet the cost of non-urgent or elective hospital care, such as cosmetic surgery, hip replacements and terminal care. After all, the OECD figures show that the public share of our health expenditure is higher, at 83 per cent, than in any other developed country except Sweden; a more normal figure was in the range 70–75 per cent, and it was under 45 per cent in the United States.

Limiting unnecessary demand

Though they are often confused, there is a distinction between the need for health care and demand for it. Repeated studies have shown that the NHS treats only a very small proportion of those who have symptoms requiring medical treatment. At the other extreme, the 'worried well' account for a disproportionate share of demand for care – general practitioners regularly suggest that as many as half those visiting their clinics do not need medical care. Unnecessary demand for care is generated in other ways as well – by doctors referring and/or admitting patients to hospitals who do not need to be there, unduly complex or defensive diagnostic procedures, and by keeping patients for longer than their condition warrants (although, overall, the NHS compares favourably in this regard with other countries). And in the strictest sense of the term, excessive smoking, drug or alcohol abuse generates unnecessary need for care.

With resources under strain, it is clearly essential to ensure that, as far as possible, NHS care is focused on those who need it most. This might well require:

- out-of-pocket expenditure for visits to GPs to deter the 'worried well'. The evidence from the United States suggests that casual visits to clinics or hospitals are substantially reduced by imposing *any* significant out-of-pocket expenses, even if the cost can subsequently be recovered from insurance. The latest American health care reforms envisage a charge of $10 for every visit to a doctor. For example, doctor office visits to a Stanford University clinic fell by nearly 25 per cent when patients (who previously had not had to make any out-of-pocket payments) were asked to meet 25 per cent of the normal cost direct
- flat-rate payments to general practitioners to cover the costs of all health care treatment including hospital care. This was the basic approach incorporated into the Health Maintenance Organisation (HMO) movement in the United States and is the philosophy behind the move towards GP Fundholders in Britain. The HMO (formed by a group of physicians) enrols patients and, for a flat annual fee, provides them with all the health care they need. What is 'necessary' is determined by the physician involved, who thus has an incentive to treat patients as economically as possible – if total expenditure exceeds the annual fee, the physician makes up the difference; and any surplus becomes profit for the HMO. The benefits of widespread application of the HMO approach in the UK could be substantial. There could be a market reduction in the number of acute hospital beds needed (as the Audit Commission has pointed out). But at present no more than a quarter of general practitioners in any given authority manage their own budgets (the so-called Fundholders). Usually the figure is very much smaller than this
- private insurance to cover the cost of prescriptions for all except children and those on income support. At present the public purse bears a higher proportion of the costs of prescribed medicines in Britain (around 85 per cent) than in any other EC country apart from Luxembourg; the average figure for the rest of the Community in 1989 was 63 per cent – and in the United States it was under 10 per cent

- personal incentives to encourage behaviour likely to promote continuing good health. A medical version of the 'no claims bonus' may be needed, with reductions in health insurance premiums for those who have regular check-ups, do not smoke, take regular exercise and so forth. This seems a rather more promising approach than denying treatment to those who obviously need it because of their unhealthy lifestyle.

Finally market forces must have the room to work. There is an obvious danger that the reforms will be stifled at birth by the existing and redoubtable NHS bureaucracy.

Streamlining the structure

Just as in the United States, a managed market system is evolving in Britain. Across the Atlantic the problem was, and is, one of escalating costs. The world's richest nation can no longer afford universally available high technology medicine; the free market is effectively out of control. Here, on the other hand, policymakers must deal with the after-effects of over forty years of central planning which, however enlightened, has resulted in gross inefficiencies. But the planners and their bureaucracies will not go 'quietly into the night', as it were. And too much management and not enough market could result in the worst of both worlds.

A bewildering array of publicly-financed organisations is responsible in one way or another for different aspects of the management of the National Health Service: Regional, District and Family Health Services Authorities, Community Health Councils, Local Authority Social Services Departments, not to mention the semi-autonomous NHS Trusts that are increasingly responsible for providing health care. The whole system (if that is the correct term) is supervised by the Department of Health and a separate management executive.

The situation is, if anything, more complex than it was in the days of central planning, before market forces were introduced to secure a less wasteful allocation of scarce resources. The questions posed twenty years ago in the aftermath of the 1974 reorganisation are even more relevant today: should the Secretary of State for Health continue to be accountable to Parliament for every detail of the delivery of health care, as well as for national health policy?

Are Regional Health Authorities necessary? Should District and Family Health Services Authorities be merged? Should local authorities play a greater role in purchasing health care for local residents, complementing their role with respect to care in the community?

There is a strong case for further streamlining the management structure. The National Health Service should be set up as an independent agency, entirely separate from the Civil Service; Parliament and ministers could safely rely on the professions, the Audit Commission and the media to monitor its performance and draw any shortcomings to their attention and that of the public. The service should have its own board of expert and independent non-executive directors, appointed for a single fixed term of, say, five years.

Once the bulk of the NHS hospitals is managed by trusts and most general practitioners are Fundholders, the trend towards merging District and Family Health Services Authorities could, and should, accelerate. Eventually, local authorities could take over the role of purchasing primary and general hospital care, complementing their new role in securing community care for local people. But specialist (or tertiary) hospital care will always need to be planned nationally if unnecessary duplication of scarce resources is to be avoided.

In any case, health authorities must be in a position to insist that the management of the new NHS Trusts with whom they contract pay due attention to the improvement opportunities identified by the Audit Commission. It is simply not acceptable that trusts should vary to any great extent in how well they use the public funds available to them; still less should we be willing to condone significant variations in the quality of the care they provide. Trusts should explain publicly what they are doing to follow up the opportunities that the Audit Commission has identified. Before any contracts are placed, health authorities should be satisfied that trust managers have followed up each and every Audit Commission report, and that its services meet (and preferably exceed) the agreed performance benchmarks. National league tables of trust performance should be published at least annually. The directors and management of those trusts that persistently fail to improve should be replaced. Forty years of inward-looking bureaucracy is, surely, enough.

Finally, Regional Health Authorities should disappear as soon as possible. They have evidently not been particularly successful in providing a buffer between ministers and politically embarrassing situations in local hospitals and trusts. Nor have they been able to prevent waste and inefficiency over many years, on a scale that can reasonably be described as scandalous. In any event they are likely to be rendered progressively redundant by a combination of an independent National Health Service, a clear distinction between the roles of purchasers and providers, and a greater role in purchasing and planning health care for local authorities.

Between 1980 and 1990 the average expectation of life improved by around two years (slightly less for women and more for men). Meanwhile annual expenditure increased in real terms by around £340 a household. So the tensions ignored by the visionaries who created the National Health Service are not going to surrender to a combination of technology, investment and market forces. Public expectations are too high, potential demand is too great and the available resources are too limited. Rather, the twenty-year-old challenges must be managed: how to moderate the expectations of patients and their families; how to contain demand while meeting genuine need for health care; how to generate more money from a general public averse to paying higher taxes; and how to galvanise the management of the service to make the improvements that are plainly possible.

Pretending that these challenges have never existed or have gone away will not make it any easier to meet them successfully. Confronting the health care dilemma, and the ingrained prejudices resulting from decades of loose political rhetoric, will be one of the elements of any blueprint for the new era. This will also need to include a much broader understanding of the importance of investing in the nation's future. This is the theme that Part II now takes up.

PART II

A NATION OF INVESTORS

INTENSIFIED COMPETITION from the Far East, elsewhere within the European Community and ultimately central Europe will require a change in national attitudes. In place of a culture of speculation in property and spending we will need to become a nation of savers and investors in our collective futures.

This shift entails reversing a well-established trend. From 1985 consumer spending in Britain has taken a steadily greater share of our national income, rising from 60 per cent of Gross Domestic Product in 1980 to over 66 per cent in 1993. This is in marked contrast with Germany and Japan where consumer spending has been more or less stable at around 57–59 per cent of GDP. In other words Britain's consumers are spending over £40 billion a year – or £35 a week for the average household – more than their German or Japanese counterparts.

What we spend they save and invest. As a result a massive investment gap has opened up, constituting a serious competitive handicap for the economy as a whole. The National Institute of Economic and Social Research estimates that British industry has to make do with machines that are, on average, seven years older than those of their United States and French competitors, nine years older than those to be found in a typical German factory, and no less than fourteen years older than the equipment in Japanese factories. There is only so much that the British genius for invention and improvisation can be expected to make good.

Creating a savings culture – for that is what is needed in the new era – will be difficult. It will entail exorcising inflation from our economy, as well as a different attitude to housing and home ownership. It will also be necessary to eliminate waste in the public services in order to finance the necessary investment in their futures.

Saving and investment are not ends in themselves. They are essential to our ability to compete internationally. We need to invest in our human capital in particular. Without world-class education, as well as a well-motivated work-force equipped with world-class skills, Britain's manufacturers stand little chance of closing the trade gap, however 'competitive' sterling may become. We will never be able to compete with the economies of the Far East in terms of costs; we must have the technology and skills to compete on the basis of quality and value with our competitors within the developed world.

But human capital and technology will not be enough. As is daily more evident, Britain has the worst transport infrastructure in northern Europe with an out-of-date rail and inadequate motorway network each pointing in the wrong direction. We also have a serious emerging problem in our social infrastructure: once an urban underclass becomes established the situation is extraordinarily difficult to reverse, as experience in north America and parts of south London bear all too evident witness.

Part II addresses each of these themes in turn.

Even before I became a director of Tarmac, the role of housing in the British economy had long held a particular fascination for me – perhaps because it struck me as being unsustainable for one of the most highly-paid public servants in Britain to be able to make more money sitting on a house in Berkshire than working. In addition, about a quarter of all homes in Britain are in one form of public ownership or another; so the Audit Commission was directly concerned with how some four million dwellings were managed and maintained. This led me to give a series of keynote speeches to the Institute of Housing Annual Conferences.

While at the CBI Douglas MacWilliams and Andrew Sentance helped me understand the nature of the damaging link between inflation and housing; and the dangers in letting house-price inflation act as a substitute for personal savings came into sharper focus. Another CBI task force in which I was involved studied the steps needed to broaden and deepen individual share ownership; their report led to the formation of Proshare, an organisation set up to encourage individuals to hold shares in publicly-quoted companies.

6
Inflation, Housing and Saving

Inflation in house prices is no substitute for saving, but a cancer gnawing away at the competitiveness of our economy. The celebrations at Britain's forced withdrawal from the Exchange Rate Mechanism may turn out to be premature.

'You should live your life as though you will die tomorrow; and farm your land as though you will live for ever.' So runs the Norfolk saying. It could as well apply to businesses and the nation as a whole. Sadly inflation and the expectation of inflation have caused us to be prepared to mortgage the future rather than invest in it. Literally as well as figuratively. The essential first step towards encouraging saving and investment must be to exorcise inflation from our economy. When, in the aftermath of yet another devaluation of sterling, the commentators pronounce that we have managed to shake off our seeming addiction to inflation, it is wise to be cautious. The disease is of long standing and rooted deep in our society; it will not remain quiescent for long. That is why the present window of opportunity must not be missed. The low levels of inflation that have been achieved at such cost provide an opportunity to rebalance the economy – to spend less and save and invest more. This will not be before time.

Exorcising inflation

Inflation has been described as a cancer that for years has been gnawing away at the international competitiveness of our economy: every point of inflation costs business in the order of £5 billion a year. Although the inflationary problem is of long standing and regularly identified by politicians and business leaders as 'public enemy number one', there has been no authoritative academic study of why inflation matters, or why Britain's record has been so poor. So four years ago the CBI's council asked its well-regarded economic staff to study the underlying causes of the UK's disappointing performance in controlling inflation. The conclusions are even more important now, in the aftermath of the removal of the sheet anchor of the UK's counter-inflationary policy, ERM membership; and in light of what appears to be a widespread conviction in the public sector that the costs of containing inflation are simply not worth the pain involved in terms of wage increases forgone. Even though millions of people have already suffered grievously as UK price inflation has been forced back into line with that of our principal competitors, there is a risk that we will give up the battle just as we are in sight of winning the war.

UK consumer price inflation averaged 8 per cent between 1960 and 1990, compared to 3.5 per cent for our principal competitor (and largest single export market) West Germany. Over this period German inflation fluctuated between a peak of 7 per cent in 1974 and price stability in 1986; whereas our rate fluctuated within a range three times as great. Inflation-induced uncertainty has important economic effects. It diverts people from the creation of wealth to the need to protect against inflation. As the former Governor of the Bank of England, Robin Leigh Pemberton, put it:

> The higher the inflation rate the less stable it is likely to be; and the less stable the inflation rate, the greater the uncertainty that is generated. The upshot is that contracts are written, and behaviour is modified, to minimise the effects of the uncertainty. In other words, we find ourselves worrying about how to protect wealth, rather than how to create it.
> Zero inflation is likely to be more stable and credible than any other level – and more consistent with a society where contracts mean what they say and the financial system supports enterprise.

One particularly important result of the distortion created by high inflation in the UK has been to focus people's attention on the housing market as a means of protecting the value of personal wealth. For companies, the uncertainty created by inflation reinforces the concern for short-run results at the expense of longer-term growth. The more uncertain the future the more expensive it will be to borrow money, and the shorter the time in which individuals and companies will be looking to see a return on their investment. Typically, British companies will not contemplate an investment that will not be completely paid back in four years; an absurdly ambitious target in almost any technology-intensive industry.

As if these were not problems enough, high inflation means higher nominal interest rates. While, theoretically, this should not affect investment decisions if the inflation-adjusted cost of capital does not change, the reality is somewhat different, particularly for smaller companies who do not want (or are not allowed by their banks) to increase their borrowings.

Moreover the tax system is not fully indexed. Depreciation allowances are calculated in money terms and corporate tax liabilities are not adjusted for stock appreciation. As a result the effective average corporate tax rate will be some three percentage points higher with inflation at 8 per cent than at 4 per cent. This difference alone would add some £2.5 billion to the annual corporate tax bill. Differential inflation also means an increasing cost disadvantage against a lower inflation economy, directly and indirectly via a weakening currency. The impact of costs in the UK rising 5 per cent faster than in West Germany would be to eliminate a 10 per cent profit margin on sales in two years and to translate this into a 10 per cent loss in four years. The consequences of this are felt particularly by manufacturers exposed to international trade. If the exchange rate does not reflect differences in inflation (as happened in the early 1980s) the effects can be catastrophic as exporters' profit margins are wiped out.

Business, therefore, has a very strong interest in low inflation. It is no coincidence that the nadir of the fortunes of Britain's manufacturers coincided with our worst relative inflation performance – in the 1970s and early 1980s. Though there are costs attached to achieving low inflation, these do not appear to have damaged the longer-term growth prospects in countries such as Germany, Japan and Switzerland. The underlying rate of inflation in the United Kingdom come down from the excessive levels of the 1970s back into line with our competitors. By late 1993 it was running at under 3 per cent per annum. This achievement does no more than bring us down to French and German levels. West Germany has consistently been one of the lowest inflation countries in the world; but during the 1980s the Franco-German inflation differential reduced to under one percentage point in 1990, from eight points in 1980. Our target must be to match the best of our European competitors. This means keeping our inflation rate in the range 0–3 per cent. Alan Greenspan, Governor of the United States Federal Reserve, has suggested that 'for all practical purposes, price stability means that expected changes in the average price level are small enough and gradual enough that they do not materially enter business and household financial decisions'.

This has never been the case in Britain since 1945. And it will not be possible if we continue our habit of devaluing the currency rather than facing the economic realities of life. The celebrations at Britain's forced withdrawal from the Exchange Rate Mechanism may turn out to be premature.

The CBI study concluded that what went wrong in the late 1980s was the rate of growth of domestic demand, rather than the performance of British business. Between 1984 and 1988 consumer spending grew more than twice as fast as the sustainable growth in output. Personal borrowing increased by two-thirds between 1984 and 1988 in real terms with the bulk of the increase made up of loans for house purchase (these account for around 80 per cent of total personal sector borrowing). At the beginning of the decade, on average personal debt amounted to 49 per cent of the borrowers' annual income; ten years later the figure was over 107 per cent.

Even aside from these problems, the government put less weight than our major competitors on securing low inflation as a policy objective. Too often policy decisions were taken which accommodated inflationary pressures rather than resisted them:

- borrowing was allowed to grow at an unsustainable rate without corrective action. In particular, interest rates were cut in early 1988 when they should have been raised
- the exchange rate was allowed to fall sharply in 1985–6, when unit costs were rising more rapidly than our competitors and the UK did not join the Exchange Rate Mechanism
- privatisation issues and sales of council houses at below their true market value, combined with personal tax cuts in every Budget from 1982 to 1989 and with particularly large reductions in 1988, fuelled expectations of rising living standards that did not have to be earned
- inflationary 'own-goals' resulted from the process of raising

nationalised industry prices, both prior to and after privatisation of electricity in particular and the introduction of the community charge as part of the reform of local government finance.

By contrast, in France in the mid 1980s the need to drive down inflation overrode other policy priorities. The OECD reported in 1989:

Over and above the role played by the rise in unemployment and the interaction between wage and price trends, the roots of the disinflation process lie in the changes in the stance of economic policy, both in France and in the rest of the OECD area. In France, the restrictive thrust given to demand management policy as of March 1983 influenced the labour and goods markets, and so affected wage and price developments. Contributing further to this movement were France's decisions with regard to Exchange Rate policy. The desire to keep the franc in the European Monetary System (EMS), where parity adjustments occasioned by the various realignments have been minimised, helped to increase the effectiveness of anti-inflationary policy by reducing inflationary expectations and limiting imported inflation.

Also, the policy of wage stringency adopted in the public sector no doubt made it easier for private sector wage earners to agree to wage concessions. From 1983 on, the practice of taking official inflation expectations into account in wage settlements became more common, also helping to slow wage costs. Lastly, the policy of controlling the prices of private services had a moderating effect on inflation from 1983 to 1985, but at the expense of growing distortions.

Unfortunately inflationary expectations appear more deeply embedded and are generally higher in the UK than in other OECD countries. A decade of seeking to raise the skills and motivation of the long-term unemployed, decentralisation of pay bargaining and the improvement in manufacturing productivity had not altered attitudes sufficiently.

Examples of this 'inflationary psychology' can be seen in the attention paid to rises in the cost of living in pay negotiations, as employees seek to preserve living standards; and the indexation of benefits and tax reliefs. The commercial world is also not immune from such arrangements. Most commercial rent agreements cannot be revised downwards and there is an inflationary bias in the system by which new rents are set at the highest level recently achieved in the locality. One way or another, most recently privatised utilities have their price linked to the RPI by their regulators. The Uniform Business Rate is also linked to the RPI.

Once again the contrast with attitudes in Germany and, more recently, France is instructive. Not only is a strong counter-inflationary psychology firmly established in Germany, but indexation in labour contracts is actually illegal. By contrast, in Britain public and union reaction to the government's determination to prevent public sector wages fuelling inflation again suggests that there is a long way still to go to convince the British public that the price of low inflation is worth paying: pay freezes, deferrals of pay settlements, even pay cuts. By late 1993 as many as one manufacturing settlement in four, and one in six in the services sector had been deferred for up to twelve months. However, freezing pay makes no sense in isolation. It simply builds up pay pressures in the future, as successive governments discovered in the various bouts of pay policy in the 1970s. Rather, the emphasis should be on securing stable payroll costs. But this will only be sustainable if improvements in productivity and profits are shared with employees through performance payments and wider share ownership. Such an approach is already in place in many companies. It will need to become the rule rather than the exception, in the public as well as the private sectors, in services as well as in manufacturing, and at all levels from the boardroom to the shop-floor, if inflation is to be truly exorcised from the British economy.

Low inflation will bring with it important benefits, besides making it possible for UK companies to compete more effectively. It will lead to changed attitudes both to housing and to saving by individuals, companies and the government.

Cooling the housing market

Almost 70 per cent of British families live in their own home; a higher figure than in almost any other developed country. The attraction of home ownership in times of high inflation has been considerable. Housing has been an excellent hedge against inflation in the past; during the 1980s those fortunate enough to be already on the housing ladder could safely ignore the need to save: inflation in house prices was doing their saving for them. The buyer of an average price new home in January 1980 would have paid around £23 thousand and could expect to sell it for a profit of some £55 thousand in December 1990, with no tax on the gain. Small wonder that the average family was only saving around £1,400 a year in 1990.

Now, however, the situation has gone into reverse. By late 1993 the house price index was 10 per cent below its 1989 peak. A home owner who had bought a typical new home in January 1990 would be looking at a loss of £5,500 by the end of 1993 – the equivalent of over two years' savings. In June that year over three hundred thousand people with mortgages were more than six months behind with their payments. One in ten home owners were effectively trapped with mortgages for a greater amount than their house was worth.

Decline in housing values is not without precedent. Indeed it seems to be characteristic of low-inflation economies; in West Germany average house prices fell by over 40 per cent in real terms during the 1980s, and in France they fell by a third. But the turn-round has come as a very considerable and unpleasant shock to home owners in Britain. It has prompted calls for action to treat this symptom of the shift from high to low inflation and a reappraisal of the economic benefits of home ownership.

In fact the immediate cause of inflation in house prices was not a shortage – the usual cause of price increases in any market. Throughout the 1980s there were more properties vacant than homeless families. Neither did the cost of new building account for the increase in the average price of new houses between 1985 and 1990: the average construction output price index rose by only 47 per cent during this period. In any case new homes accounted for only one purchase in seven during the boom years of the late 1980s.

Rather, the escalation in house prices during the 1980s was due to a combination of the artificial restrictions on the availability (and thus price) of building land resulting from the planning system, and a willingness of home owners to treat housing as a form of speculation – as a one-way bet on which no one could lose. Exactly the same attitudes were evident in other markets too, such as antiques, fine art and rare stamps.

However, as interest rates and fear of unemployment rose in the late 1980s, speculative demand for housing vanished. The bubble burst, with effects on the national economy and consumer confidence which are only now becoming apparent. Most of the national news is written or broadcast by people living in the south-east; and in the early 1990s housing values fell in money terms in London and the south-east for the first time in the memory of almost all householders. (During the 1970s real housing values fell, but the impact was masked by inflation.) Not unnaturally, the commentators regarded their personal experience as representative of the situation across the nation as a whole, even though it has generally been the case in recent years that 'the further you go from London, the better things look'. In fact house prices in Scotland, Northern Ireland and the north of England rose between 1989 and the middle of 1982; and they were more or less stable in Wales and the Midlands. But in London, East Anglia and the south prices fell by about 20 per cent on average. As a result a national mood of gloom and despondency radiated from London, and by the end of 1992 had reached virtually every part of the United Kingdom.

The aftermath of the housing boom is therefore both a serious loss of consumer confidence and an inadequate base of personal savings. Between 1982 and 1988 personal savings as a proportion of disposable income fell from 11.2 to 5.6 per cent – the low point was 5.4 per cent in the third quarter of 1988. While the international comparisons show that during the 1980s personal savings as a proportion of GDP in the UK accounted for nearly two points less than in West Germany; three and a half points less than USA, over four points less than France; and a staggering twelve points less than Japan. Each point represents over £5 billion a year that is saved and invested in other developed economies and spent in Britain – often on imported goods, as the car park in any suburban shopping centre will demonstrate.

The problem posed by inadequate savings will increase as the world moves from an era of capital surplus to one of capital shortage. The demands for capital from the former Soviet Union and eastern Europe – not to mention the Pacific Rim, India and Saudi Arabia – coincide with a likely fall in the ability of the Japanese economy to generate savings on the scale of the past; while the US appetite for Japanese capital seems likely to continue unabated. The implications for the UK are serious. We will not achieve the economic prosperity that we need and want in the 1990s without investment. And to pay for that investment we need again to become a nation of savers. When economists talk about savings, they are referring to *net* savings minus borrowing. And, compared with the rest of the world, where we are out of line in the UK is not in our direct saving but in our borrowing. Our investments in building societies, bank deposit accounts and pension plans bring the UK level of savings pretty well into line with the international average. But whereas private individuals in the UK borrowed an amount worth 15 per cent of their personal disposable income last year, in France and Germany borrowing averages only half as much as this.

Why do we borrow so much? The answer is clear. It is a myth that credit cards are mainly responsible. On the whole, British people use credit cards as a means of payment, not as a means of borrowing. Credit card borrowing accounts for only some 2 per cent of total personal borrowing in the UK. The bulk of the borrowing is ostensibly for house purchase; about half of that was taken out and spent on other items, the so-called phenomenon of 'equity withdrawal'.

So through its effect on consumer confidence and borrowing, and hence on financing the growth of consumer demand, housing is right at the centre of the twin economic issues of inflation and a balance of payments deficit. And it is these twin problems that caused the government to raise interest rates from $7\frac{1}{2}$ per cent in May 1988 to 15 per cent in October 1989; while over the same period producer price inflation rose from around $4\frac{1}{2}$ per cent to a little over 6 per cent.

There are two other ways in which the housing market has affected inflation. The cost of housing contributes directly to inflation through its impact on the RPI, which directly determines many benefit levels as well as acceptable price increases for electricity, telephone and water charges, and many pay settlements in the public sector – not to mention the Uniform Business Rate. On average, during 1989 and 1990 mortgage interest payments and the community charge added nearly two points to the RPI. This alone meant additional public spending of over £2 billion a year: some £650 million a year on pensions and family benefit payments in 1991 and £250 million on the Uniform Business Rate. To the extent that public sector wages are largely determined by reference to the RPI, the inclusion of housing costs probably increased the public sector pay bill by a further £1.3 billion in 1993.

Moreover, as we move into a world where economic prosperity is heavily based on the availability of skills, it becomes ever more important that people with scarce skills can move around the country to the places where these skills are needed. Yet the dearth of suitable rented accommodation makes it very difficult for people to move to take up new jobs. The private rented sector accounted for 8 per cent of housing stock in 1991 compared with 19 per cent in 1971 and 53 per cent in 1951; public sector housing had declined from 30 per cent in 1981 to 22 per cent a decade later. As a result, in the 1980s, while firms were short of labour in Surrey or Hampshire, where unemployment was often around 2 per cent, people with the necessary skills were out of work in the north or Scotland.

Addressing the Institute of Housing's Annual Conference in mid 1990, the author insisted that:

> We should stop playing Monopoly with the roofs above our heads. The basic, but essential, service of providing accommodation should not be confused with the type of speculative investment well known to the players of this game. Because of the myth that house prices are a safe hedge against inflation, people in Britain devote an immense proportion of their income to purchasing houses. If you take out a mortgage of three times your income you will end up spending 48 per cent of your pre-tax income on interest alone.
>
> If people want to spend their own money on housing, then that is their choice and it should be respected. But they should not be encouraged to do so by developing a casino mentality where they are encouraged to gamble ever more on house prices in the vain hope that it is a one-way bet.
>
> Permanent one-way bets do not exist this side of heaven. And the bigger your stake when the roulette wheel moves the other way, the more you stand to lose.
>
> The tax system should not be used to distort investment into housing rather than into other forms of assets. It is outrageous that those who buy a stake in British business through buying equities directly should receive inferior tax treatment to those speculating in the property market. If we make it more 'tax-efficient' to borrow than to save, we should not be surprised that this is precisely what has happened during the 1980s.
>
> While personal savings have fallen in the boom years, the market values of the nation's housing stock rose by perhaps £100 billion annually. But let us not forget that 'genius is a short memory and a rising market'. There is no reason in economics why housing should never decline in real value. I suspect that many people will be badly hurt in the years ahead because of unthinking acceptance of this conventional wisdom.

Unfortunately not enough people outside the conference hall were listening. By late 1992 the University of Hard Knocks had graduated over two million home owners. But the general lesson has surely been learned by home owners generally.

With low inflation, an expected surge in inter-generational bequests over the next decade and pressure on government spending, this must be the best possible moment to eliminate tax incentives designed to encourage home ownership as an appropriate vehicle for saving and investment, just as it makes no sense to provide tax incentives to encourage ownership of cars as opposed to any other consumer durable that people might wish to own. Mortgage interest relief should be phased out by the end of the century; and, when houses are sold, they should be subject to capital gains tax, as would be levied on any other asset sale. The rate of taxation on capital gains should be reduced in any event, and the annual exemptions increased to encourage people to invest in assets which increase in value, rather than deterring them from doing so.

A savings culture

Obviously it would be wrong to blame all the problems in the UK economy on the housing market. But equally, for too long, we have ignored the connection between inflation, housing and our poor savings performance. The savings gap is large. We should aim to increase personal savings by some £35 billion at today's income level. This means every employee saving an extra £130 a month. It also means a change in our national culture of borrow and spend.

It is easy to see how this developed. For at least three decades after the Second World War the relatively high personal tax regime in the UK prevented individuals from saving out of income to create capital. Capital gains tax was introduced and income derived from personal investment was additionally penalised from time to time. It is hardly surprising that tax-efficient saving through housing and pensions assumed such importance.

The same three decades saw the rapid and effective expansion of employer-promoted pension schemes which are now the norm rather than the exception they once were. Continual inflation – with only brief periods of comparative respite – has enhanced the attractions of final salary pensions which only collective schemes can provide; and their convenience only serves to reinforce their perceived advantages to employees. Pension funds grew as individual share investment declined; their influence is now dominant in the UK securities market. Other forms of pooled investment have also developed to attract personal savings, including life assurance and unit trusts. For the individual investor these provide the combined advantages of portfolio diversification and professional investment management in an easily accessible way.

There is thus formidable competition for personal savings and we are still a long way from the share-owning democracy where most people feel that they have a direct personal stake in the success of British business in general and manufacturing in particular. The relationship between profits and investment is not well understood – judging by popular reaction to the trading results of the banks and newly-privatised companies. Direct investment in company shares provides individuals and their families with a personal stake in the nation's economic future and makes them more aware of the realities of economic life. At present most voters have only the haziest understanding of the extent of corporate profitability (it is generally thought to be much greater than in fact it is); and an even hazier appreciation of the relationship between pay, profits, investment and jobs.

However, there are some formidable barriers to changing attitudes to investment so that direct share ownership becomes part of our culture. It will be necessary to secure more even tax treatment for all forms of saving. Experience in France and the United States has shown that giving a tax-free allowance for savings in equities – that is, front-end tax relief – is the most effective way of attracting long-term savings to the stock market. For example, in France the Loi Monory scheme was established in 1978 for a period of four years to provide tax deductibility for investment in shares or collective investments up to FFr6 thousand a year. This would be worth around £1,500 today. The investment had to be held for a minimum of five years and there were tax penalties for early exit. The scheme was extremely popular, with some two million investors taking advantage of it. In the United States individual retirement accounts (IRAs) were introduced in the early 1980s to encourage retirement savings. Employees could save up to $2 thousand a year with penalties for withdrawal before retirement age. The amounts saved were typically invested in shares or collective investments. They too have been an immensely popular and important form of savings – research shows that they attracted 'new' money. In mid 1985 nearly two-thirds of all shareholders (some 12 per cent of the adult population) had an IRA or similar account, and in 1986 it was estimated that they accounted for about a quarter of all personal savings.

A tax-free allowance for a limited period only, coinciding with the run-down period in mortgage interest relief – now costing the Exchequer some £4 billion a year – would serve to underline the importance of a 'save and invest' culture, in place of the old one of 'speculate and spend'. Tax relief at the basic rate could be given for direct investment of up to £5 thousand a year in ordinary shares of listed companies (including those of the company in which the taxpayer works).

It is not only private individuals who need to spend less and save and invest more for the future. The same applies to governments, which always seem to find it easier to cut capital projects rather than their day-to-day expenditure. During the annual round of ministerial discussions of future public spending plans we are invited to believe that there is no more waste to be eliminated within the public services; and the government pleads poverty as it mortgages the future. These pleas should be discounted. There is more than enough waste and inefficiency in local government and the National Health Service to finance a major expansion of investment in those aspects of the public service vital to our future in the new era.

One of the most impressive achievements of Japanese management that I saw when advising Nissan on their European investment strategy was their ability, continuously, to eliminate waste – of time, people or resources. Just-in-time inventory management systems, 'lights-out' machining centres working round the clock, often unmanned, 10 per cent annual productivity improvements, right-first-time quality, partnership sourcing philosophies, were practical realities.

The Audit Commission provided an opportunity to see whether these approaches could be applied to the public sector. The scope for improvement is great: in almost every aspect of the public service improvements of 20 per cent or more are possible without compromising service standards, just by applying proved good practice more widely. But implementing the changes has proved distressingly difficult. So much of the potential remains untapped; and waste in local government and on the NHS on a massive scale – costing perhaps as much as £10 billion a year – is still endemic. Meanwhile the rhetoric about 'cuts' continues. As Controller of the Audit Commission I oversaw studies into the economy, efficiency and effectiveness of some £25 billion of annual public expenditure and the efforts to apply the lessons nationwide.

7

Waste and the Public Finances

Waste in local government and the National Health Service is costing over £10 billion a year – sufficient to finance a doubling of public sector construction work.

'But in this world, nothing can be said to be certain except death and taxes,' wrote Benjamin Franklin to Jean-Baptiste Le Roy in November 1789 in the aftermath of the French Revolution. In reality there are other certainties in the world of political economics. In particular, it is certain that politicians and the voters enjoy spending money more than they do raising and paying taxes.

Well-attested legend has it that, late one autumn evening after school, a fourteen-year-old girl was riding her pony home through one of those villages in the Home Counties where ponies outnumber people. Suddenly a flasher appeared out of the hedgerow; the horse reared, nearly unseating the rider, who was, naturally, frightened and distressed. By the time her father had returned from his office in the City his household was in uproar – his wife was in tears with anger and frustration, his daughter hysterical.

Fortunately they lived in a close-knit community and it was clear what was needed to prevent a recurrence; street lighting must be installed in the village streets forthwith. A community action programme was launched, and within a month a protest meeting was arranged with the leader of the county council to call him to account, and to insist that street lights were installed. So great was the interest in preventing a similar outrage in future that the meeting had to be moved from the village hall to a nearby secondary school with an assembly room large enough to accommodate the crowd.

The county council leader had a torrid time, as is common on such occasions (it is said that only two events would fill the Empire Ballroom in Skegness: a Miss England contest and a meeting to protest against the closure of a local secondary school). The leader concluded that street lighting was indeed the answer and that it would be installed within six months, at a cost of £23 thousand. This would be possible by re-ordering the county's capital programme; and he assured the meeting that the necessary steps were already in hand. But before confirming the order the councillor wanted those present to be aware that the cost would fall on the parish rate, and would amount to £460 for every household.

When it came to a vote, not one person wished to proceed with a cause they had all supported when it seemed that someone else was going to pay for it. 'I have seen the enemy, and he is us,' as one of Sherman's officers is said to have remarked on returning from a reconnaissance of the Confederate lines in the closing stages of the American Civil War. He could have been talking of the prospects for victory in a war on public waste.

The anecdote illustrates the reality of public expenditure in Britain. Analysis of the trends shows that in the past thirty years public expenditure has fallen significantly in real terms on only three occasions – in 1976, 1977 and 1978. In each case the fall was accomplished by massive reductions in capital spending. Currently general public expenditure (including privatisation proceeds) is more than double the level in the mid 1960s, after taking account of inflation; in the year ended 31 March 1993 local authority expenditure amounted to nearly £3,000 per household (that is, £58 a week), a real increase of very nearly £300 per household compared with the situation five years earlier.

Meanwhile in recent years tax revenues have not increased as fast as government spending. The difference now amounts to around £2,050 a year per household, adding to the national overdraft at a rate which has alarmed the nation's collective bank managers: the international financial markets. Interest payments on central and local government debts are now running at not far short of £20 a week for every household in the United Kingdom; and if the debt burden continues to increase at this rate, this figure will rise by around £3 a week every year. Despite this, it is one of the rites of autumn for Downing Street to let it be known that 'this year's public spending round has been the toughest ever'; while ministers generally emerge with their existing budgets intact. Attempts at so-called zero-based budgeting or in-depth programme analysis have long been abandoned.

Every householder knows from experience that this situation

cannot be allowed to continue, and that the longer no action is taken the more difficult and painful it will be to balance the books. Meanwhile real interest rates for would-be borrowers remain at an historically high level, acting as a brake on needed investment by smaller businesses particularly. Indeed there has never been a sustained economic recovery with real interest rates above 2 per cent, less than half their level at the end of 1993.

Moreover most of the obvious ways of avoiding tackling the problem only serve to make it worse. Central government and local authorities have both resorted to what might be described as 'creative accounting' on a grand scale. Since the early 1980s privatisation proceeds have exceeded £50 billion; and these have been used to finance general government expenditure – thus helping to mask the true state of the public finances. Similarly local authorities have indulged in a whole range of dubious accounting practices, often with the support of major financial institutions. Sometimes these are exposed to public scrutiny, as in the case of the Hammersmith and Fulham interest rate swaps which cost the shareholders of the banks involved some £500 million. But often they remain safely out of the public gaze: few council tenants in one inner London authority can have been aware that their bath taps were owned by a well-known merchant bank (the council had concluded a sale and lease-back deal in an attempt to circumvent the then government's spending targets and associated penalties for over-spending).

The failure to distinguish between day-to-day revenue and long-term capital investment means that it is all too easy to mortgage the future by cutting capital spending and maintenance in order to sustain benefit and public-sector employment levels. By the end of 1992 the backlog of maintenance expenditure on the local authority housing stock, schools and NHS hospitals amounted to over £20 billion, a figure that appears nowhere in the nation's 'books', so beloved of Leaders of the Opposition at election time ('we cannot give any commitments until we have had a chance to look at the books'), for the simple reason that there is no public sector balance sheet. Up to now, Whitehall has operated what one leading businessman has described as a 'shoebox' accounting system which fails to distinguish – as every business must, by law – between current and capital spending.

It is clear that the government's objective must be to ensure that, over the economic cycle, tax income and public expenditure are in balance. This will entail a war on waste throughout the public sector. Moreover there is general agreement among informed observers about how the war can best be prosecuted: eliminating the automatic indexation of benefits and targeting them more effectively on those in need, and realising the opportunities to reduce waste and inefficiency within the public services.

Targeted benefits

In 1992 social security benefits accounted for nearly a third of general government expenditure on services – £79 billion, or around £3,400 for *every* household in the United Kingdom. So any moves to contain growth in public spending must look at the benefits system, particularly since the cost has increased in real terms by almost 60 per cent since the beginning of the 1980s. So much for the cuts that feature strongly in political rhetoric at election time.

Successive generations of politicians have recognised the dangers of seeking to confront the welfare industry, which is both well-organised and has a remarkably effective publicity machine. It is generally thought too that every pensioner is living in abject poverty, part of popular mythology which politicians seek to debunk at their peril. Yet currently some 55 per cent of pensioners have a private pension, compared with 41 per cent in 1979. According to Salomon Brothers, real personal sector wealth in the United Kingdom in mid 1992 was £100 thousand per household. Excluding houses and land, it had increased by nearly £15 thousand a household since 1987 alone. It is among the long-term unemployed, single parents and the very old that poverty is greatest and where public support needs to be concentrated.

The painless political answer is to promise a further campaign to reduce fraudulent benefit claims. But even the most enthusiastic members of the Anti-Fraud Squad do not claim that annual savings from any crack-down on scroungers will exceed more than £1 billion a year, barely scratching the surface of a budget of nearly £80 billion, unless the government and employers are willing to tackle the growth in claims for sickness and disability benefits which now cost over £5½ billion a year – more than double the level six years ago. But this seems unlikely given the political risks that would inevitably arise: hard cases may make bad law; but they certainly make very effective television sound-bites.

So there is simply no alternative to looking at benefit levels and entitlements. Of the total, old-age pensions account for 38 per cent, income support and housing benefit 28 per cent, unemployment benefit 12 per cent and family benefits 10 per cent. Several possibilities have been canvassed by those rash enough to confront the issues and the special interests involved:

- concentrate all social security payments on those demonstrably in need, and eliminate all universal entitlements not covered by individuals' contributions. There is something absurd, as well as remarkably inefficient, about wealthy families sending their children to private schools and simultaneously receiving family benefits now costing over £7.6 billion a year in total; there is no good reason, either, why people in receipt of private pensions should have their state pensions topped up by the current taxpayers
- equalise the state pension age for men and women at sixty-five which estimates have suggested would save the Exchequer £3 billion a year. Some commentators have even suggested, from the safety of their commentary boxes, that state pension retirement age should gradually increase to sixty-seven, as is the case in America
- outlaw indexation of benefits; this is simply an accommodation with the enemy of inflation and a convenient way for ministers and Parliament to avoid hard choices. Contributory benefit payments should be frozen at current levels until the government actuary judges that current National Insurance contributions are sufficient to fund the future payments
- encourage opting out of the publicly financed pension scheme so that the majority of people make their own provision for their old age and do not have to rely on their neighbours and fellow taxpayers. This will become progressively easier as inter-generational bequests treble over the next decade, to some £24 billion a year – close to the total current annual cost of state retirement pension payments
- expect individuals to take out insurance against short-term unemployment, just as they can do for longer-term sickness.

As patterns of work and careers change, people can expect to have more spells between full-time employment – for lifestyle reasons, for training or simply because they seek new directions. Unemployment benefit could then be focused on the long-term unemployed.

If taxpayers are to see their 'benefits' reduced, they are entitled to look for a contribution from the bureaucracy. This means a more effective war on waste and inefficiency in the public services.

Less waste and inefficiency

The Japanese industrial hegemony has been based on a simple concept: the elimination of waste – of time, capital or people. That is why Japanese companies pay such attention to just-in-time manufacturing techniques, to minimise the need to have parts or components lying around on the factory floor. For instance, car seats for Nissan cars built in Sunderland are ordered, from an independent supplier, only on the day that they are required: they are delivered not to the factory gates or stores, but to the production line; and to the precise station and at the exact time that the car for which the set of seats is destined is arriving – so that the seats can be installed without any wasteful delay. That is why, too, world-class companies operate the most expensive equipment continuously; and why productivity improvements of 10 per cent a year are commonplace – reflecting an attention to minute detail as well as teamwork to identify and implement necessary changes.

The same attention to the elimination of waste could be worth £10 billion a year in local government in England and Wales alone, a figure so massive that it challenges credulity. However, local government revenue spending rose in real terms by 15 per cent between 1986 and 1993 and the potential value improvements represent only 15 per cent of total current expenditure on these services – a modest improvement target by private sector standards.

The potential is already on the public record in successive reports by the Audit Commission since it came into being just over exactly a decade ago, in April 1983. Unfortunately, however, these have not received the public attention they deserve. The public and Parliament seem more interested in pursuing wrong-doing than managerial incompetence. Incidents like the recent £50 million hole in the BBC's management accounts tend to catch the headlines, while far more substantial waste elsewhere in the public service goes virtually unnoticed by those who are paying for it. The average Audit Commission report would sell no more than around four thousand copies, though each report usually receives an initial burst of publicity: articles in the 'heavy' newspapers; an interview on the BBC Radio 4 *Today* programme; even conversations with Jimmy Young. But very soon the spotlight of public attention moves on, leaving those providing a service and their constituents well able to cope with external irritants like the district auditors, who are required to follow up each report at the local level.

Since successive Audit Commission reports have not been challenged, let alone contradicted, in any significant particular, the best way to illustrate the scale of the opportunities is simply to quote from the summaries of successive reports from 1983 onwards:

local authority purchases, excluding utilities, now approach £3 billion a year; and the Commission's survey suggests wide differences in the prices paid for the same items which cannot be explained by quality, volume or distribution factors. [Some authorities were spending twice as much as others on the envelopes in which their rate demands were sent out, for instance.] There is potential to secure better value for money in local government by bringing prices paid closer to those secured by the most successful authorities. If this can be achieved, a gain for local government of as much as £200 million [a year] may be possible

refuse collection productivity has increased in real terms by 25 per cent since 1978 [but] investigations show that with no changes to existing standards of service, further improvements worth £20 million are possible. If all authorities were willing to accept the lowest cost collection methods (and accept the service standards involved) a further saving worth some £50 million would be possible

the Commission's auditors examined in detail the way resources are being used in 165 out of 550 polytechnics and colleges of further education. The local projects identify value improvement opportunities worth over £50 million a year, over £300,000 per college [around 8 per cent of total annual costs] local authorities in England and Wales spend around £1 billion a year on transport, of which about £700 million is on their own fleets of vehicles and major plant ... The Commission's study has shown very wide variations in practice, even between authorities known to be better than average in terms of vehicle fleet management. Numbers of vehicles, maintenance costs and operating costs all vary by factors of 2 or more, even after differences in local conditions are taken into account. The study suggests that an annual saving of £130 million or more is possible if authorities adopt practices designed to reduce the number of vehicles and reduce maintenance costs per vehicle without compromising service or safety standards

removing 2 out of every 5 surplus places [in secondary schools] will mean that the potential cost savings available are between £100 and £150 million per annum. Changes in teaching staff costs have not been included. Cleaning costs could be reduced by around 25 per cent (or some £50 million a year) without unacceptable consequences in terms of quality or service

at present, a typical shire county might spend £9 million a year on services for the elderly and a metropolitan district £6 million. Managing these services well would result in better social services for the elderly, in some cases at lower cost to ratepayers. In a number of authorities, the Social Services Department could support 15–20 per cent higher service levels within existing resources at the same time as improving the quality of services

heating and lighting non-domestic buildings cost local authorities £800 million each year; and reducing energy usage offers a ready opportunity to save money without cutting services or jobs. The study revealed a 2:1 range in energy efficiency of buildings, after taking account of such factors as floor areas, exposure of buildings, local climate and hours of use. Most authorities can reduce consumption by 15–20 per cent, some by as much as a third; a determined effort could eventually yield savings of as much as £100 million a year

falling [secondary school] rolls present an important opportunity to redirect investment over the next three to five years that will not come again. The scale of the resources available is very considerable: £500 million to £700 million a year by the end of the decade, or £2,500 to £4,000 per teacher. But major change will be necessary if the opportunity is to be taken: new incentives are needed to encourage authorities to reorganise their secondary schools; the way teachers are assigned to schools needs to be changed; more effort needs to be devoted to assessing individual schools' performance in adding educational value to their pupils; maximum authority should be delegated to the school level the cashflows handled by local authorities amount to some £60 billion annually in England and Wales. Managing these payments and receipts is also a major administrative task costing some £500 million annually and involving 400 million transactions a year. Some £60 million of annual savings could come from better management of cash flow. A further £40 million to £50 million a year could be saved by general application of current good practice in administering cashflows

despite annual expenditure of over £2 billion a year, a backlog of maintenance work [on council houses] has built up which could well cost £10 billion to clear. Tenants are often, and with some justice, dissatisfied with the standard of services they receive: repairs which should be done within days often take weeks, if not months ... The benefits of improved management of the maintenance effort are likely to be substantial: a shift from the current pattern of work to the ideal could generate something of the order of an extra 30 per cent in improved maintenance value; this could be worth perhaps as much as £700 million a year

the current arrangements for managing local authority roads in England and Wales are a mess. In many parts of the country, tax and ratepayers' funds are not put to best use because of lack of communications, or even open hostility, between County and District Councils. This is not solely, or primarily, a political problem. Relationships between the staffs of the different Councils are often very poor. Changes are urgently needed if potential value improvements of over £100 million in highways maintenance are to be achieved.

In total, these value improvements amounted to some £4 billion (in 1992 prices) or around 15 per cent of the costs examined. By the end of 1987 the Audit Commission had only examined less than half of local government expenditure in England and Wales, and had not covered such areas as police services, primary education, leisure and recreation or central management overheads. So £8 billion of annual value improvements would seem a perfectly reasonable target for local government in Great Britain to aim at, of which less than £1.5 billion has so far been achieved.

Meanwhile the scope for improvements elsewhere within the public service is becoming more apparent. The scale of the opportunities in the NHS is also illustrated in summaries of the Audit Commission's recent reports – the commission took over responsibility for the external audit of the NHS in 1991:

if all District Health Authorities performed day surgery consistently at readily achievable levels for each of 30 common procedures, an additional 186,000 patients could be treated each year without increased expenditure. And many other procedures are suitable for day surgery, offering potential for 300,000 additional patients to be treated annually. This is the equivalent of about 34 per cent of existing day case and in-patient waiting lists in England and Wales

general nursing on wards in acute hospitals costs some £1.2 billion a year... Hospitals vary significantly in the length of the overlap between morning and afternoon shifts, in the extent to which nurses perform clerical and housekeeping duties and in the costs of managing nursing. A reduction in the overlap to a maximum of one hour throughout the country could theoretically release resources of £50 million; reducing the proportion of nurses' time spent on non-nursing duties to 8 per cent would release £40 million; while containing the costs of managing nursing services to no more than 2 per cent of the nursing pay budget would release £35 million

correcting the inefficiencies [in admission procedures, placement in the wrong ward, excess length of stay, poorly organised discharge procedures, mis-allocation of beds to clinical specialties] would result in reduced need for in-patient beds. If these were combined with investment in community services allowing a shift in clinical practice towards shorter lengths of stay, the reduction in beds would be substantial... The current level of medical in-patient treatment in England could be provided with 27,000 or almost one-third fewer beds.

If all the value improvements identified by the Audit Commission over the last decade had been realised – and proved good practice had become common practice – total current spending by local authorities in England and Wales and the NHS could be as much as £10 billion lower than was the case in 1993 without any reduction in the quality of the services provided.

Although the figure appears very large, it should come as no surprise. Local authority and health services are particularly people-intensive, employing over three million between them. So improvements in labour productivity will have a dramatic effect on aggregate spending levels, as well as the balance between day-to-day (revenue) and capital expenditure. A saving of £5 billion would represent an annual improvement of no more than 2 per cent in labour productivity in local government since the beginning of 1984, when the Audit Commission first began to follow up its national studies at the local level. To set this figure in context, productivity improvements of 3 per cent a year would be the minimum acceptable in the private sector; in industry 5 per cent annual gains are commonplace and 10 per cent is by no means unheard of.

Notwithstanding the evident scope for achieving substantially improved value for money in the public services, progress has been disappointingly slow. Ministers have been unwilling to assume an improvement of even a single point in productivity in their annual round of negotiations over public spending. The agonisingly slow pace of change is illustrated in the 1992 Annual Report of the Audit Commission. This shows that in the past six years total specific local value for money opportunities identified in local government in England and Wales were worth under £1.2 billion a year, of which only around £600 million had been set aside as fulfilled. And of these well over three-quarters of the improvements were attributable to national studies carried out prior to 1987. Currently value improvements identified by the commission's auditors are running at under £100 million a year, of which, on past form, around half only will be fulfilled within five years. Performance in the past five years, when the Audit Commission has avowedly been 'working with the grain of the public service', has been particularly disappointing. It is evidently difficult to secure changes in the way public services are managed without creating more enemies within the bureaucracy than most people are prepared to accept.

So it seems that between £5 billion and £10 billion of public money is being wasted annually which could be spent on investment in our national infrastructure without any extra call on taxpayers. The sheer scale of the private poverty that is resulting from this public waste is considerable:

- the difference between the value of all work at the peak of UK construction activity in 1990 and forecast for 1993 is under £10 billion. So it is arguable that at least half the recent increase in unemployment in the construction sector could have been avoided – the equivalent of well over a hundred thousand jobs
- total public sector capital expenditure on transport (including roads), housing, health services and education is estimated at £13 billion at current prices; so re-allocating £5 billion of the wasted day-to-day spending to capital would

entail an increase of some 40 per cent in public construction activity.

The slow pace of change is not an inevitable consequence of the human condition, or even of management within the United Kingdom's public services. But too often those involved simply do not consider that the effort (and pain) that is involved are justified by the benefits that seem to be on offer. And unless there is a more definite and obvious will to manage at all levels in the organisations in question, institutional inertia will ensure that no significant change takes place. A combination of concern for the interests of the providers of services, creative accounting and a manipulation of the tendering process itself, can usually be relied upon to see off any serious attempts to introduce competition in public services. Indeed the conventional approaches of managers in Britain's public sector – the search for consensus and avoidance of conflict, management by committee, government by amateurs referred to earlier (Chapter 3) – have created the inertia in the first place.

There will need to be much sharper individual accountability, such as is beginning to emerge in the NHS Trusts. This approach will need to be mirrored within local government, where too often accountability is confused by the bureaucracy and committee structure to the point where no individual – member or paid official – can reasonably be held responsible for any particular service. And with sharper individual accountability should go greater rewards for success and penalties for failure. So far the public service has been sadly faint-hearted in its attitude to performance-related pay. Even the most exceptional performers do not earn more than an additional 10 per cent over and above their regular salaries, compared with a ceiling of 30 per cent or more in comparable private sector positions.

The public sector needs to become more proficient at applying both the carrot and the stick. There is a strong case for all future changes in management compensation to reflect individual and collective performance. In the private sector an outstandingly successful manager can expect the combination of annual performance payments, longer-term incentives and share options to double his or her salary over a five-year period; a manager who persistently fails to meet budgeted performance can expect to have no future. Within the public sector the carrots are not sufficiently attractive; and one of the most attractive potential carrots, the honours system has seemed largely divorced from assessments of individuals performance; while sticks remain in their respective ministerial cupboards unless individuals become too 'difficult' to handle. Public sector managers are dismissed (if they are), not for failure to achieve stretching management targets but for embarrassing their political masters in one way or another.

But accountability and rewards and penalties will only be effective if the information available to the stakeholders in local government or the NHS is comprehensive, comprehensible and timely, as well as accurate. Too often citizens are deluged with facts about inputs to services that are of dubious relevance and doubtful accuracy; while they receive very little understandable information about results achieved. The Citizen's Charter has an important role to play filling this information gap and thus enabling citizens (as well as the local media) to call those responsible to account. It would be particularly necessary to ensure that any league tables are at once easy to understand and soundly based (as well as accurate), so that the special interests do not have the opportunity to criticise the messenger rather than address the message.

At the same time, all public accounts should distinguish between revenue (day-to-day) spending and capital investment for the future. Every authority or trust should be required to present not just an annual statement of its cashflow but also a balance sheet showing its assets and liabilities. This is now the case in New Zealand, so it is perfectly feasible.

Indeed the cost of failure to tackle the existing waste and inefficiency in present services needs to be greater, and clearer to all local stakeholders. Every citizen should understand that the reason why their local tax is too high, the local public infrastructure is in poor shape, or their local hospital lacks the latest diagnostic equipment is that services are not being well managed. This will only be the case if systems for allocating Exchequer funds to NHS Trusts and local authorities are much more transparent and understandable than at present. In local government the complex grant allocation and expenditure-capping arrangements simply provide local councillors with the excuse to blame the government for shortcomings in local services; while controls over capital spending in the NHS, local government and the remaining nationalised industries introduce rigidities which were designed to meet the needs of a bygone era. Provided the private sector is prepared to accept the risks involved, there seems no reason why sale and lease-back arrangements should not be far more wide-spread in the public sector, or why British Rail should not be able to tap the world's capital markets to finance its development plans.

Finally, for the foreseeable future, the public sector pay bill should not increase at all in money terms; pay increases for individuals should be earned by improved performance. This does not imply a pay norm. It simply reflects the basic principle that pay must reflect individual and collective performance – from the boardroom to the shopfloor, in services as well as in manu-facturing, in the public as well as private sectors. Similarly the government should be able to insist that its suppliers of goods and services do not increase their prices in money terms – a discipline many major companies are imposing on their suppliers.

Since the central and local government pay bill (£66 billion in 1990–1) and expenditure on goods and services (£39 billion) has been rising at the rate of around 9 per cent a year over the last four years, the scope for savings is immense. The planned annual increase by central government for these two categories of expenditure was £2.1 billion a year over the period April 1993 to March 1996, when the government's plans were announced in November 1992. Total public expenditure in 1994–5 would be nearly £3½ billion lower than planned if the central and local government pay bill did not increase overall and if the cost of external supplies of goods and services could be contained.

These are realistic targets. Indeed they have been bettered regularly by virtually every UK manufacturing company that has survived the last two recessions: pay freezes and deferral of pay settlements have become commonplace, while productivity has been growing faster than pay in many cases. Even large service organisations like the UK clearing banks have begun to commit themselves to achieving flat costs in money terms (and thus real reductions) year after year.

Apart from questions about the morality of waste, the cost of failure to eliminate £10 billion a year of waste will be serious. Continued pressure on public expenditure is bound to mean that as a nation we will continue to invest less than is necessary in those parts of the public sector vital to our competitive future: education, skills, the transport infrastructure and in our deprived inner cities.

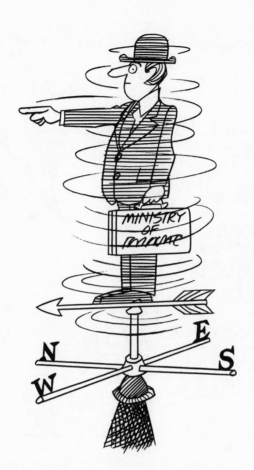

Over half of all local authority expenditure is devoted to education. So the Audit Commission inevitably concentrated considerable effort in its early years on various aspects of the management of secondary, further and higher education. Local management of schools was one of the results.

But the commission was not empowered to examine the quality of teaching, although it came perilously close to doing so on occasion. None the less it is evident that world-class education requires world-class teachers.

Business leaders had formed the same views. So, a CBI task force was set up, chaired by Sir Adrian Cadbury, to strengthen the links between business and secondary schools. I was also involved in a number of seminars contemplating education policy issues including two convened by Professor Sir Douglas Hague at Templeton College, Oxford. Here I was particularly struck by some innovative ideas presented by Professor David Hargreaves of Cambridge University, about the structure of the teaching profession. This chapter is based on material prepared for an after-dinner speech to the Secondary Heads Association at its Annual Conference in Scarborough. Discipline on that occasion was not good.

8
Towards World-Class Education

World-class education requires world-class teachers.

Every student of military or business strategy knows that timing is everything: doing the right things in the wrong order or too late invariably leads to disappointment and often to failure to achieve the original objectives.

So it has proved with national education policy, perhaps because there have been no less than four Secretaries of State and Permanent Secretaries since the latest round of educational reforms was launched with the Education Reform Act 1988.

Each of the initiatives that has been undertaken makes sense by itself. There is indeed a strong case for a National Core Curriculum; and parents and teachers, as well as pupils, need to know how well they are progressing in mastering it. There should be greater emphasis on mathematics and sciences, and on technical and vocational education. Schools need greater autonomy to manage their own affairs. There needs to be a closer relationship between the public and private sectors in education; it makes sense to involve the private sector in establishing 'beacons of technical excellence' in education in the form of City Technology Colleges.

Revolution at risk

But these initiatives do not appear to form part of a coherent strategy for creating world-class education. Rather it seems as though they have happened in response to political pressure. So they have been introduced in the wrong order. In particular, eliminating the waste and inefficiency resulting from a failure to close redundant schools has been made more difficult by the erosion of the Local Education Authorities' (LEAs) role and the ability of schools threatened by closure to opt for grant-maintained status. The introduction of the core curriculum has been marred by inadequate preparation and an over-prescriptive approach reflected in mutual suspicion among the three so-called partners involved in the enterprise: government, LEAs and teachers. An over-complex curriculum cannot be tested in ways that teachers find acceptable and parents can understand. And so on.

Perhaps the worst mistake has been to ignore the needs of teachers – the 'poor bloody infantry' on whom the success of the whole range of initiatives will depend, no matter how elegant the strategy or impressive the equipment at their disposal.

First World wages cannot be sustained without world-class education, and a world-class teaching profession to make it possible. So the 1990s must be the decade of engineers and teachers, just as the 1980s was the decade of consultants and the 1970s the decade of accountants. At present this is only a distant dream. Serious shortages loom, particularly in those inner city areas where education is most important as a means of escaping from the cycle of deprivation, and in subjects of greatest importance to the economy: mathematics, sciences, craft design technology and foreign languages. The measures taken by the trade unions involved to deal with the situation appear only to have made matters worse. This is partly because they have devalued the teaching profession in the eyes of the general public and probably of many of its members as well.

Despite all the recent reforms there remain serious grounds for concern about public education in Britain: low staying-on rates, the relatively low attainment of British schoolchildren by international standards, the disciplinary problems in many schools, the empty desks in many classes, dilapidated buildings, lack of sufficient books and equipment. More than 375 out of the top five hundred secondary schools in terms of 1993 GCSE Grade A passes were in the independent sector.

As long ago as 1987 the Audit Commission noted that the proportion of students leaving at the age of sixteen was very high by OECD standards; yet in the more deprived areas especially, absence levels of 25 per cent or more were not uncommon in some classes. Sickness absence among teachers – a barometer of staff morale – often exceeded 10 per cent on a typical school day, well over three times the level most private sector employers would expect to see. Teachers rarely received any formal feedback on their performance. There was a failure to reward talented teachers properly and there had been a notable increase in the number of younger teachers leaving the profession to take up other employment. Partly as a result there were shortages of teachers for mathematics, physics and technology-based subjects in particular, and it proved difficult to fill many head teacher posts.

As if these were not problems enough, the local management of the education system faces continuing uncertainty. The future role of Local Education Authorities is far from clear – in most cases they would continue to be involved in planning and funding the system, working with a new Schools Funding Council. The extent to which schools decide to opt out of local authority control seems to be more a matter of local political speculation than national education policy; and the method by which schools will be funded in the future is still evolving – with the possibility of government-appointed regional funding councils already being canvassed.

Treating the symptoms rather than the underlying causes will not meet the needs of the present situation. Not surprisingly, in a society where, until very recently, most (literally) of the 'products' of the education system emerge with no recognisable qualifications, the value of education is not generally appreciated. Most people have got by fairly well without them; after all, the purchasing power of the average after-tax wage is higher in the United Kingdom than in most other European countries and we are more likely to have the latest technical wizardry in our homes. In the meantime differentials in wages to reflect skills are relatively low in the United Kingdom; the wages that unskilled people can earn are twice as high (relative to the skilled rate for the job) as in West Germany, for example.

Moreover, as in so many other aspects of the public services, there is no agreement on how the education system should be judged. The focus has been on inputs not outputs – on economy and efficiency rather than effectiveness. Thus for decades the pupil:teacher ratio (PTR) was generally accepted as a surrogate for the quality of the nation's education system – even though no relationship has been established between the ratio and educational outcomes. Indeed concern about the quality of the nation's education system increased even as the PTR improved – and expenditure per secondary school pupil rose by over 50 per cent in the 1980s in real terms. Only very recently has attention focused on attainments relative to those of schoolchildren in other countries, and on the possible reasons for the poor position of the UK in any international league table. Interestingly, the pupil:teacher ratio in the UK is, if anything, rather more generous than in most other European countries.

In such confused circumstances both central and local government have benefited from the lack of clear accountability for the quality and cost-effectiveness of the education system. This is a further problem needing to be addressed. Each level of government can plausibly blame others for any shortcomings in the system – and continues to do so. Parents dissatisfied with their children's education cannot sensibly call the school governors to account; outside the private sector governors do not generally employ the teachers or determine their pay. Nor can the Local Education Authority reasonably be accountable, when the schools can opt out of their control and the bulk of the funding for education comes from the Exchequer via the Revenue Support Grant or from business via the Uniform Business Rate. The Secretary of State cannot reasonably be called to account either, because in most schools he does not employ teachers or appoint the authorities or governors that do. Nor does he determine how the local education system is organised, although he can, and regularly does, delay any proposed reorganisations.

As if all this were not sufficient, the teachers' unions have tended to focus on pay negotiations and have used strikes and the threat of strikes as a means of forcing concessions from their employers. This tactic has not succeeded in halting a long-run decline in teachers' pay relative to the average for non-manual workers. In 1974 the average teacher's pay was some 35 per cent above the average; currently it is only around 7 per cent higher, despite the large increases awarded in 1980 and 1987. (In 1986 the Audit Commission observed that experienced teachers in the UK were paid over a third less than a police sergeant; in West Germany and France they were paid at least 45 per cent more.) The focus on raising teachers' pay rather than their performance has ensured that economies have been greatest in the area of books, equipment and 'learning technologies' – just those items which are so essential if pupils are to have the opportunity of learning to learn and to work by themselves.

But union tactics were successful in one respect: they served to undermine the public standing of teaching as a profession. Entry standards to teacher training establishments are well below those for entry into other professions, such as, medicine, law and accountancy. It is far easier to gain entry to a teacher training college than to virtually any university or polytechnic.

In short, we are attempting to reform an education system which is not regarded as central to the national quality of life, whose low relative effectiveness is neither understood nor a particular cause for concern within the service or outside it, where accountability is confused to the mutual benefit of those who might be called to account for this state of affairs, and where trade unions' unsuccessful attempts to improve the situation of their members has served to make matters worse. Parallels with other parts of the public sector and with most of British industry in the 1970s are inescapable. Teachers are employed in a service characterised by low investment, low productivity and thus low pay relative to their continental counterparts.

The result is a looming crisis in the nation's classrooms that could completely offset the benefits to be derived from the recent reforms. Some estimates have suggested that within five years one secondary class in three would be without an appropriately qualified teacher, and perhaps one in four pupils would have to be sent home because there would not be a teacher in place at all. This would mean that an existing national competitive disadvantage for the economy would worsen. Apart from any considerations of quality, in a school year a Japanese pupil will receive as many as 1,500 hours of lessons compared to 950 hours in England (seven hours a day for 240 days including Saturday mornings, compared to under five hours for 190 days in the United Kingdom). This could well be another instance of the golfing adage, 'the more I practice, the luckier I get'.

A world-class future

None of these problems is insurmountable, provided suitable action is taken in time. After all, there are many strengths to build on. The best of British education – at the primary, secondary and tertiary levels – is already widely regarded as world-class; if 10 per cent of the population, from a wide cross-section of the ability range, can enjoy these benefits, surely the majority could do so as well? We are pioneers, and probably world leaders, in the open and distance learning field pioneered by the Open University. We are used to applying technology successfully in the education sphere: investment in information technology in UK schools compares favourably with that in most other developed economies.

But although the problems should not be insurmountable, there is no 'quick fix' available. Rather, a number of steps might be needed. There will have to be closer links between schools and the local community, so that parents and employers recognise the importance of continuing education. A new structure for the teaching profession is needed; improving pay will not solve the problem by itself. Greater use should be made of technology so that teachers focus on individual tuition rather than class instruction, and young people progressively take responsibility for their own learning. Accountability for different aspects of the education system should be clearer. And there needs to be more local determination of teachers' pay and conditions; national negotiations must leave room for flexibility to meet particular local needs. Finally the continuing role for Local Education Authorities needs to be clarified.

Closer links with the local community

It is commonplace to suggest that most learning takes place outside the confines of schools. Or, as Professor Charles Handy puts it more graphically, 'there is plenty of education going on; much of it just happens not to be in schools'. So by definition the community has a key role to play in education; and the strong links between schools and local businesses can be expected to develop further, as employers feel the effects of the demographic time-bomb of a sharp decline in the number of school-leavers. Eventually every secondary school (at least) will be linked with sufficient local businesses to offer a range of worthwhile work experience to every pupil during their school career and to at least 10 per cent of teachers every year.

Valuable though all this is, and will continue to be, much more is needed. Parents must be involved to a greater extent in the education of their children, and not merely in the governance of their schools, which would inevitably be a minority activity affording opportunities to relatively few parents. The rights of all parents to free primary and secondary education for their children surely imply duties greater than securing their regular attendance. Yet even this duty is readily ignored. On a typical school day in many inner city schools as many as a quarter of fifteen-year-olds who should be at their desks are likely to be absent; truanting is a word dreaded by the police, who are only too aware that sixteen is the peak year for committing crimes.

And head teachers of all types of schools regularly observe how difficult it is to engage parents in their children's education – encouraging reading and academic attainments, supervising homework, attending parent-teacher meetings. The contrast with the situation in Japan could hardly be more striking. There, pressure from mothers (particularly) is widely regarded as excessive; early on in their nursery school career Japanese children are likely to be introduced to the proverb that 'the nail that stands out from the floor gets hammered in'.

At present there are too many false antitheses that British parents must be helped to recognise, such as the need to choose between the academic and the vocational; the tension between education for life as opposed to education for making a living; the distinction often drawn (wrongly) between knowledge and skills. Dr Arnold who was quoted earlier as observing that 'we over-value doing' had obviously forgotten the advice of Aristotle: 'What we have to do, we learn by doing.' Moreover the culture of continued education through life needs to be established more widely.

The experience of Education 2000 – a business-led and financed charity working in Hertfordshire – suggests that community links can be facilitated by steps such as the following:

- a secondment of 15 per cent of teachers every year into local companies, to enable them to study the use they make of the skills of young employees
- establishing study groups drawn from local interests such as the Chamber of Trade, local churches, etc., with an equal number of teachers meeting over an extended period to create a 'mission statement' for the local education system to which the entire community could subscribe
- extensive programmes mounted through each school to assist parents to partner their children on particular projects
- exploration of the way in which informal learning opportunities within the community could be better identified, and then used in partnership with formal education
- regular discussions between teachers and representatives of

the local community leading to the shadowing of teachers in schools by employers and others, involving perhaps one teacher in three.

Closer links between schools and teachers and their local communities could help to bring about another needed change in the system: a complete restructuring of the teaching profession.

A restructured teaching profession

It is inescapable that the future of the nation's education system depends on the availability of able and qualified teachers. However, the competition for graduates is certain to intensify, not least from the education system itself: the necessary expansion of higher education will act as a drain on those who might otherwise be teaching in secondary schools. Across-the-board pay increases will not prevent shortages. Not only will they be expensive (a flat rate increase of £2 thousand a year per teacher would cost almost £1 billion) but there is no guarantee that the other professions, industry and commerce will not match any pay increases awarded to those schoolteachers that they particularly want to attract.

There seems no alternative, therefore, to considering ways of restructuring the teaching profession itself. At present the vast majority of secondary schoolteachers are graduates who qualify through the one-year Post-Graduate Certificate in Education (PGCE). However, many qualified teachers choose not to teach (as many as 20–30 per cent) while over half of new recruits are leaving the education system before they are thirty – even though experience at the 'chalk-face' is agreed to be vital to teachers' effectiveness. Radical thinking is long overdue about how teachers are trained, how they are rewarded, and their career pattern. For example, in the future there could be three different types of teacher.

Career teachers would have a very short basic initial training of, say, three months following their graduation from university. This training would be based on schools, organised by senior teachers as supervisors or mentors, supported by staff of teacher training institutions to nationally agreed standards. This basic training would focus on the fundamental practical skills and the capacity to cope in the classroom. It would be followed by a carefully structured induction programme, largely based in schools, to promote professional development. At the end of five years the teacher would be eligible for an advanced teaching certificate.

Career teachers could then take a third-stage qualification as a new teacher supervisor with responsibility for the basic training of new teachers and the supervision of induction. Career teachers (only) would be eligible to go to staff college to qualify them for roles as head teachers. Each extra stage in their career would be reflected in higher pay and would be an incentive to the career teacher.

Assistant teachers could be a second type and support the qualified teacher by undertaking those tasks important to the successful operation of schools but not requiring the expertise of the career teacher. In practice teachers spend a surprisingly low proportion of their time and energy teaching, simply because so much is expended on managing pupils and classrooms – calling registers, controlling corridors and playgrounds and lunch arrangements, preparing equipment and materials, caring for the personal needs of pupils. In secondary schools (excluding head teachers and deputies) non-contact time – that is, time not spent in the class-room – takes up 20–25 per cent of a teacher's average working day; even in primary schools up to 15 per cent of teachers' time is spent on administrative duties of one form or another. Assistant teachers would require a sound education but not recent or relevant higher education. Young people with A levels, married women looking for part-time work with children and the early retired might well be attracted to the work of assistant teachers, some of whom might subsequently enter higher education and/or take the short basic training to become career teachers.

Associate teachers would be the third type within the restructured profession. The associate teacher would take the short basic training but without ever intending to become a career teacher. He or she would, from the beginning, see teaching as a short-term commitment before moving on to another career. Associate teachers could hold two jobs simultaneously, part-time in school and part-time in some other occupation. Increasingly, business is sympathetic to such approaches, with almost half the work-force in a position to 'telecommute' for part of the week. At present many people are employed in the private sector for work-based training, and have considerable teaching skills even though they are not qualified teachers; the education of many young people is shared with trainers and further education colleges. This is a huge potential source of associate teachers and would bring much experience and credibility into schools.

Such a system would depend on a supply of sufficient 'good' schools, where teachers under training learn the best of evolving practice, rather than simply perpetuating traditional teaching strategies. City Technology Colleges and schools that have successfully 'opted out' could provide a panel of excellence in education, which could serve as exemplars for the rest of the education system and to people training to be teachers in particular.

Assistant and associate teachers could also form a core of people to expand nursery education. Experience in the United States and elsewhere shows that children who have been to nursery school tend to do better, and benefit more, from full-time education. This is likely to be particularly true of children from lone parent households. So nursery education should be a priority in those areas where there is a concentration of single parent families.

Greater use of technology

Technology has an important role to play, not only in linking pupils to the community, but also in ensuring that teachers are able to focus on the needs of individual students – rather than keeping order, instructing whole classes and compensating for the lack of books. It means that pupils can learn at their own pace and in private, without the fear of being shown up in front of their peers as stupid. Lao Tsu could have been writing of teachers: 'The wicked leader is he who the people despise. The good leader is he who the people revere. The great leader is he who the people say "we did it ourselves".'

Experience has shown that imaginative use of the latest information technology can bridge the gap between different schools in the local community, maximise curriculum choice and bring the strengths and traditions of each to the service of every pupil. Indeed interactive videos could mean that every child has the opportunity to learn mathematics from a world-class teacher – just as every would-be Walker Cup star can be coached, on film, by the greatest players on the international golf circuit. Technology can also link the world of education to that of business. Already, for example, engineering students on Ford-sponsored courses at Loughborough University can access technical drawings at Ford's Technical Centre in Brentwood 'down the line'.

But new technology (perhaps one computer terminal for every four students) will mean investment. Including the extra staff required, the experience of Education 2000 indicates that the extra cost would be around £150 for every secondary school pupil annually. This is around 10 per cent of the average annual cost of educating a secondary school pupil and far outweighs most authorities' present spending on books and equipment. Some Local Education Authorities spend under £15 a year per pupil on textbooks, thus further increasing dependence on teachers for instruction and increasing the likelihood of bored classes.

Called to account

Finally the present confused accountability for the nation's education system may lie at the heart of its poor performance. Responsibility cannot safely be divorced from authority if people and organisations are to be held to account for their actions and the results they achieve with the resources at their disposal. Yet this divorce has characterised the British education system at all levels. The contradictions are numerous:

- under the 1944 Education Act boards of governors were nominally responsible for what was taught in schools; but in practice they had little influence, let alone authority, over the curriculum, which was in the hands of the teachers and the teaching profession
- the organisation of the local schools system was a matter for the Local Education Authority; but in practice this was influenced, if not determined, by the Secretary of State who enforced the change-over to comprehensive education, and had to approve any school closures. As a result the equivalent of over a thousand fully-staffed secondary schools are standing completely empty
- the Department of Education and the Secretary of State are nominally responsible for funding education on a national

scale; but in practice the funding depends on the Department of the Environment (which determines the level of grant to individual authorities), the Treasury (which determines the level of the Uniform Business Rate), local authorities (which determine the community charge and the education budget) and LEAs which allocate budgets to individual schools that have not opted out
- meantime the child-centred learning philosophy which the UK education establishment adopted depended for its effectiveness on outstanding teachers; but the same establishment could not deliver the salaries necessary to attract or keep sufficient teachers of the required calibre.

Clearer accountability for different aspects of the education system is urgently required. As was proposed earlier (Chapter 4), secondary education (at least) should be funded in full by the Exchequer in the form of a grant to each LEA or school judged sufficient by Parliament to fund an education system of the desired quality, and in particular to deliver the National Curriculum. The grant would need to take account of the particular problems of teaching, both in inner cities and deprived rural areas, as well as the higher accommodation costs that teachers were likely to incur in London and the south-east in particular.

The Department of Education will also need to devote resources to curriculum development and to the management of the education system. It comes as something of a shock to learn that much of the vital work of developing the curriculum taught in our schools is not even financed by the Department of Education. Rather, it has fallen to private charities like the Nuffield Foundation, whose resources are inevitably limited. Better management training for head teachers is also an urgent need. The courses now on offer have been described by an independent and knowledgeable observer as 'patchy, mediocre and inward-looking'. Yet there is no staff college to help potential head teachers acquire the skills and knowledge they will need in what is a new management era for education.

Meanwhile the Local Education Authorities should concentrate on quality assurance and on eliminating the waste and inefficiency that goes with teaching empty desks. The planning and consultation procedures involved should be streamlined further to remove the scope for bureaucratic foot-dragging in Whitehall and at the local level. The national educational establishment cannot be allowed to continue to play snakes and ladders with the way our local schools are organised. The analogy was chosen by the Audit Commission to describe the process or 'game that can take five years to play, with no guarantee of success'.

It is clear what needs to be done: around a thousand secondary schools – ten in a typical Local Education Authority – need to be closed over the next four years, more than twice the current rate of closures. But the political process locally and nationally renders progress difficult, if not near impossible at times. Virtually all the vested interests oppose change; too often the interests of current and future pupils and taxpayers are subordinated to those of local politics, parents of current pupils and teachers.

A shift in the balance would require such moves as:

– streamlining the required consultation procedures which were framed to deal with the problems of a different (and more benign)era, and require only ten local electors to object before the Secretary of State 'called in' reorganisation schemes

– exempting receipts from the sale of school land and buildings from the controls limiting local authorities' capital spending, so that LEAs are both enabled and encouraged to help themselves by disposing of under-utilised school buildings and property and recycling some (at least) of the receipts into capital improvements in the schools that remain. Capital expenditure of the order of £3 billion will be needed over the next few years if the potential school closures are to take place – several times the expenditure now planned

– providing more incentives for local communities to press ahead with reorganising local secondary provision – for example, through a capital grant to cover reorganisation costs or at least some of them; and reducing the scope for those protesting against reorganisation schemes agreed by the local authority to impose what are, in effect, extra taxes on their fellow citizens without the latter's agreement. One method of 'encouraging' local people to accept sensible proposals for changing their local secondary school systems would be for the extra cost of keeping a redundant school open to fall on the local parish or town rate.

If Local Education Authorities are to be left to wither on the vine, as it were, they will have to be re-invented. On past experience, this will be a painfully slow and messy business. One possibility would be to encourage the evolution of federations of opted-out schools, along the lines of the NHS Trusts. In addition to attracting private sector funding and sponsorship, with the agreement of the schools involved, some of the additional Exchequer funds for opted-out schools could be channelled through the trusts. This would have a powerful incentive to encourage the closure of redundant schools. But such trusts take time to set up and even longer to acquire the necessary local support for painful changes to the local school system. Meanwhile the quality of local education will continue to suffer as resources are still wasted teaching empty desks.

Finally new arrangements for determining pay and conditions of service for teachers will be needed. The Burnham system has outlived its usefulness and is itself a source of some of the present management problems, blurring accountability and distorting management structures and career progression within schools. Pay and conditions of service should be negotiated together; and there should be substantial local flexibility within the nationally agreed terms and conditions of service, in particular to determine the appropriate arrangements for recruiting teachers for shortage subjects; managing teacher absence; providing cover for lunchtime supervision; and recognising superior teaching performance.

If boards of governors are to be held accountable for delivering the National Curriculum to their pupils, it follows that they must employ the teachers directly, as is the case with private schools. Indeed this is the logical extension of local management of schools. Moreover, since every local labour market differs, it makes little sense to try to determine nationally how much should be paid to recruit teachers to particular areas of shortage subjects. Nor does it make sense to negotiate the details of conditions of service nationally. Rather, like every other sizeable local employer (on average a secondary school might employ fifty people and have an annual operating budget of over £1 million), the governors of every secondary school should be free to agree what individual teachers should be paid and their conditions of work, subject only to nationally negotiated minimum payment levels for each category of teacher.

Specifically, within its overall budget allocation from the LEA or (regional) funding council, every school's governors should be able to determine the appropriate mix of staff (as between, for instance, the categories of teachers mentioned), the total compensation for each of its employees (including any performance payment that might be appropriate) and any particular payments for 'out of hours' activities or extra responsibilities. It is worth recalling that there is no 'standard rate' for solicitors or accountants. Their pay is a matter for individual negotiation with their employer. This approach implies that national negotiations would be restricted to determining the minimum national payment for the different grades of teacher. It does not necessarily follow that there need be incremental pay scales or anything of the like. Any pay above the minimum could simply reflect the performance of the individual teacher; more experienced teachers could be expected to receive higher performance awards than their less experienced colleagues.

Such an approach will result in higher, rather than lower, pay for teachers overall – which is why the Treasury is certain to oppose it. What local determination of pay should help to deliver is improved performance.

Moreover it should not be assumed that the abolition of detailed grading structures would automatically be opposed by staff who previously 'enjoyed' such a system. Experience of setting up the Audit Commission suggests otherwise. There the Civil Service pay and grading structure, as well as inflation-proof pension arrangements, were abolished. The new package included a basic rate for every job with no annual increments, an annual payment based on assessed performance in the past year, and a fully-funded pension plan with no guarantee that payments would be increased in line with inflation. The result was minimal staff wastage and hundreds of graduate applications for training posts; under the old regime there was just one qualified application for every opening.

As the Audit Commission concluded over five years ago:

> Falling school rolls provide a considerable opportunity to devote more resources to teaching and less to maintaining, cleaning and heating buildings. In this, as in other aspects of local government, the need is for clear National strategic direction (e.g. over the Secondary Curriculum, examinations, the governance of schools and the education/training of 16– 19-year-olds) combined with more scope for local initiative

in the management of teachers and schools and less detailed intervention by ministers in local affairs. It should be clear where responsibility, authority and public accountability for the quality of the Local Education service lies: at present the responsibilities of ministers, LEAs and governors are still not sufficiently distinguished. Partly as a result, the prospects for closing schools on the scale required – of perhaps one in five – are poor. And without school closures, the consequences will be serious: some combination of a continued under-rewarding of teachers, more limited curricula and higher costs than necessary for tax- and ratepayers.

⋆   ⋆   ⋆

So it has proved. And as a result the ability of Britain's businesses to compete with the world's best has been further compromised. The director of one of the most deprived school districts in New York City once remarked that 'when I want to know what to do about the education of poor kids, I simply look at the education of rich kids'. Britain has some of the finest secondary schools in the world. The opportunities now available to perhaps one in ten of the school population must become available to all if the British economy is to prosper in the new era of low inflation and intensified global competition. Until this dream is a reality, a greater burden will fall on the employers of school-leavers and on the skills revolution which is now under way.

My interest in the so-called national skills gap is long standing. In the mid 1960s I was an early beneficiary of the interests of the then Chairman of Reed International (Lord Ryder) in developing young managers. McKinsey has always believed in developing its own people, and virtually all the partners are elected from among the firm's associates.

Moreover no management consultant can be unaware of the damage that incompetent management can cause, or of the difference that professional competence can make to any business.

So it was natural that on arriving at the CBI I should take a particular interest in promoting management development and skills training more generally. The Management Charter Initiative and the skills revolution described here are two of the results. Both are subjects providing serious competition for Mogadon on the national lecture circuit. The situation is much better than is generally recognised, thanks to the skill and dedication of the likes of Sir Bryan Nicholson and Sir Geoffrey Holland within government, and Sir Bob Reid who has led the Management Charter Initiative with his own particular blend of vision and tenacity. Tony Webb and John Cridland of the Confederation of British Industry made a major contribution to the work of the CBI task force which effectively launched the skills revolution with its 1989 report of that name.

9

The Skills Revolution

**The future will belong to companies and economies
which compete on the basis of superior skills, responsiveness and innovative capability. Technology can be
purchased or copied. Finances are rarely a constraint.
Ready access to raw materials or the advantages of
geographic location will seldom compensate for competitive shortcomings. What cannot readily be bought
are teams of skilled, committed and experienced
people.**

One of the most pressing challenges facing the governments of
Europe is unemployment. In the autumn of 1993 over sixteen
million citizens of the European Union (EU) were looking for
work, an increase of five million in a decade. In the United
Kingdom the unemployment rate may be lower than in France,
Germany, Italy or Spain; none the less, close to three million
people who want work cannot find it; and half of them have been
on the dole for over six months. The picture is particularly bleak
for young men and ethnic minorities. This is only partly because
women are more likely to be working in Britain than in any other
EU country except Denmark; in 1990 the difference between the
proportion of women in paid employment in the United Kingdom
and Germany represented some one and a half million jobs. (We
are also second only to Denmark in the EU league tables for
divorce and illegitimate births.)

The largest loss of jobs in the recent recession has been in those
industries which are particularly likely to employ unskilled or
semi-skilled men. Thus, over half of all unemployed men in 1992
were manual workers and the unemployment rate among young
Afro-Caribbean men is over twice the average. Between the middle
of 1990, when employment was at its post-1979 peak, and the

trough of the recession two years later, employment in manufacturing, construction, the coal, oil and gas industries, fell abruptly. The declines were as follow:

manufacturing	598,000	12%
construction	172,000	16
coal, oil and gas	26,000	17

Over the same period the overall reduction in employment for the economy as a whole was 5 per cent; in most public services employment was stable (the number of Civil Servants, excluding defence, actually rose slightly).

In a world where unskilled labour is cheap and getting cheaper the only realistic prospect for competing with the Far East or North Africa, and for achieving anything close to full employment at home, must lie through improving the skills of everyone in the work-force. It is no accident that the advanced economies with the lowest unemployment rates, West Germany and Japan, have traditionally invested very heavily in technical education and training. In 1991 OECD figures showed that Japan had an unemployment rate of 2.1 per cent and West Germany 4.3 per cent; the UK figure was 8.7 per cent.

Sadly, however, for generations we seem to have forgotten the wise words of Elizabeth de Burgh, Foundress of Clare College, Cambridge, writing in the aftermath of the Black Death:

Experience, the universal guide, plainly shows that learning is no mean advantage in every rank of life ... But so many men have been swept away by the ravages of the plague that learning has lately suffered a sad decline in number ... Desiring to further the public good we have enlarged the revenues [of Clare College] from the wealth God has given us and have increased the number of students ... And to enable the scholars residing in our said College to live in harmony under the protection of a firm discipline and so enjoy greater freedom to study we have, with the advice of experts, made certain statutes and ordinances, set out below to stand in perpetuity. [Preamble to the Statutes of the Foundress of Clare College, Cambridge, 1359]

Over six centuries later the problem remains. Although we have long aspired to a high skills, high-productivity, high-wage economy, for decades we looked for the higher wages forgetting (or at least ignoring) the need for the skills and productivity to earn them. Apprenticeships – whether to crafts or professions – were often designed as much to protect the living standards of today's work-force as to equip people for the challenges of tomorrow; while the industrial relations history in the post-war period was dogged by seemingly endless disputes over 'who does what'.

One of the successes of the past few years has been a transformation in national attitudes towards skills, at least outside the professions, where restrictive practices still seem to abound. Manufacturers have continued to increase their already considerable investment in training throughout the recession, in notable contrast to their investment in plant and equipment, while their productivity in the trough of the recent recession was some 4 per cent above its level at the peak of the economic cycle two years earlier. And by mid 1993 Britain's unit labour costs – the cost of the labour for every unit of output – were actually falling by around 2 per cent a year. This is a notably better performance than most of our principal international competitors.

It would be wrong to take this success for granted. A similar revolution in attitudes has not taken place elsewhere within the European Union. Indeed the social chapter of the Maastricht Treaty rests on the proposition that it is possible to legislate an improved standard of living for employees generally. This is no doubt one reason why Britain remains the favourite destination for investment in Europe from north America and Japan. Similarly it is evident that the necessary revolution in Britain's education system has a long way still to go before it can be seen as a success.

So we should learn the lessons from the success of the skills revolution. To do so first requires an understanding of the challenges facing the would-be revolutionaries as well as an appreciation of their strategy.

The challenge

In the winter of 1988 a group of leading business people assembled to consider what needed to be done to tackle the so-called skills shortage that had contributed to the boom and bust cycle of the

157

post-war era in Britain. Repeated studies had shown that Britain's work-force was undereducated, undertrained and underqualified. A third of school-leavers had no useful qualifications to show for at least eleven years in full-time education. Despite the massive investment in education over the last generation, nearly half the employed people in Britain had no qualification equivalent to the old GCE O level. Nearly two-thirds had no vocational qualification, compared with 26 per cent in Germany. Just over half the work-force received no formal training in 1987 and that figure rose to two-thirds in manufacturing. Fewer than one employer in three had a training plan or a training budget, only one in five evaluated the benefits of training in any way; and even fewer had formal training targets for their whole work-force or measured the benefits of training against the costs.

It was clear to the CBI's Vocational Education and Training Task Force that many training providers did not respond to employers' needs speedily, because there was little incentive for them to do so. Rigidities, particularly where educational provision and business needs meshed, undoubtedly caused waste and inefficiency. Faced with these difficulties, many employers preferred to poach instead of train people only to lose them to a higher bidder before their investment had paid off. With limited expectation of what individuals could achieve, the result was lower levels of attainment and narrower competence. The education system had bowed to the needs of the more academic, leaving the potential of the majority as an untapped national resource. There was a tendency to undervalue skills and professionalism; vocational training favoured lower-level qualifications for traditional jobs over high-level skills for newer industries.

Employers were evidently ready and willing to respond to this challenge. In 1987 they spent £18 billion on training and the numbers of employees receiving training had increased by half in the previous five years. Yet these moves were not sufficient, nor in time, to address the problem. The decline in the number of school-leavers was already stoking up youth wages. Taking a short-term view could still lead employers to concentrate on narrow job-specific training rather than the broader approach that was needed. For many young people, especially for those disillusioned with full-time education, a higher wage at sixteen was often more attractive than continued learning. Also, there was little evidence that training aimed at the adult work-force would counter the pressures on the overall skills base. Indeed skills shortages were – and are – a significant constraint on business efficiency.

These trends were of great concern. The prospect of more young people entering the labour market directly at sixteen or receiving narrow foundation training was simply unacceptable at a time when German employers, for example, were calling for further strengthening of their own system. Indeed most international comparisons gave no cause for comfort. On average, British children were two years behind the Japanese in terms of basic mathematical competence; less likely to develop foreign language skills than the French, Germans or Scandinavians; had a lower level of economic awareness, and had fewer and lower-level educational qualifications than was the case for most of our major European competitors.

It was not difficult to see why. Britain had one of the lowest rates of participation in post-compulsory education and training of all the OECD countries, producing a much smaller number of school-leavers educated to the standards required by a modern economy.

The position was equally disquieting for adults. Comparisons by the National Institute of Economic and Social Research showed lower levels of education attainment, fewer qualified workers and narrower vocational training here than in Germany, France and Japan. For example, new mechanical and electrical engineering training regulations introduced in Germany in 1987 included explicit outcomes in decision-making, stress acceptance and team spirit as well as knowledge of machine tools and skills in computer technology. The size of the skills gap was perhaps most worrying in engineering, where the number of craftsmen and technicians qualifying in France and Germany every year was more than *double* the UK level, after adjustments for the size of the population. Even in the newly-industrialising nations in the Pacific Basin, far more people remained in education and training after the end of compulsory schooling, failure rates were low and vocational courses were held in high esteem. South Korea was aiming for 80 per cent of its young people to reach university entrance standard by the end of the century. The figure for the UK was only 30 per cent.

It was evident, then, that a revolution was required in the delivery and financing of vocational education and training. Foundation skills were the priority. The transition from education to work had been the weakest element of Britain's skills provision and this had made the updating of adult competence both difficult and expensive. All sixteen- and seventeen-year-olds in employment needed to be undertaking education and training relevant to their needs. The idea of lifetime learning also needed to be promoted. Only when skills were enhanced throughout working life would each employee's full potential be realised. All employees needed to be involved in training or developmental activities as a matter of course. At least half the employed work-force should be aiming for updated or new qualifications.

The strategy

Thus the challenge facing the CBI's Vocational Education and Training Task Force in late 1988. The group was aptly named. The task it faced was formidable. After all, many businesses had manifestly failed to take training seriously, preferring to let others incur the expense and to poach trained people. The government was understandably concerned mainly with training programmes for the unemployed and looked to the forces of the labour market to solve the problem; if employers faced skills shortages through their own shortsightedness, that was, and should be, their concern.

So it was evident that the 'normal' approach for business of demanding more public money for vocational training was unlikely to succeed. Rather, the task force resorted to a distinctly unfashionable approach to the problem. In an era when strategic thinking was frowned upon, it developed and put forward a strategy for public discussion. This put individuals first. It sought to improve employers' performance, rather than whingeing at the government of the day. And it aimed to create a real training market.

Individuals first

It was clear that skills levels would only be improved if individuals were helped and motivated to make fullest use of their talents. Their horizons needed to be broadened and their expectations of themselves raised. Yet the current vocational education and training system had never put individuals first – the needs of providers had higher priority.

A new culture was needed in which the school-leaving age ceased to be an end to education and in which the development of skills and knowledge continued as a matter of course throughout working life. This implied a self-development ethic which built on entitlements and responsibilities. It required an overall framework in which all learning took place, bridging education and training provision. Coherence had long been an objective of policy-makers; but the pursuit of clear objectives which accentuated career choice and availability for all could make it a reality.

The concept of 'careers for all' and creating more demand for education and training was not a new one. Career choice was an occupational theory developed in America in the 1950s which envisaged individuals choosing between a range of offerings. What was new was for employers themselves to focus on individuals rather than on groups. As jobs are upskilled there is more scope for career progression within work for a larger proportion of the work-force. With the accelerating pace of change in the labour market there will be many opportunities for important career choices throughout a working life. These, in turn, should generate more interest in, and demand for, learning, give attainment more overt recognition, improve the quality and the content of education and training provision and provide incentives for its take-up. It should provide a single framework to guide and structure the development of foundation skills from fourteen to nineteen and a basis for continuous learning and training throughout working life.

These ideas for change already had substantial support among the people who would be most affected. A survey of seventeen- and eighteen-year-olds in England and Wales in 1989, before the recession began to bite, showed a demand from young people of all backgrounds for more training and support for training entitlements; 60 per cent of respondents were already thinking in career terms rather than expecting merely to have a job, and were prepared to spend considerable time planning for their future. Support for careers and training came both from boys and girls with non-academic backgrounds, and from those following pathways leading to the professions and management. There was also evidence of support for training and career development among older employees. Research showed that for 40 per cent of the work-force there had been occasions when they would have liked more training but did not receive it; almost 60 per cent was considering or could imagine undertaking training in the future. This research emphasised the positive links between demand for training and the existing education and skills level of employees.

The strategy proposed for realising the untapped potential of individuals involved:

- one national system of Records of Achievement and action plans to be used both in schools and employment. This would require a coming together of school records with the National Record of Vocational Achievement and the embracing of records and action plans within one profile for every individual. All young people would then be treated equally, irrespective of the route of their learning, and the profile would emphasise that structured learning should take place throughout the fourteen to eighteen age range and beyond
- top quality independent advice focused on the individual and available to young people, and to a lesser extent to others in working life. Careers guidance required a new rationale, reinvigoration and extra investment. Pupils in their final three years would receive at least one period of teaching a week as part of a co-ordinated careers education and guidance programme, reported to parents and governors regularly. Each school or college would make adequate provision for careers co-ordinators and careers teachers who must receive adequate training and updating. Ultimate responsibility for careers education and guidance and securing the above would rest with a nominated member of the senior management team within the school or college. This might involve the separation of responsibility for professional direction from that for service delivery. Services to schools and colleges would be negotiated and paid for individually; and basic service to employers (for example, for vacancies and referral) specified and funded in a contract with, for example, Training and Enterprise Councils
- individual Training Credits for young people. A credit or voucher would be available for all sixteen-year-olds to enable them to buy learning associated with courses leading to National Vocational Qualification (NVQ) level III or its academic equivalent (A levels). Neither individuals nor employers alone can be expected to meet the full costs of

investment in skills and training before the deficiencies of the education system have been remedied

- incentives for adults. A personal income tax allowance of, say, £1 thousand per annum could be made available to anyone working towards a nationally recognised qualification in their own time, where a credit was not also being used. The short-term loss of tax revenue would be more than outweighed by future higher earning power, and the reduced risk of long-term unemployment

- transferable skills and relevant qualifications. Britain's education and training has been relatively weak because of the inadequate levels which it has reached and the narrow foundations on which it is built. Learning through training should be concerned with an appropriate balance of skills, knowledge and understanding; and the core skills should be transferable from one job or employer to another: effective communication, numeracy, applications of technology, understanding of work and the world, personal and interpersonal skills, problem-solving, positive attitudes to change. The new NVQs should be broadly based on a national consensus on what all trainees should be able to do, as opposed to what exams they should have passed – 'learning outcomes' in the jargon of the training world.

The task force expected that putting individuals first throughout the education and training system would go a long way towards raising skills levels. Individual profiles and credits supported by careers advice, transferable skills and high quality qualifications could eventually have a major impact on foundation skills in particular. But meeting the training needs of current members of the work-force was, to a much greater degree, the responsibility of employers.

Investors in people

In the late 1980s there seemed a realistic prospect that more employers would regard skills training as an investment essential to their future competitiveness, not simply as a current cost to be minimised. For the returns from investment in training were clear. Employers who invested in people enhanced their competitive performance: productivity was higher, unit labour costs lower, staff turnover and sickness absence less and skills shortages more manageable. Moreover it was clear that in the 1990s and beyond the future would belong to companies and economies which can compete on the basis of superior skills, responsiveness and innovative capability. Technology can be purchased or copied, as can productive capacity and market access. Finance is rarely a constraint. In the absence of protectionist measures, ready access to raw materials or the advantages of geographic location will seldom compensate for competitive shortcomings. What cannot readily be bought are teams of skilled and committed people.

Yet some organisations are notably more effective in managing their skills needs than others. Too many employers seem to think only about today's skills needs without taking effective steps for the future; they expect that people with the right skills will always be available in the labour market; and they rely on 'poaching' from other firms which train skilled labour – 40 per cent of employers who did no training claimed that they only recruited experienced people. The result: lower productivity and quality and higher labour turnover, absenteeism and recruitment costs. The more successful companies make sure of their supply of new talent through well-established links with local schools and colleges. Yet few employers will be able to rely completely on the recruitment of young people in the years ahead, particularly at a time when there are fewer school-leavers and more young people choose to go on to higher education. The more far-sighted employers – and the only ones with a future – invest in their people just as they invest in technology, new equipment and marketing.

A characteristic of the Investor in People is that each sets targets to raise the skills and qualifications of all members of their workforce. They have a training budget, and aim to deliver the equivalent of ten days in relevant off-the-job training every year to every employee. They encourage individuals to help themselves through, for example, open and distance learning centres.

Finally Investors in People demand value for their investment with systematic and thorough evaluation of the training to ensure its effectiveness and to highlight the benefits. For too long it has been too easy for top management to say that, as with advertising, 'we know that half the money we spend on training is wasted; we just do not know which half'. Not any more. By mid 1993, 3,500 organisations were working towards the Investors in People designation. More than seven out of ten employers claimed to have a formal quality management programme with people at its heart. Over fourteen thousand sites have earned the highly-prized, and very demanding, British Standards Institute Quality Award, BS 5750.

A training market

While in theory planning and taking appropriate steps to meet future skills needs is obvious enough, the practice is far from straightforward in an era of volatile exchange rates and rapidly changing technology – not to mention pressures from the financial markets for immediate profits. It would be unwise in such circumstances to assume that good management sense and generalised exhortation alone will prevail. It seems that almost every possible approach to tackling the skills shortage has been tried, from benign neglect, to the regulatory approach of the grant and levy system run by industrial training boards, and to the central planning that still characterises much of the public sector (and the NHS in particular).

But one approach has never been tried: creating a market for skills. Only a market can correct the basic weaknesses of the current system: an employer tendency to 'buy' rather than 'grow' the skills they need; the difficulty of predicting medium-term skills requirements with confidence; the limited incentive of training providers in the public sector to respond quickly to changes in demand; and the lack of influence by the ultimate customer – the individual – on their local supply of training courses.

The task force thought that a market could be developed by channelling as much as possible of the public funding for the education and training of young people through individual credits, with employers paying their wage costs. Colleges and other training providers would then have every incentive to respond promptly and effectively to new demands from a market.

At sixteen *every* young person would receive, in writing, financial credit entitling them to the cost of approved learning where a course leading to a nationally recognised qualification relates to needs identified in their individual action plan. Studying full-time in a sixth form or further education college would count against the credit. Any individual entering employment would receive a wage from that employer or trainer at the competitive market rate. They would then jointly agree a programme of education and training by producing an action plan. Where this led to a recognised qualification, the employer would be able to apply to the local Training and Enterprise Council for the learning costs to be paid against that individual's entitlement.

Beyond individual credits and pump-priming such as Business Growth Training, there is no case for new grants or tax incentives for employers to train their own work-force. It is far more important to bring about a reduction in corporation tax rates and other elements of the burden on business so that companies can afford extra investment in training. Employers should fund the relevant training of adult employees and the job-specific training and wage costs of youth trainees; and adult employees should fund the cost of training not relevant to their current employment, perhaps encouraged by tax incentives (as explained above).

The Exchequer contribution would only be available for the off-the-job learning costs, and the employer would normally pay a market wage to the trainee. This would concentrate current Exchequer funding on improving skills levels and allow wages to find their own market level.

The new training market could be regulated by the eighty business-led Training and Enterprise Councils (TECs) in England and Wales (and by twenty Enterprise Companies in Scotland). They are ideally suited to give strategic leadership at a local level to these initiatives. However there are challenges that will need to be managed if the TECs are to realise their full potential. Although initial progress with TECs has been most encouraging, it would be all too easy for them to regress to little more than reconstituted Area Manpower Boards of the old Manpower Services Commission. These would be of little attraction to local business leaders, who will not be attracted to serving as (unpaid) non-executive directors of agencies responsible for implementing government training programmes for the unemployed, in the face of their other priorities. An erosion of support from local business leaders would then be represented as evidence that business is not able or willing to step up to its responsibilities in the training field. And it would be a short cut to reviving the failed corporatist solutions of the past; with training levies and grants and the whole expensive and ineffective panoply of Industrial Training Boards.

The role of TECs must be strategic and they should act as regulators of the kind of training market described above, rather than as providers of training. They must also give sufficient attention to their role of leading the regeneration of local economies.

There is considerable potential to build on the local Business Leadership Teams set up under the aegis of Business in the Community. These teams comprise senior members of the local business community and are adopting the strategic role necessary to their task of rebuilding the economies of their communities. Similarly TECs will need to include community interests and link closely with local business/education partnerships which share a common purpose in raising education standards and aspirations. Each locality has only a limited number of business leaders with the time to devote to such initiatives and it will be essential to avoid confusion and duplication of effort.

This means that TECs could be structured along the lines of a 'holding company' with subsidiaries responsible for different aspects of their activities. Conflicts of interest between the funding and delivery of training programmes will have to be avoided. TECs will need to have an overview of all local programmes (including those of employers) that relate to vocational education and training. They will need scope to adapt national programmes and sizeable discretionary budgets to meet local needs. In particular TECs would have a bank of 'credits' to pay for the supply of courses, allocating these to employers to allow them to pay colleges and other providers for courses supplied to individuals pursuing appropriate and nationally recognised qualifications as part of an agreed individual action plan. They would also ensure that employers and training providers offer quality training where each individual's choices of training are well-informed.

The strategy put forward by the task force was timely. It was both coherent and comprehensive – in marked contrast to the piecemeal approach to other national strategic problems. Remarkably soon it was accepted as a sensible way forward by all the special interests involved.

Lessons learned

Five years later, and not withstanding some academic turbulence the skills revolution seem to be well under way. Investment in people has continued to increase even though skills shortages were a problem for only one manufacturer in twenty in mid 1993 compared to nearly one in three when the task force began its work. Almost all elements of the strategy have been taken up in one way or another: National Records of Achievement, better careers guidance, focus on transferable skills and relevant qualifications, individual training credits, the Investors in People programme and a broader strategic role for TECs.

The Management Charter Initiative, to improve the competence of managers of all levels throughout the economy, is now gathering momentum. The movement, launched in 1988, has the support of over 1,500 corporate members from the private, public and voluntary sectors. Detailed management standards have been defined for first-line supervisors (an historic weakness in the British economy), as well as middle and senior management. A nationwide network of management development centres is in place. Over twelve thousand managers are working towards nationally recognised qualifications in management, gaining credit from the competencies they have already shown in their various jobs.

All this happened during a period of turmoil in Whitehall and at Westminster, with particular pressure on the Employment Department's budget. In the five-year period involved, there have been no less than four Secretaries of State for Employment, though for most of the time there was only one Permanent Secretary, whose creative thinking and ability to manage challenging ideas through the machinery of government were of critical importance. Moreover the subject lacks much political and media appeal unless and until the whiff of 'scandalous waste' of public money surfaces; so two of the recognised ingredients for successful policy change were not in place. Neither has the honours system been used to particularly marked effect to reinforce the revolution.

So what can account for this apparent miracle? The most important factor was the calibre and motivation of the revolutionaries. The members of the CBI Task Force comprised busy people at or near the peaks of their respective careers who could not expect to benefit personally in any way from their involvement in its work. They agreed to become involved because their own experience had convinced them that the future of the nation's economy was at risk if we continued along the same old path. And they recognised too the need for a comprehensive and strategic approach to the problem, rather than the more traditional reaction by business in such circumstances of generalised exhortation to government and employers alike.

The second secret weapon was the group's Chairman, Sir Bryan Nicholson. He was (and is) one of the very few business leaders with a close understanding of the way Whitehall and the trade union movement thought and worked. His network of contacts among the educational and training establishments was wide and put to excellent use to manage expectations, diffuse potential problems and avoid surprises. There was no attempt to secure a consensus among the very many special interests involved. Indeed it is difficult for anyone familiar with the way the National Economic Development Council worked to believe that the skills revolution could have emerged from tripartite discussions between government, employers and trade unions, however compelling the need. The various interests nominally represented around the council table could not 'deliver' their members' support for any measures that might be agreed; and some important interests – notably the owners of small businesses and training providers – were not present in any case. But it was important to ensure that there was no public opposition to the proposals.

But none of this would have been sufficient without the ability of the task force to set the policy agenda rather than simply reacting to proposals from elsewhere. This was not easy. On the one hand there was persuasive evidence that Britain's international competitive position was at risk without a skills revolution. But on the other hand government was not keen (or able) to pay for it; and in any case, it had a range of existing programmes to defend politically. Employers were scarcely more enthusiastic, having increased their investment by over half to not far short of £20 billion a year. The trade union movement and the Labour Party were more concerned with unemployment than the skills of those in work. So there could be no question of doing good by stealth. Every available platform therefore had to be used to change attitudes and perceptions; and, of course, in many instances, the medium was part of the message.

But it had to be the right message, at the right time. None of the key ingredients in the strategy for the skills revolution was news. There was no single 'big idea'. After all, individual training credits were (perilously) close to the educational vouchers that had been on the right wing agenda for at least a decade; the leadership teams of Business in the Community provided a role model for the TECs; while the British Standards Institute's quality assurance philosophy, embodied in the world-class standard BS 5750, was a useful parallel for the Investors in People programme. What was new was bringing these ideas together in a coherent and integrated approach to a national problem, while avoiding the impression that this was happening in an era in Whitehall when strategic planning was deeply suspect: two achievements that required staff support of a very high order.

Finally the revolutionaries needed persistence. The attention span of ministers, Parliament and indeed the media is remarkably short. The pressure on new Secretaries of State for something new to say or initiatives to announce is unrelenting. And few are content simply (and it is usually far from simple) to see through a strategy that is unlikely to bear obvious fruit during their time in office. So, perforce, it has been individual members of the CBI's Task Force and their associates who have carried forward the ideas in countless articles, speeches, seminars, weekend conferences and in their day-to-day professional lives; for the most wounding accusation of all is 'physician, heal thyself'.

The skills revolution therefore carries some important lessons. Contrary to the received wisdom, there *is* a market in Britain for ideas on public policy issues; and it is possible to change the ingrained habits and attitudes of decades. The private sector can supply the ideas and lead the changes, provided always that the would-be revolutionaries share a common vision of the future, are well-led and supported, stick together and have the courage of their convictions. These lessons need to be applied in rewriting the nation's economic geography as well.

The state of the nation's transport infrastructure is a major preoccupation of CBI members, since distribution (or logistics) costs amount to over 20 per cent of the retail prices of many product categories. But British public investment in roads and rail has lagged behind our international competitors.

The CBI report, Trade Routes to the Future, published in November 1989, was the first comprehensive attempt to set out a possible way forward. I was invited by the Royal Society of Arts, the Institute of Transport and the Road Haulage Association to speak on the issues involved; and I chaired an international conference on the transport infrastructure at Ditchley Park. I owe to Peter Bottomley, MP the notion of the need to rewrite the nation's economic geography; and to Derek Palmer of the Institute of Transport (formerly of the CBI) my enthusiasm for a problem that is costing the economy in the order of £18 billion a year in waste.

10

Rewriting the Economic Geography

Britain has long invested substantially less than our principal competitors in both road and rail infrastructure.

When the Channel Tunnel opens for business, the contrast between the British and French approaches to planning and implementing major infrastructure projects will be all too apparent. Once again, too late, there will be the cry, 'What went wrong?' Those responsible will not be called to account, since they will no longer be on the scene. A further blow to national self-esteem will be rationalised away.

Yet it is clear that Britain has demonstrably the least competitive transport infrastructure in northern Europe. Furthermore it is pointing in the wrong direction. Over half of UK non-oil exports are now sent to the Single European Market, compared to only 13 per cent that go to north America. But the lack of effective transport links to the Continent creates the prospect of the United Kingdom – which only accounts for around 10 per cent of the combined Gross Domestic Product of the European Union – becoming economically marginalised on the fringes of a market whose centre of gravity is moving steadily south and east and whose epicentre is within 200 km of Düsseldorf. By failing to capitalise on our geographic position within the Atlantic Arc and the opportunities that the tunnel represents for Britain to compete with Rotterdam as an entry port for Europe, we could lose out in the growth stakes to northern France, Spain, Italy and ultimately eastern Europe by our failure to invest in a world-class transport infrastructure.

None the less the case for a further massive increase in public investment – in rail as much as road – is not generally accepted; government is seeking to limit its role to the regulation of a transport market, leaving investment to the private sector. An apparent allergy to strategic thinking, fragmented responsibility for planning and action, a planning system designed to prevent (or at best delay) major developments is likely to ensure mounting congestion, not to mention increasing environmental damage, as well as lost opportunities for ports along the south coast and in the north-west. Meanwhile the City of London's position as the European financial services centre will be threatened by Frankfurt, Zurich and possibly even Paris.

There is an urgent need to rewrite the nation's economic geography. This will entail setting clear national priorities for infrastructure development. It will mean changes in the way we plan and manage our national transport network. It will require the nation's investment in the transport infrastructure to double over the next decade, simply to contain the costs of congestion.

The cost of neglect

Demand for all types of transport rose sharply during the 1980s. Car ownership increased by 29 per cent between 1981 and 1990; in Great Britain as a whole the proportion of households without regular use of a car fell from four in ten to one in three. Passenger traffic on the roads increased by nearly 40 per cent, faster than any other western European country. Freight carriage rose by almost a quarter over the same period.

The railway share of this traffic is relatively modest. In 1991 rail accounted for under 6 per cent of total passenger miles and 7 per cent of freight carried (including loads carried by water and pipelines). Moreover the rail share fell during the period. So even the most fervent advocate of railway privatisation – and there seems to be remarkably few of them in evidence – must recognise that a railway renaissance will not meet the nation's transport needs. Even in France where there has been massive investment in the railway system, as we shall see, the rail share of passenger traffic in 1990 was under 10 per cent.

So if mounting congestion is to be avoided there is no alternative to increased investment in our road system. During the 1980s this was neglected, and the cost is rapidly becoming insupportable. Already road congestion, with its attendant economic and environmental costs, has risen sharply. Few companies keep detailed accounts of the costs of congestion because there is little that they can do about it. However, as a result of studies carried out by the CBI, it is now possible both to identify the sources of congestion – induced costs – and to assess the impact of congestion in more detail than from the previous rough estimates based on motorway traffic flows. Moreover managers are devoting more time and attention to logistics. And for good reason. Transport and distribution costs are around £50 billion a year – a sum that amounts to some £40 a week per household and represents two-thirds of company trading profits.

The spread of 'just-in-time' manufacturing strategies, the increasing emphasis on fresh and perishable food in retail outlets and the tighter control of stock made possible by recent advances in information technology have combined to make suppliers very sensitive to being able to meet their delivery promises. Rather than run the risk of failing to meet their customers' increasingly stringent requirements, suppliers simply allow more time for journeys from their factories or depots to retail stores. This means more vehicles and drivers.

For example, there are some 125,000 multiple retail outlets in Great Britain, of which perhaps fifty thousand are in London and the south-east. Nearly half the products sold in a typical multiple retail outlet are likely to be perishable (for example, sausages, meat, fish, garden and dairy produce and bread) with tight sell-by dates on their packs. To meet the demands of customers – not to mention the law – retailers operate systems which enable every shop to order daily supplies sufficient to meet customers' needs for the following day. Deliveries are planned to ensure that perishable goods arrive at each branch before 7.30 in the morning. The longer-life and non-perishable products arrive during the course of the same day, up to eight o'clock in the evening. To achieve the required service standards, depots work around the clock. In such circumstances, apparently small differences in journey times make a substantial difference. At an average speed of 16 mph – the average speed in London before 7.30 – one vehicle/driver can often meet the daily delivery requirements of an individual store (of three loads a day) within the store delivery 'windows' for different types of products. But problems of congestion seem to be worsening, in the London area in particular. One supplier has reduced his scheduled speed for journeys in the London area from 8 to 6.5 mph in the last three years. Another routinely adds 25 per cent to journey times after 8 a.m. when 60 per cent of trips are made. With average speeds of 7 mph many stores will need an additional vehicle, or even two, even though over 50 per cent of their deliveries are made by 7.30. Thus, for the grocery sector alone, congestion could well be putting an additional fifty thousand lorries on to already overcrowded roads in London and the south-east.

One leading transport company calculates that in the congested areas of the south-east its vehicle fleet is 30 per cent greater than elsewhere, a figure confirmed by a leading frozen foods company which finds that its vehicles in the south-east carry out only two-thirds of the work possible in other parts of Britain. A major brewer confirms that distribution costs in the south-east are 22 per cent above the rest of the United Kingdom, with productivity (tonnes per man year) 15 per cent lower. The need for more drivers and vehicles is not the only congestion-induced cost that business has to bear:

- fuel consumption will be higher, as will maintenance costs as tyres and transmission systems wear out more rapidly. The brewer observes that average fuel consumption (in a comparable fleet mix) is 12 per cent higher in the south-east than in the Midlands, for example. Tyre and maintenance labour costs per vehicle mile are 30 per cent or more lower in depots outside the south-east
- the strain on drivers will inevitably be greater, leading to more sickness absence. Every percentage point of sickness absence for drivers (which averages 5–6 per cent) could well be costing business over £100 million a year
- the productivity of sales forces is lower. Sales representatives in the London area can take twice as long to travel the same miles between calls as those elsewhere in the south-east, and two and a half times as long as those in the rest of the country. As a result sales people in London often average 25 per cent fewer calls a week than the national average
- the inability of staff to predict their time of arrival at the office with any accuracy – and the stress that this uncertainty often induces – means that the productivity of office staff is lower: meetings have to be scheduled later; time is wasted as people express their frustrations to those around them. One major company has put the annual cost at around £1,000

for every one of its five thousand employees in central London (in 1991 British Rail carried over 40 per cent of commuters into Central London, and the Underground a third; only one in seven commuters came into central London by car).

The impact on business of road congestion is not simply a question of extra costs, although these are certainly important. Opportunities for savings are missed as well. Motorways can allow companies to reduce their number of depots by two-thirds if they are able to rely on the kind of road infrastructure available to competitors on the Continent. For example, a major food manufacturer has been able to service the same customer base in the London area with two depots rather than the six previously required, because of the availability of the M4, M40 and M25. Even the most efficient operators would be able to reduce their costs by 10–15 per cent if they could rely on a network of reasonably congestion-free motorways.

Finally there are public expenditure implications as well. More lorries than necessary mean that roads are likely to break up more quickly, adding to maintenance costs. Overall it is now generally accepted that road congestion is costing the economy in the order of £18 billion a year, adding over £60 a month to the average household shopping bill.

Long-standing weaknesses

How did waste of this magnitude apparently creep up on us? There are long-standing weaknesses in the current approach to planning the infrastructure which must be tackled. To start with, forecasting must be improved. The methodology of road traffic forecasting in the UK has been somewhat primitive. Forecasts made as recently as 1984 were badly out. By 1988 traffic volume (vehicle miles) was 27 per cent higher than in 1983, compared with a forecast increase of 9–16 per cent. The latest national road traffic forecasts for Great Britain have suggested that, although the number of vehicles on the road will more than double by 2025, the increase in volume over the period is expected to be lower than the (wrong) forecasts in 1984. But it is not clear that they take adequate account of the underlying forces at work in the economy. For example:

- the scope for increased car ownership in the United Kingdom, which is relatively low by continental standards; it was 363 cars per thousand population in Great Britain in 1990, compared with 468 in France and 486 in West Germany
- the continuing shift to a service economy and the growth of self-employment, with a greater proportion of staff 'on the road'. Sub-contracting by business, especially of catering, cleaning, equipment servicing and security, has caused a rapid increase in the volume of commercial traffic. In the period 1983–7, for example, there was a 30 per cent increase in the number of light goods vehicles entering London every day. In the year to the end of the first quarter of 1989, light van traffic grew by 9 per cent – half as much again as the increase in all road traffic during the period
- heavy inward investment by companies using Britain as a manufacturing base from which to supply Europe. Investments by the likes of Honda, Nissan and Toyota, all of whom expect their components to arrive just in time to be assembled, have inevitably added to road traffic
- the trend to out-of-town shopping and to even larger stores, combined with ever-more demanding delivery standards for suppliers
- the trend to heavier vehicles to increase productivity within the road haulage industry
- the impact of de-regulation of buses on the frequency and demand for bus services. Long-distance commuters and Londoners will find a zero growth forecast for buses and coaches particularly open to question
- the shift of much bulk freight from rail to roads, as British Rail increases its freight prices ahead of privatisation.

The problems of the M25, which accounts for 14 per cent of the UK's motorway traffic, illustrate the need to plan roads well ahead of demand. It is now clear that the road should have been built as originally suggested, with four rather than three lanes in each direction. But the road planners were instructed to reduce their forecasts, because the ministers at the time saw no possibility of securing planning approval for four lanes. As a result, apart from the current congestion (which could well be costing over £1 billion a year), there will be further delays to traffic while the extra lane is added. Meanwhile the cost of the work will be approaching £10 million a mile – close to the cost of building a new four-lane motorway.

Overcrowding is not confined to the road system. Fifteen stations of the London Underground are critically congested and twenty-five stations are operating at or beyond their notional full capacity. A further ten to fifteen stations are expected to become seriously congested by the end of the century if demand continues to grow as forecast. While off-peak demand has grown by 80 per cent since 1980, the major problem has been the 35 per cent growth in peak traffic over this period. Similar problems face British Rail. The opening of the Channel Tunnel will create new opportunities for international rail transport, especially for passengers between London, Paris and Brussels, as well as freight. Steady growth in rail commuting is also anticipated. Morning peak rail traffic entering central London is forecast to rise by 15 per cent by the year 2001, with British Rail trips growing by nearly 20 per cent and those on the Underground by 13 per cent. Underground journeys from British Rail stations within the central area are forecast to increase by 20 per cent during the morning peak.

But by far the most rapid increase has been that of air travel: 87 per cent from 1977 to 1987 in terms of terminal passengers, both international and domestic. Whereas from 1977 to 1983 the average annual rate of increase in the number of visits to and from the UK was around 6 per cent per annum, since then it has almost doubled. Growth has been particularly rapid at four major airports where the number of international passenger movements has more than doubled over the past decade: Manchester, East Midlands, Gatwick and Birmingham. Meanwhile air freight since 1983 has grown by an average of 8 per cent per annum, reversing a decline over the six previous years.

All this suggests the need for a massive infrastructure investment programme, covering road, rail and air services. Yet Britain has long invested substantially less than our principal competitors in both road and rail infrastructure. Traditionally, we have allocated far less of our revenue from motoring taxation to the provision, improvement and maintenance of our road system. In 1987 expenditure on roads accounted for less than a quarter of the taxes paid by motorists; the figure was over 60 per cent in West Germany.

France, for example, is already committed to expanding its

motorway network by three and a half times between 1987 and 1997. In addition, Charles de Gaulle Airport is to have a third runway and has the capacity to be expanded to five runways to cater for ninety million passengers per annum, two and a half times the current size of Heathrow. Furthermore continued substantial investment is occurring in the high-speed Train à Grande Vitesse (TGV) network, which will eventually be 7,000 km long including 2,300 km of new line, allowing running speeds of up to 300 kph. The TGV Sud-Est has been operating since 1981 and the TGV Atlantique has recently opened. In addition the TGV Nord Européen will link to Brussels, Amsterdam and Cologne, with a branch to the Channel Tunnel from Lille. Studies are under way for linking Paris with Strasbourg and with Marseilles/Cannes by TGV. Charles de Gaulle Airport will be fully integrated into the TGV network via a station at Roissy.

The Federal Republic of Germany intends to put both public and private money into a rail modernisation plan. Plans for a 'Transrapid' electro-magnetic hovertrain costing DM 30 billion to link seven major airports from Hamburg to Munich along a 640-mile corridor are being developed. The project is designed to reduce road traffic by 8 per cent and air traffic by 35 per cent by the year 2000. The heavily subsidised German rail network (30,600 km) is almost twice the length of ours, while its motorway network is almost three times longer – 8,400 km compared to 3,000 km in the UK. Germany, Austria, Italy and Switzerland are considering the construction of two new rail tunnels through the Alps, one of which would relieve pressure on the Brenner Pass. These would link in with the proposals for a European high-speed train network which would connect the industrial and commercial centres of the Continent: Paris, Amsterdam, Brussels, Hamburg, Cologne, Frankfurt, Munich, Basle, Milan, Lyons, Barcelona and Madrid.

Continental companies also have the benefit of an extensive network of rivers and canals which offer cheap transport. To this will be added another advantage: the Rhine–Danube canal will create a waterway corridor allowing vessels up to 1,350 tonnes dead weight and barges up to 185 metres long carrying 3,300 tonnes to cross Europe from the North Sea to the Black Sea. Thus North Sea ports will be open for direct traffic to Austria, Hungary, Romania, Bulgaria, and ultimately the Near and Middle East.

Meanwhile, even before the projected increase in traffic (which suggests that there will be five vehicles on the road by 2025 for every two now), traffic density on the UK's motorways and main roads is 70 per cent more than in West Germany, twice that in France and five times that in the USA.

So major improvements in the motorway and primary route network are needed, pointing at Europe, including south and east coast motorways. The south-east need not be covered in steel and concrete. The priority schemes would occupy the equivalent of less than 1 per cent of the farmland in Dorset, Wiltshire, Hampshire, Sussex and Kent – considerably less than has already been 'set aside' from agricultural production or has already been earmarked for housing development in these counties.

However, investment in roads alone obviously will not cater for the forecast growth in traffic. Investment to capitalise on the potential that the Channel Tunnel affords for a railway renaissance will provide a valuable alternative to road freight for middle- to longer-distance international haulage trips. It will also remove some of the lorries that are currently clogging up our inter-urban motorway network. A recent report in *Time* magazine describes the renaissance that has taken place in the United States rail freight industry:

> In any given 24 hours, there are 20,000 freight trains moving somewhere in the US, growling over the great Plains, clanging through urban switches and labouring up mountain passes carrying 37 per cent of the stuff that America produces and consumes. Their long tails, sometimes stretching 3 km behind, are mostly hidden in the swells and crevices of the land ... The 12 great freight routes which bear 90 per cent of the business of the 535 surviving American railroads are all profitable these days ... Rails transport two-thirds of the new cars from factories to dealers and piggy-back 6.5 million truck trailers a year. [*Time*, 23 August 1993]

If the railway renaissance is to come, the privatisation of British Rail should focus more on international freight and London suburban services than on the Inter-City service which is well run and profitable. Ultimately a new Berne gauge line spine link as the backbone of the rail system will be needed. Even though this would take many years and be very costly, it will be essential if the UK is to become part of the European rail freight network.

Investment in air transport is also needed. Quite apart from other considerations, UK tourism is a major industry that warrants modern infrastructure support. The European Community was created almost thirty-five years ago. Yet the European Air Traffic Control uses twenty-two different systems, operating from forty-five different ATC centres; inefficiencies in the system probably cost the European economy some £3 billion a year. In the USA the volume of traffic is three times greater but is handled by only twenty centres. In Europe there could be a single unified system operated from six centres if there were the political will. Euro-control is gradually improving harmonisation and integration. But at the present rate of progress it will take another two decades to achieve full unification of air traffic control.

This is not the only problem. More terminal and runway capacity with suitable surface access is also urgently required in the south-east. The business case for another runway at Heathrow, as well as another terminal, is overwhelming if it is to remain the pre-eminent international hub airport in Europe. According to one estimate, Heathrow now accounts for business turnover equivalent to over 15 per cent of Britain's international trade.

An integrated approach

The need for massive investment in the transport infrastructure presents particular difficulties for a government faced with a combination of a strident environmental lobby and even more strident opponents of any local infrastructure developments, a £50 billion public sector borrowing requirement, and a commitment to privatising a loss-making British Rail in such a way as to avoid damaging its electoral prospects in the London commuter-belt. The temptation to hope that market forces and the private sector will somehow come to the rescue must be very great.

But they will not. Government must take the lead in the thinking about our future infrastructure needs, and in the planning to meet them – even if some of the funding is to come from private sources. Only government can introduce the measures necessary to divert traffic from road to rail and to speed up a planning process which can delay needed developments for decades. This requires strategic oversight which is presently lacking; no one is in charge. Responsibility for co-ordinating infrastructure planning must be undertaken by the Department of Transport. But the department is only responsible for transport in England, with the Welsh, Scottish and

Northern Ireland Offices governing their own transport networks while the Treasury controls the financing of public investment. The fragmented approach to planning and implementing infrastructure projects, with no fewer than ten Whitehall departments, not to mention 128 highway authorities in Britain alone, as well as BAA, BR, CAA and LRT all directly involved, is a recipe for confusion and delay.

And so it has proved. The last overall strategic plan for the nation's roads was published in June 1971, setting a target network of 3,500 miles of new roads by the early 1980s, of which 2,000 miles would be motorways and the rest dual carriageways. Much of this plan has yet to be implemented. There is little thinking about how to improve the links between different transport modes. Co-ordination of London's infrastructure needs represents a particular problem. The solution must lie in clear assignment of lead responsibility to the Department of Transport, whose Secretary of State should be answerable to Parliament for:

- developing a national strategic infrastructure programme for the United Kingdom as a whole, and covering air and rail as well as major roads and ports development. The recent White Paper, *Roads for Prosperity*, is an important step in the right direction – but it only refers to roads in England and does not address the issues of how the programme will be financed or the timing of the various projects concerned. Nor does it cover such questions as how the privatisation of British Rail will affect road traffic levels; when and where new airport capacity in the south-east will be needed; what impact the Channel Tunnel will have on south and west coast ports
- proposing how the programme is to be financed, and the implementation timetable, taking due account of the potential for attracting private capital and the implications of privatising British Rail
- putting forward changes to the planning system to speed implementation of national priority schemes. Still better compensation, combined with limits to the ability of local planning enquiries to hold up priority national projects, must come higher on the political agenda. Much could be achieved by improving the levels of compensation of those adversely affected by new road or rail schemes; these have been far too

low to encourage the ready acceptance of change. Recent improvements in reimbursement (to 110 per cent of property values) are a step in the right direction. But British practice still compares unfavourably with France, both in terms of speed and generosity – there, affected householders can receive up to 140 per cent of their properties' market values as compensation

- refining the existing investment appraisal methods, including cost-benefit analysis, used by the Department of Transport to take greater account of environmental benefits. Rail and other public sector investments should not be obstructed if they fail to meet the required rate of return when clear environmental advantages can be identified. Even if these are difficult to quantify or do not appear in the public sector profit and loss account.

In any event, urban public transport must be greatly improved. Clearly, the problems in London are in the most urgent need of attention. The costs of the necessary improvements could be financed through the introduction of road pricing in some form. Surely this is an idea whose time has come now that the technology is available to 'tag' individual drivers using particular roads at a given time of day. At present it seems considerably cheaper to travel by road than by rail; few drivers take account of the value of their own time and many tend to regard the costs of their car as being fixed: there is no point in having a car and not using it. But it must be sensible to reduce congestion and marginal use of roads (and motorways in particular), so that the economic cost of congestion is reduced. Moreover road space in many areas and during peak periods is a scarce resource. Yet drivers can use it without any direct charge. Thus, the costs of congestion imposed by any one individual car driver on other users, particularly emergency services and businesses, are not borne by that individual who may well have an alternative means of transport.

To overcome these problems, one approach would be to price road space to discourage non-essential users at certain times and in certain places. Introducing charges for road use using automatic vehicle identification (AVI) technology for toll collection is quite feasible. The system is already in use in the United States as well as in Hong Kong. It comprises vehicle-borne tags, roadside reader units, and a computer system. Customers joining the scheme fit an electronic tag to their vehicle and drive through, without stopping, in dedicated lanes, on the side of which are reader units which register as cars pass. Linked to a central computer, customers can either be billed monthly or they may pre-pay into their account.

Carefully controlled experiments should be set up in and around London, in areas where public transport is considered adequate, to see whether direct charging is a practical proposition, how much income can be generated and whether it has the expected impact on congestion – some estimates have suggested that tolling motorways for private motorists could generate as much as £10 billion a year in extra revenues.

The presumed opposition to road pricing may not materialise if the proceeds are seen to be spent on improved roads and public transport and if there were some offsetting reductions in the taxation of unleaded petrol or ownership of motor vehicles: motor vehicle Excise Duty generated less than £$1\frac{1}{4}$ billion in revenue in 1991. But this would require removal of another Treasury shibboleth: the aversion to 'hypothecating' tax revenues.

Finally, new and better ways must be found to put private funds to work financing more major infrastructure projects. For many years the private sector has urged the Treasury to facilitate private investment in the national infrastructure. In vain until very recently. With the sole exceptions of the Dartford river crossing and the second Severn Bridge, the mandarins have so far shunned private capital. The Ryrie rules have seen to it that private investors should not profit from the provision of better roads, modern schools, improved housing or more up-to-date hospitals and adequate community care facilities.

The economic justification for the Treasury's reluctance to see British Rail lease rolling stock or borrow on the international money markets to finance major projects has always seemed questionable to this author. There is ample evidence that the private sector is able, and willing, to finance major capital infrastructure projects where the financial pay-off may be well into the future. The £10 billion Channel Tunnel project is the most obvious example. There is no need to be concerned about the implications for the Public Sector Borrowing Requirement either. After all, recently privatised companies such as BT, BAA, National Power and PowerGen between them sustain a capital expenditure programme of well over £4 billion a year (the same order of magnitude as annual public investment in road and rail). This expenditure would have appeared as part of the Public Sector Borrowing Requirement before the companies concerned were nationalised; but it is now sustainable without any apparent impact on the standing of sterling in the international financial markets.

There must, surely, be scope for the private sector to build hospitals, schools, roads and bridges, and lease them to the relevant public sector bodies at a rate which provides an appropriate return to investors. The French railways are able to raise finance on international money markets, secured against projects such as the TGV line from Paris to Lyons which now has some 50 per cent of the combined air-rail market between these two cities, which are over 400 km apart. The original fifteen-year loan was repaid within seven years. Indeed it is often said that French railways represent better security than French government bonds; after all, governments may come and go, but no one is about to remove the track and rolling stock.

Only now is the general public beginning to perceive the costs of our past failure to invest on an adequate scale and to plan rail, road and air transport – not to mention our ports – together. For the United Kingdom as a whole the embarrassment associated with the inadequate links to the Channel Tunnel will stir public opinion further. For the first time, perhaps, the political cost of doing as little as possible will begin to exceed that of confronting local opposition to investing in this aspect of the nation's economic future.

The mid 1980s were a time of turmoil in English local government. *The Audit Commission, and its Controller, were in the middle of these events; and the state of some of our inner cities became a preoccupation of mine. This preoccupation was in no way lessened when I visited Atlanta, Chicago, New York and Washington in late 1986. In early 1987 the Audit Commission published a report drawing attention to the emerging problems,* The Management of London's Authorities: Preventing the Breakdown of Services.

But there was hope in the example of the turnaround in Glasgow in which I had played a part at McKinsey, as well as in the private sector role in north American cities such as Cleveland, New York and Pittsburgh. So when I moved to the CBI in the spring of 1987 an urban regeneration task force was set up, chaired by Tom Frost, the then Chief Executive of the National Westminster Bank. Its report, Initiatives Beyond Charity, *summarised the lessons to be learned from experience of innercity renewal in both the United Kingdom and across the Atlantic. It owed much to contributions from Norman Blackwell and Duncan Campbell-Smith of the* Economist *and formerly at McKinsey, who contributed to the work* pro bono publico.

11

The Urban Underclass

The South Bronx in New York and the Southside of Chicago represent a future to be avoided at all cost.

'It took a riot,' wrote the then Secretary of State for the Environment, Michael Heseltine, in the aftermath of the Toxteth and Brixton riots in the early 1980s, to galvanise the government and nation into action to prevent further deterioration in our inner cities and to set in train what was then seen as a concerted programme of urban regeneration. Urban renewal was, and remains, a noble cause. The combustible mixture of social and economic deprivation in some parts of London in particular represents one of the most difficult management challenges facing the public sector. And it is a challenge which it is failing. Despite annual expenditure of some £4 billion a year, the government was told recently that it faced a choice between gun law and regeneration:

> segregation of poor and disadvantaged people into ghettos guarded by armed police or better-off neighbours hiring their own armed guards ... could be a realistic end product if there is continued failure to address the problems faced by too many people in our cities ... when too many inhabitants of a city are without money, without work, without homes and, worst of all, without hope, then cities as entities must inevitably flounder.

It is indeed a terrible prospect, one that is already a present reality in some parts of our inner cities. The underlying problems must be tackled aggressively and the lessons of the 1980s, good and bad, learned well. These come not just from our own experience but from across the Atlantic.

A terrible prospect

Those who have visited the South Bronx in New York or the Southside of Chicago invariably return appalled by what they have seen, depressed about the prospects for beneficial change and determined to do all in their power to ensure that similar intractable problems will not be allowed to afflict our own inner cities. An introduction to a twenty-four-year-old grandmother and the very idea of 'babies having babies' frightens the most hardened observer. According to one recent report, in Baltimore a quarter of all teenage girls, and almost half of teenage girls from ethnic minorities, have been pregnant by the time they are eighteen; nearly one in ten of all fifteen- to seventeen-year-old girls in the city became mothers during 1990.

In inner London the writing has, literally, been on the wall for at least six years. Concerned about the situation facing the inner London authorities and a looming shortfall in income of about £400 million (as much as 40 per cent of current revenue expenditure in some authorities) and over £700 million of creative accounting measures that would load extra costs on to future generations of ratepayers, the Audit Commission examined the situation in late 1986. It found that there were very disturbing parallels with the situation in parts of New York and Chicago in a number of boroughs in inner London, ten of which head the league table of urban deprivation in England (in order: Hackney, Newham, Tower Hamlets, Lambeth, Hammersmith and Fulham, Harringey, Islington, Brent, Wandsworth and Southwark).

Indeed the sheer scale of the challenge and the unacceptable costs of failure were of sufficient concern to the Confederation of British Industry that in 1988 it set up a special task force to consider what needed to be done. Its report, *Initiatives Beyond Charity*, painted a bleak picture:

The South Bronx and the Southside of Chicago represent a future to be avoided at almost all costs. There, a combination of poor housing and education, high crime rates, much of it drug-related, large-scale immigration and associated racial tensions, an exodus of jobs and the more well-off to the suburbs, high youth unemployment and welfare dependency and the break-up of traditional family structures (with a very high proportion of single parent families), have served to create what some commentators in the United States have described as an 'urban underclass'. Each of these factors tends to reinforce the others, creating a vicious circle. Once such a situation develops it is extraordinarily difficult to retrieve, as American experience over the last three decades demonstrates. So preventing the further growth of an urban 'underclass' in the United Kingdom must be a national priority concern.

By the mid 1980s many of the factors that created an 'underclass' in a number of north American cities were already present in large parts of London. There had been a decline in opportunities for semi-skilled and unskilled employment. Over the period from June 1982 to June 1986 the number of jobs in manufacturing and construction in Greater London fell by 126,000. This was particularly serious when around half the 95,000 leaving school every year had no O level or equivalent CSE passes and on a typical school day around one pupil in three was playing truant. Unemployment was relatively high especially among young men from ethnic minorities. In October 1986 unemployment among men in inner London was 21 per cent. At that time 34 per cent of all men aged twenty to twenty-four were registered as unemployed (the figure was 46 per cent in Hackney and 44 per cent in Lambeth); for young people of Afro-Caribbean origin the figure was higher still – in 1984 the unemployment rate among West Indians was double that for Greater London as a whole.

Nearly 40 per cent of families lived in council-owned accommodation, much of it in poor condition. In April 1984 over one in five of the 444,000 council dwellings was considered unfit, lacked some basic amenities or was in need of renovation. (The commission had already shown that the backlog of maintenance and improvement work on council houses in inner London was double the national average and averaged over £4,000 per dwelling.) There was an increasingly serious problem of homelessness. On a typical night, over five thousand families were accommodated in bed and breakfast accommodation at council expense; and there was a council house waiting list in inner London of over 150,000, partly caused by the difficulty young people experienced in buying their first house.

Crime, much of it drug-related, was high and rising. The number of serious crimes reported per thousand residents in inner London was 56 per cent above the average for metropolitan areas outside London; and it had increased by over 90 per cent since

1971. In the most deprived boroughs the crime rate was a third above the average for inner London generally.

The number of single-parent families was also high and increasing; in inner London as a whole in 1984, 31 per cent of children were born to single parent families. (The figure was 39 per cent in Southwark and 42 per cent in Lambeth). In more than one in five cases, the mother was under twenty years old. Racial tensions and problems between the police and ethnic minorities were evident – and not just from the Brixton riots and the events on the Broadwater Farm Estate.

This catalogue of problems was so serious as to be difficult to comprehend by those who had never lived in a rundown inner city area. The following quotation from a report prepared by the Department of the Environment describes the reality then facing many people in inner London:

> Many (estates) have become 'dumping grounds' for the poorest, most disadvantaged families, as 'better' tenants have moved. Very modern estates with the more up-to-date amenities are also hated for their long dark corridors and balconies and monolithic style. They provide havens for skateboarders, go-kart fans, and, in some cases, young muggers; they echo noise; they invite abusive graffiti; the lifts are regularly smashed. Some modern estates also suffer from physical defects, of which the most notorious are water penetration, condensation and unsuitable heating systems.

Since these initial warnings, there have been substantially larger government grants to the local authorities concerned, as well as some £1.5 billion of expenditure in Docklands and from the Urban Programme between 1986 and 1991. (Between 1987 and 1990 annual government grants of one kind or another to the ten most deprived London boroughs increased in constant (1990) prices by some £85 to £785 for every resident; the comparable figures for Manchester – which faces similar problems – were an increase of £9 and total grants/subsidies of £459.) There have also been a series of new initiatives to add to what seems like an alphabet soup of Urban Programme Authorities (1978), Priority Estates (1979), Urban Development Corporations (1981), City Action Teams (1985), Task Force Areas (1986), Estate Action (1987), Training and Enterprise Councils (1988), City Challenge (1991), and the Urban Regeneration Agency (1992).

But despite all this effort, in 1991 in the twenty-five most deprived council wards in England unemployment was over 30 per cent and half of the children were living in single parent households. Educational results remained poor, with fewer than one in five pupils leaving school with five or more GCSE grades A–C and six out of ten leaving school just as soon as they could. Around a quarter of the adult population was receiving income support or supplementary benefits; in some areas the proportion was well over one in three.

Partly because of the continuing low level of social housing construction, homelessness increased almost fourfold; one in every fifty households was in temporary accommodation of one form or another, a third of which were bed and breakfast hotels. In urban programme areas two out of three people who had completed Employment Training were still unemployed three months after leaving the scheme. Crime rates had risen as well. The deterioration in the condition of local housing was continuing, piling up bills for the future which will have to be met eventually by residents and taxpayers.

The problem is not going to solve itself, however successful the economy may be. Between 1979 and 1989, a period of unprecedented overall real growth for the British economy, the proportion of households with below half average income more than doubled to not far short of one household in five. During this same period the disposable income of the poorest one-tenth of households actually fell slightly, even as the average rose by almost 25 per cent. The costs to the taxpayer of a disaffected urban underclass are huge: a family with one member in prison, another receiving unemployment benefit and one child in a residential home run by the local authority, while the whole household is in receipt of full housing benefit, would now be costing the public purse over £50,000 a year.

So the challenge is going to have to be managed very effectively.

Underlying causes

The underlying causes of the national failure to come to grips adequately with the problems that will assuredly come to haunt us sooner rather than later are many and complex. They include incompetent local authorities, perverse social policies, fragmented government efforts and lack of effective local strategic leadership.

The management problems were evident to the Audit Commission seven years ago. It pointed out that:

> Not to put too fine a point on it, large parts of London appear set on precisely the course which will lead to financial and management breakdown. In the Commission's view, the problems now facing some London boroughs are not due solely to social and economic factors over which they have no control. Of course these constitute a daunting management challenge. But management makes a vital difference – for good or ill: there is a marked contrast between the performance in terms of economy, efficiency and effectiveness of similarly deprived authorities in London and the provinces.

The Audit Commission cited detailed evidence comparing three groups of authorities, all with similar levels of social deprivation. This showed that the eight boroughs of Brent, Camden, Hackney, Haringey, Islington, Lambeth, Lewisham and Southwark spent substantially more money, employed more people and performed significantly less well than comparably deprived boroughs in London or in metropolitan areas facing similar difficulties, such as Bradford, Kirklees or Knowsley. Compared to the latter group, the eight boroughs spent three times as much per resident in 1985, employed almost 80 per cent more people (when the size of the resident population is taken into account), and performed worse on every available indicator. For instance, in the housing field their rent arrears were nearly three times higher, it took them more than twice as long to re-let a vacant property and the management cost per dwelling was also twice as high. The precise figures were as follows:

	The London eight	The provincial eight
Rent arrears (as % of annual rent)	20	7
Time to re-let vacant properties (weeks)	20	9
Management cost per dwelling managed (£)	201	101

To mask their inefficiency, as in New York, local authorities had turned to creative accounting. The London eight had negotiated over £700 million in capitalised maintenance and deferred purchase arrangements; those represented over £1 thousand per household, compared with under £350 in their provincial counterparts.

As if that was not bad enough, as was observed earlier a practice of 'management by members' had evolved, whereby members sought to do officers' work for them. Their officers were seen as part of the problem rather than as part of the solution; and in any case local government salaries and conditions made it difficult for inner London authorities to compete with the private sector or less stressful authorities in the provinces – where housing and travel to work costs are generally much lower. This was particularly true in the information technology field, where senior council staff in London were paid around a third below the rate necessary to attract the very best qualified people, as the jobs demanded.

Relations between members and senior officers were further compromised by labour relations problems. Members often found it difficult to distinguish between their roles as politicians, employers and trade unionists. It had proved extremely difficult to secure changes in the face of trade union opposition, often supported by members; and attempts at any kind of performance review all too often resulted in demands for extra services which were countered by claims from the trade unions for additional staff and salary regradings. As a result auditors' reports were peppered with references to industrial relations difficulties. The following quotations provide a flavour of the situation; each came from a different deprived London borough:

... the Council has a 'no redundancy' policy for its employees. Such a policy might be expected to lead to harmonious industrial relations but in fact this is far from being the case ... Staff operate a policy of no cover for vacancies or sickness. Staff in the public libraries have also imposed minimum staffing numbers; when numbers on duty fall below levels set arbitrarily by the staff side, libraries are closed to the public ... There were numerous days when area offices of the Social Services Department could not open to the public ... Implementation of new technology generally has been subjected to delays due in part to the protracted negotiations (required by the New Technology agreement) for each work area affected ... Staff side [Trade Union] representatives are normally able to attend and speak at committee meetings [of the authority].

... action should be taken to secure more effective working relations
with Trade Unions, to ensure that prolonged disputes or negotiations
do not arise ... [I am] concerned at the lack of progress concerning
bonus schemes ... closures delayed by the effects of industrial action.

... because of Trade Union resistance, no work has yet been undertaken on the electricians and plumber [incentive] schemes; while what
little work has been undertaken on the highways and sewers schemes
has been hampered ... Supervisors [are] refusing to co-operate with
work study [of work inspection arrangements].

Not surprisingly in such circumstances, turnover among senior
executives was very high. During the three years to the end of 1986
over half of the senior officers in the eight boroughs had left; and
recruiting adequate replacements was proving far from easy. It was
the same story in council house maintenance, social services,
refuse collection and vehicle management. Internal financial controls were a cause for particular concern. Commenting on the
internal audit arrangements in the London eight, the Audit Commission drew attention to the fact that four out of five of the staff
were unqualified, some 15 per cent of the posts were vacant, and
minimal effort was devoted to professional training. The contrast
with the rest of inner London and comparable deprived metropolitan districts was notable. And subsequent allegations of widespread corruption come as no surprise.

There is little evidence of the situation in inner London improving in any material respect since the Audit Commission's warnings
were first issued. Indeed in the period 1988–92 twenty-three out of
thirty-three London Chief Executives had changed. The problems
have been compounded by what was described in 1989 as a 'patch-
work quilt' of government and support programmes for urban
regeneration that remain only loosely sewn together – to borrow
the Audit Commission's metaphor. In a report on Britain's
deprived urban areas, the Policy Studies Institute draws attention
to nine separate and distinct initiatives aimed at urban renewal
sponsored by four different central government departments. The
institute could have added City Technology Colleges (and the
Education Department) to the inventory of programmes designed
to tackle the problem of inner city regeneration.

In such confused circumstances, leadership for local regeneration initiatives has been difficult. Usually business has taken
the lead in forming a high-level partnership between the private

and public sectors locally. There have been some notably successful results in Glasgow, Newcastle and Birmingham in particular. But in London, too often local initiatives have been plagued by funding problems, local jealousies and competing calls on the time of the executives concerned – not least from the new Training and Enterprise Councils. There are some important lessons for the new Urban Regeneration Agency to learn from the successes and failures of the past. Lessons that must be learned well, if the terrible prospect of Baltimore and the Bronx is not to be visited on Birmingham, Bradford or Brent.

A future that works

It is always comforting to have the feeling that 'I have seen the future, and it works'. The most obvious sources of encouragement for the new Urban Regeneration Agency and for those contemplating the problems of inner London are to be found in Glasgow and Newcastle. During 1982, with the co-operation of Glasgow District Council and Strathclyde Regional Council, the Scottish Development Agency commissioned a major study into the potential for Glasgow city centre, which resulted in the identification of three key areas of economic opportunity: attracting and developing headquarters activity; developing exportable business services; and building the city's tourist potential. To help with the realisation of these opportunities, Glasgow Action, an independent group of private and public sector leaders, acted as the guardian of a vision of Glasgow's future as well as a catalyst for actions to renovate the city centre environment, expand the city's service industries and generally build up Glasgow's external image. Some of the symptoms of a resurgent Glasgow include the 'Glasgow's Miles Better' campaign; the 1988 Glasgow Garden Festival; the city's designation as the 1990 European City of Culture; a £60 million shopping and leisure complex in the city; and over a million square feet of new office space completed in the city centre in a recent twelve-month period.

It is evident that although every city is different, all problem cities and areas share the same need for a process of renewal to get sound economic development under way. Following a study of the situation in Newcastle, the CBI Urban Regeneration Task Force defined this process. Highly visible 'flagship' projects are needed to break into the cycles of decline; numerous features of depressed urban areas were reinforcing each other, so conspicuously successful initiatives were needed to arrest the downward spiral. Any early wins must be reinforced. The impact of the initial projects must be exploited to attract private capital into land and property development, to disarm sceptical critics of the process and to lift the pride of the local community. The momentum must become self-sustaining, integrating the many individual efforts comprising a city initiative, removing any obstacles to recovery.

While promoting these individual phases, however, the task force also concluded that local business leaders needed to be particularly conscious throughout the process of the need for:

- promoting land and property development: physical rebuilding must be a key element in many cities. Attracting development capital is all about restoring confidence in the future. Local authorities are inevitably major players in this context. They need to approach the challenge in partnership with private developers
- creating appropriate job opportunities: demotivation, alienation and low skill levels make urban unemployment immeasurably harder to tackle. A new approach is needed, both to create appropriate jobs and to help the long-term unemployed take advantage of them. Service industries will be more important than manufacturing as a source of future jobs. New training and recruitment programmes will open up valuable opportunities for employers. Universities, polytechnics and science parks will become increasingly important catalysts. Self-employment and start-ups will continue to draw heavily on support from enterprise agencies and managed workshops, supported in some instances by special loan funds
- involving the community: successful urban programmes must win the participation of local people. Valuable precedents have been set by community enterprise schemes, especially in Scotland, by new crime prevention tactics, by educational compacts between businesses and schools, and by charitable trusts to green the urban environment
- creating a partnership between the public and private sectors: business, local authorities and central government all have

crucial and complementary roles to play. Both central and local government initiatives are already widespread. They need to be closely integrated with the business community's efforts. Council executives can provide invaluable staffing support for private sector city initiatives.

The process plainly works well, as experience in Newcastle and Liverpool as well as Glasgow demonstrates. For instance, the most recent brochure for Business Opportunities on Merseyside portrays a situation very different from the time of the Toxteth riots.

The development of the Albert Dock re-introduced Merseysiders to the river as a source of entertainment and local history. The development corporation's ability to attract private investment on both sides of the Mersey to build new homes, refurbish factories and promote leisure facilities demonstrated beyond doubt that Merseyside had re-emerged in the eyes of investors, and its track record in combining government investment with private capital helped give Merseyside a more positive profile nationally and locally. One of the most obvious examples of successful partnership on Merseyside, and perhaps the most dramatic example of an initiative to promote high technology and related businesses is Wavertree Technology Park, a development originally launched by a partnership between Plessey, English Estates, Liverpool City Council and Merseyside County Council. Within the space of a few years a deserted sixty-four-acre site close to the centre of Liverpool has been transformed into a parkland setting for major manufacturing and commercial operations, supported by amenities such as a health centre and dental surgery, on-site bank and comprehensive security arrangements. Some thirty-eight enterprises employing 1,500 people are now located in the technology park which has developed into one of the north-west's most conspicuous success stories.

Meanwhile in Knowsley the News International development attracted a total investment of £200 million and incorporates the latest, most technologically-advanced printing and newspaper-publishing facilities in the world. Also in Knowsley, Kodak has already committed £8 million to its photographic chemicals plant at Kirkby; Delco Electronics continues to service the General Motors network in Europe; and BICC Cables has opened its first purpose-built optical cable factory at Whiston.

In St Helens, Pilkington and other public and private sector interests have joined forces to form Ravenhead Renaissance – the first UK public-private sector inner city development company promoting the economic and social regeneration of 250 acres of derelict land just south of St Helens town centre. Already the results are evident in the shape of new retail activity, new hotel facilities and well-serviced sites for high technology industry. The local Training and Enterprise Council share the borough's technology campus with St Helens College and the borough's Economic Development Team. Sefton is the third Merseyside district to secure 'City Challenge' status along with Wirral and Liverpool. The transformation of Birkenhead Centre as well as the Wirral Freeport and the Maritime Development Zone in Wallasey anticipates £190 million of investment from the public and private sectors to create six thousand new jobs, establish Birkenhead as a major shopping centre and regenerate the area's docklands.

Of course the desperate problems facing the residents of the most deprived areas on Merseyside – which included thirteen of the twenty-five council wards with the highest unemployment levels in England in 1991 – require a concerted national effort. But at least an organised framework is now in place to spend the available funds productively.

Applying these lessons in London, where the problems are greatest, will require some uncharacteristic actions by both government and local authorities. First, the regeneration of inner London needs the leadership to ensure that public funds are put to best use. London First, a group of business leaders committed to tackling the situation in the interests both of their shareholders and their community, is well placed to provide it. The present situation is fragmented. In an account in the spring of 1993 of what was being done in London, the then Secretary of State for the Environment mentioned a Cabinet Sub-Committee on London, EDL(L), a transport working group to co-ordinate London's transport services, the London Forum to promote London overseas, the London Docklands Development Corporation and seven successful City Challenge bids (from local authorities) which will result in some £1 billion of investment in urban regeneration.

However, letting 'a thousand flowers bloom' is not a certain way of achieving an orderly herbaceous border. In particular, London First will need to concentrate on developing a regeneration strategy. Once this is in place and agreed, all public funding designated for the areas in question could be channelled through London First. It would then be evident 'who is in charge' and to whom local people can look for action. It could become a superTEC for London.

Next, the management of the local authorities most directly involved must be improved dramatically. Arguably the most challenging jobs in public education, police, social housing, management or social services are in inner London. The scale and urgency of the challenge demands the very best from local government. Too often authorities have fallen short, often by a wide margin, of the very highest standards. In particular, in most authorities the organisation structures still need to be streamlined, seven years after the Audit Commission identified the need for urgent action in the following terms:

- elected members should determine council policies and priorities and (of course) the budget and the community charge decisions which flow from them; and subject to the safeguards against politicised appointments discussed below, they should appoint the chief officers of the council
- chief officers should have delegated executive responsibility, without the need to refer back to the committee or council for authority to take operational decisions – as long as these are consistent with the agreed policies and priorities, and can be met within the approved budget
- management responsibility should be devolved to the community level, in urban as well as rural areas – the so-called urban villages that can recreate the community spirit that is essential if social problems are to be tackled successfully; local government needs to rediscover general management, and the skills of managing local communities rather than services and bureaucracies
- sub-committees should be wound up, except under exceptional circumstances. Where they are established, they should have a specific task and a limited life
- 'back-bench' councillors should have the officer and other support necessary to enable them to deal effectively with 'case-work' from their constituents
- a single, flat-rate, allowance should be paid to members for the totality of their council work to discourage unnecessary committees and meetings.

At the same time it is essential that all possible steps are taken to reverse the present trends which make it difficult to attract the very best people to the areas facing the most serious problems. Interview panels should be limited in size (normally to no more than five people) and should include at least one independent external assessor and a member of the local opposition for all Chief Officer appointments. The assessor should be in a position to prevent what appears to be an inappropriate appointment going ahead. Rolling four- to five-year contracts, renewable only by mutual consent, should be considered to safeguard Chief Officers' professional independence. And there should be an independent element in the procedure for hearing appeals against dismissal; in this case too the independent assessor's ratification should be mandatory.

The standard chief executive's contract should define his (or her) authority vis-à-vis other Chief Officers and, in particular, specify the chief executive's role in selection, promotion and compensation decisions. (In New Zealand, following recent local government reforms, the chief executive, not the council, is the employer of all council staff.) Members of authorities should concentrate on the appointment of chief officers and those reporting directly to them (that is, first and second tiers). They should not be involved in any appointment below the third tier; and they should only become involved in the third tier appointments in exceptional circumstances.

In addition, the pay and conditions of service for first- and second-tier officers working in the most deprived areas should be reviewed independently and urgently. The review should be asked to determine the extent to which the present terms are sufficient to attract people of the required calibre and experience to these very demanding jobs where the turnover rates remain disturbingly high.

More attention will need to be paid to correcting the design mistakes committed when much of council housing was built during the 1960s and 1970s. The quality of life in many inner city areas is heavily influenced, if it is not determined, by the way in which local councils and housing associations design and manage their estates. Alice Coleman's *Utopia on Trial* should be required reading for everyone concerned with urban regeneration. Unfortunately, by giving their tenants what the housing professionals thought they ought to want without even going through the motions of asking them, serious mistakes were committed. These will have to be corrected if the crime rate is to be reduced and the quality of life improved. There is a very clear link between anti-social behaviour and the way in which housing estates or blocks of flats are designed and managed: the more design faults there are on local housing estates, the higher the local crime rate is likely to be, and the more degraded the environment – in terms of graffiti, refuse, noise and uncontrolled dogs. These are apart from the 'normal' problems faced by council tenants, of flat roofs that leak, windows that are not weatherproof, inadequate lighting of communal areas, poor heating and unresponsive maintenance organisations. Even estates that are less than ten years old and have received architectural awards have proved virtually impossible to live in almost from the moment they were first occupied. The lack of defensible space, poor control over entrances and exits, inoperative lifts, open spaces that are not properly maintained, too many places for intruders to hide, have combined to make the residents' lives miserable.

Yet over the last five years, the backlog of expenditure on improving council housing stock has increased, even though the nature of the design faults has been clear, along with their consequences, for at least a decade. The Audit Commission first drew attention to the problem as long ago as November 1986 when a backlog of maintenance and modernisation of council-owned property in inner London was estimated at over £8,000 per dwelling (or some £13,000 in 1993 prices). Meanwhile levels of new house-building have fallen and homelessness and the use of temporary accommodation has increased.

At last there is more general recognition that economic and social regeneration of communities goes hand in hand with improvements to the local environment. The large capital investment involved can stimulate local employment and training initiatives. It can draw on other organisations interested in local initiatives. It can also act as a catalyst in bringing the concept of urban villages alive. As a member of one of Edinburgh's Tenants' Associations puts it:

> We have had the master planners back in the 1960s, implementing the fashionable ideas of the time. We still suffer the consequences. We have learned that we are best placed to save what's best for our community.

Whoever manages the improvement process must be accountable to us if they are to be credible.

Finally any teacher can confirm what the sociologists tell us: many children raised by a lone parent start off with a massive handicap in building social relationships, while the parent often faces a life of degrading welfare dependency and grinding poverty. Yet we have not, it seems, learned the lessons that are freely available – about what not to do as well as more positive action. In Wisconsin, for example, which has a long-standing liberal tradition, the state penalises parents on social security if their children play truant from school. If a teenage father fails to pay child support, all four grandparents are liable until he marries or reaches adulthood. Welfare benefits are increased if couples marry; but there are no additional benefits or other incentives for a single mother to have more than one child. At the same time teenage mothers have support in the form of child minders (who can also act as mentors), so that they can return to school. Errant fathers are tracked down at the expense of other welfare recipients – benefits were recently reduced by 6 per cent to finance child support enforcement. It is a crime to cross state borders to escape maintenance payment; and non-payers have their pay docked directly by employers.

Deterrents and penalties will not always work. So it is important both to help the young mothers to cope with a very difficult situation and to avoid young people being entrapped by the welfare system. A 1990 EC study of the conditions on deprived housing estates outside Edinburgh showed that a quarter of the newcomers to the estates were aged between sixteen and twenty-one, and a quarter were also single parents. Young mothers need help bringing up children, especially if they are alone. Deprived inner city areas would benefit greatly from universal nursery education, as well as nurseries to cover after-school hours. Not only would this provide a safety net, but children would in all probability do better when they entered primary school.

But there is no point in providing encouragement for mothers to go back to school or college, or out to work, if they are penalised by the welfare system for doing so. At present a lone parent is only £15 a week better off earning £170 a week than £70. (In 1992 average gross weekly earnings for women aged eighteen to twenty in full-time employment were just under £150.)

The Southside of Chicago and Harlem and the Bronx in New York provide a foretaste of the future that is in store unless action is taken to address the underlying problems in Britain's inner cities: high welfare dependency and generation intervals of fifteen years or less; youth unemployment of 70 per cent or more; an extremely high crime rate, much of it drug-related; uneasy relations between the police and a disaffected and largely unemployable urban 'underclass' with no stake in the development of the society in which they live. This future cannot be allowed to happen.

The prospects remain discouraging. However, Glasgow, Newcastle and Birmingham show what can be done, even in the most difficult times, by a business-led partnership between the public and private sectors. Meanwhile the economic times are improving, which will bring their own benefits. We now need to seize the opportunity to turn the situation around. It must not take more riots or further horrifying examples of juvenile crime to alert the nation to the growing dangers it faces in the urban ghettos that disfigure many inner city areas, and to persuade us to mount the consistent, co-ordinated and constructive response that is needed.

PART III

A WORKSHOP FOR THE
WORLD

THERE WAS A TIME when Great Britain was known as the workshop of the world. Even in the mid 1950s the UK accounted for approximately a fifth of the combined exports of the world's major manufacturing countries. By 1970, however, our share had halved – reflecting the recovery in the war-ravaged economies of continental Europe and Japan, as well as Britain's poor inflation and industrial relations record and the relatively unattractive employment prospects in the manufacturing sector for engineers.

The decline in Britain's world market share continued during the turmoil of the early 1970s, and as a result of the capacity that was closed down during the early 1980s – when a combination of high inflation and sterling's new-found (and temporary) status as a petro currency exacted a terrible price on the nation's manufacturing base.

By 1985 Britain's share of major manufacturing countries' exports had fallen below 8 per cent. The government sought to make a virtue of the situation by arguing that manufacturing was of no special importance, provided that the deficit in visible trade could be financed through borrowing, investment from overseas and a surplus on the so-called invisible account that includes financial and other services, as well as tourism. Those who disagreed were simply disregarded by the economic policy establishment and the media as well as government, as reluctant refugees from the failures of the corporate state era; while industrialists' calls for an industrial strategy were seldom precise, and often seemed to amount to self-serving pleas for continued protection and subsidy. So the government persisted in its strategy of having no strategy, other than letting the forces of the market and international competition do their work.

The result was not at all what was expected. The balance of payments surplus on services deteriorated (in 1990 prices) from

£6.7 billion in 1980 to £5.2 billion in 1990; while imports of goods exceeded exports by almost £19 billion, some $3\frac{1}{2}$ per cent of GNP in that year. As the recession took hold, the presumed weaknesses in our manufacturing base were seen to be a cause of continuing economic difficulties which were not affecting Germany, France or Italy. The widespread belief among the general public that Britain was not able to compete with the world's best eroded consumer confidence, and thus made a difficult situation even worse.

The extent of this general lack of confidence was demonstrated in a Gallup poll in late 1992. This showed that nearly two-thirds of respondents believed that Britain can never compete with Germany and Japan and was bound to go on lagging behind. More than half expected that they or a member of their family would be 'affected by rising unemployment'. One in three knew someone with serious mortgage arrears or whose business had been lost or was at risk. Overall, by a majority of five to one, people thought that the country was not 'going forward on broadly the right lines'; half of Conservative voters agreed with this view.

Correcting this false perception must be a priority task for industry and government. At the same time there is no point in investing in industry if equivalent rewards are available elsewhere at lower risk, or if investors lack confidence in the overall direction of British business. They will certainly not want to back companies forced by regulators to rewrite the original promises made when they were privatised. Above all, investors take their lead from government and its attitudes and actions.

Part III addresses each of these problems, which must be tackled successfully if Britain is again to become a workshop for the world – as will be essential in a new era of low growth, low inflation and intensified competition.

Few people in public life or the media have any first-hand experience either of top management or of making things. So it is not surprising that a pervasive mythology has grown around Britain's past manufacturing record, and its present relative international strength – or lack of it.

I spent my early commercial career in advertising and in marketing in the manufacturing sector. As a management consultant at McKinsey I saw the problems facing a wide range of British companies of different sizes and in a wide cross-section of industries, from steel through aerospace and automotive engineering to baked beans. And at the CBI I probably visited more factories and had a better appreciation of what was really going on in the nation's manufacturing heartland than anyone in Whitehall or at Westminster.

A concern for the future of our manufacturing base led me to establish the CBI's National Manufacturing Advisory Group. Their report, Competing with the World's Best, *to which Dr Andrew Sentance and his colleagues in the CBI's Economic Directorate made a major contribution, forms the basis for this chapter.*

12

Manufacturing Myth and Reality

Britain's manufacturing record is not quite what it seems.

'We don't make anything any more' has been the refrain of innumerable radio interviews, articles and discussions at the National Economic Development Council – whose demise at the beginning of 1993 seems to have passed both unnoticed and unlamented. Since most economic commentators and interviewers have only the haziest knowledge of the realities of manufacturing, and because the state of the nation's manufacturing base has latterly become a political issue, it is perhaps scarcely surprising that myth and reality have become confused – with damaging consequences.

The mythology is relatively clear. It is generally believed that manufacturing is weaker here than in France, Italy or the United States. That the quality of British goods falls short of best international standards. That we tend to produce lower value-added products and are losing out in the high-technology markets of the future. That British management is relatively incompetent and that industrial relations on Britain's shopfloor remain in the parlous state epitomised by events that have burned themselves into the nation's subconscious, such as the picket-line violence at Wapping; during the miners' dispute; and the periodic disruption in the car industry. It is generally believed too that the dark satanic mills of the Victorian era remain. A career in manufacturing is thought likely to be dirty, noisy, brutish and short. It will not be intellectually or professionally satisfying, nor particularly well-rewarded. It will certainly not be much fun.

Even if unfounded, such beliefs can become self-fulfilling. They breed a pervasive loss of self-confidence in the nation's economic future, as we have seen. They lead parents and teachers to guide the most talented children and pupils into more obviously attractive careers. They encourage a propensity to import: imported products are presumed to have qualities which British suppliers cannot match. They even fuel speculation and inflation, because of the fear of the economic future they instil: 'spend it while it's there' is an altogether reasonable response to an economic future that looks bleak. So it is timely to review the manufacturing record and the action in hand to improve it further.

The manufacturing record

The mythology of Britain's manufacturing weakness needs to be challenged, just as the realities need to be faced: the financial markets seem to take a remarkably long time to find the incompetent out; while the national cult of the not-so-gifted amateur is not confined to Westminster or Whitehall.

Unfortunately the mythology receives regular reinforcement. The monthly trade figures deliver a regular diet of doom and despondency, causing the financial markets to sell sterling short and real interest rates to remain at punitive levels. Indeed the balance of payments on manufactured goods has become the yardstick against which the state of the manufacturing nation is assessed – even though the deficit is usually outweighed by the annual appreciation in Britain's portfolio of overseas business assets, which is worth some £150 billion (and which the trade figures do not take into account). Moreover the commentators rarely penetrate behind the headlines to examine the detail of Britain's trading performance. Analysis of the import and export statistics for the third quarter of 1992 – when our trade performance was generally regarded as disappointing – reveals some surprising facts:

- there was a positive trade balance in each of: drink and tobacco, chemicals, pharmaceuticals, power-generation equipment, scientific equipment, machine tools, aerospace and steel. Together, these sectors reported a surplus of £1.8 billion for the period
- the high-technology trade account – photographic and optical equipment, office equipment, telecommunications

and electrical equipment – was in credit for the period to the tune of some £800 million
- during the period, UK exports were at an all-time record high in volume terms, 31 per cent above the average for 1985 (they were around double their 1970 level, incidentally). They were worth nearly £400 million every working day; and exports per person exceeded those of Japan or Italy.

For the quarter 90 per cent of the deficit was accounted for by (in order of the size of the deficit): food, motor vehicles, clothing, raw materials and paper products. With the sole exception of raw materials that are not available in Britain, there is substantial scope for improving the situation in each of these sectors. Inward investment by Japanese car manufacturers has produced the prospect of a positive balance of payments on motor vehicles by the end of the century. Similarly a major expansion of wastepaper processing, taking advantage of the largest 'urban forest' in Europe in the shape of London, could result in the transformation of the adverse balance of payments for paper-based products.

Food and clothing represent a greater challenge. In both cases there are important lessons to be learned from Germany, where investment in skills, design and technology has produced one of the most successful textile industries in Europe. As far as food is concerned, the 1993 Oxford Farming Conference heard a number of specific recommendations for closing the trade gap and growing in Britain food which now has to be imported from other countries in northern Europe. In 1991 the food and drink trade gap with northern Europe (Benelux, Denmark, Germany, Ireland and the Netherlands) amounted to nearly £3 billion, of which half was accounted for by meat, fruit and vegetables which could be produced in Britain.

In short, Britain's manufacturing record is not quite what it seems. The list of companies that emerged from the 1980s able to compete with the best in the world is longer and more impressive than is generally realised. Forty British companies are included in the *Fortune* magazine list of the world's largest five hundred companies, based on market capitalisation, compared with thirty-two for Germany and thirty for France. A 1992 survey of the profitability, financial soundness and growth records of the largest four hundred industrial companies in Europe showed that the UK had easily the largest group, with 121 companies. The average UK company scored higher on the ratings used by the (German) academic conducting the analysis than the French, German or Italian contingents. British firms more than made up for their relatively poor growth performance with generally lower borrowing, higher profitability and stronger cashflow. There were six British companies in the top ten: Glaxo, Reuters, the Aegis Group (media-buying), Smithkline Beecham, Cable and Wireless, and Wellcome. The number of companies from different countries ranked in the top hundred within Europe on the basis of the survey was as follows:

United Kingdom	41
France	23
Germany	11
Spain	6
Italy	5
Switzerland	4
Belgium	3
Netherlands	3
Sweden	3
Eire	1
	100

Behind each of the British companies is a story of successful transformation under, at times, unimaginably difficult circumstances of high domestic inflation and real interest rates, volatile currency and (at least in the early part of the 1980s) difficult industrial relations.

The transformation is best illustrated by reference to an industry which came to exemplify the 'Britain can't make it' history of the 1970s. A report for the Central Policy Review Staff (CPRS) of the Cabinet Office described the situation of the motor industry in the early 1970s in these terms:

There is not the slightest chance of Britain retaining a volume car industry at anything like its present size [1.5 million cars a year] if present shop floor attitudes persist. Present trench warfare attitudes of management and labour will not serve in the assembly industries of Twentieth Century Western Europe. The British car industry's approach to quality of workmanship, to new working practices, to continuity of production and manning levels is so out of date that it cannot survive. Workers and management must see the danger and adapt rapidly or go under. They must not be persuaded otherwise by politically-motivated militants.

It is also clear that plants and product ranges must be rationalised if the industry as a whole is to be viable. The cost penalties resulting from overheads on under-utilised plant are too severe to be carried indefinitely. In addition, the gap in investment between British industry and its competitors must be made good. Nevertheless the problems of productivity are at the centre of the industry's problems.

The same study, in which the author was directly involved, showed British car manufacturers anchored firmly at the bottom of the European investment, productivity, capacity utilisation and profitability league tables.

By late 1992 the situation was very different. Britain had one of the most efficient and profitable car industries in Europe. Vauxhall's Ellesmere Port plant was producing Astras for some £350 a car less than the same model coming off the Opel production lines in Germany; the quality was comparable if not superior. A combination of inward investment by Nissan, Toyota and Honda, together with the turnaround in quality and design at Rover and continuing Ford commitment to the UK, meant that car exports rose from under 200,000 units in 1986 to over 600,000 in 1991. There is a realistic prospect that a trade deficit of over £5 billion in 1993 will be eliminated within two years. The total output of the UK car industry in 1993 will be not far short of 1.5 million units, despite very difficult market conditions on the Continent. The very idea of Daimler-Benz considering the establishment of a manufacturing plant here would have been dismissed as absurd even five years ago.

The transformation is not confined to the automotive sector. The anecdotal evidence from visits to major UK non-OECD export markets like Saudi Arabia, the Gulf, Iran, India and South Africa provided supporting evidence. Returning from a visit to these markets in early 1992, the author was able to report:

- a 15–20 per cent share for Britain of imports into almost all of these markets

- UK firms were well up with the world's leaders: Glaxo's new operation in South Africa (where the UK accounts for some 40 per cent of inward investment) serving all of sub-Saharan Africa provided a good illustration of the worldwide application of an innovation- and investment-led strategy
- there was widespread recognition of the superlative performance of British military equipment during the Gulf conflict: Tornados were flying along wadies at the speed of sound; their electronic software was rewritten in a week. Almost three times as many British firms as American were represented at an exhibition in the Gulf in 1992: in 1991 British representation was only half that of the Americans
- Rolls-Royce's share of the civil jet market had doubled in four years; South African Airways had just switched from Pratt and Whitney to Rolls-Royce. (It so happened that the Chief Executive was a former CBI scholar who had spent a period earlier in his career working in England with a UK manufacturer – an experience which he, like all such scholars, remembers with affection and pride)
- a UK contractor was involved in the former American preserve of the $30 billion Aramco refurbishment programme in the eastern province of Saudi Arabia; on one major petrochemical construction contract 55 per cent of the orders placed following a worldwide procurement trawl were with British suppliers
- a courageous team from Royal Ordnance was clearing a million mines from the desert in Kuwait; they were in the field months before their French or American counterparts
- UK contractors had a major share in the $850 million first phase of the Jebal Ali Power Station in Dubai, and were the preferred suppliers in India for major electrical engineering contracts
- a contract for a $1.5 billion aluminium smelter in Bandar Abbas in Iran had been awarded to a UK contractor subject to the availability of ECGD cover.

Of course we could do even better. There are still too many people like the manager who was reported by a major Kuwaiti importer to have said that 'things are so difficult at home we cannot afford to export', or the firm that tried to do its marketing from three thousand miles away and evidently believed that exports could be turned on and off like a tap. But there are not many such people and organisations. And not nearly as many as there were.

The mythology of Britain's supposedly inadequate and eroding manufacturing base has been explored methodically in two recent reports by the CBI's newly-established National Manufacturing Council. These confirmed that the 1980s have seen more dramatic changes in manufacturing industry than any other decade since the Second World War. Specifically, the key indicators of output, productivity and share of world trade all show an improving trend relative to our main competitors; there has been a considerable restructuring of industry, with the help of inward investment, increasing the UK presence in high-technology sectors. As the analysis makes clear, there are certainly no grounds for complacency. We still have a long way to go if our overall performance is to match the best in the world. But there is now a sound base on which to build.

Positive trends

Relatively slow growth of manufacturing output has been a persistent problem for the UK economy over the post-war period. It is a relatively poor performance in manufacturing, rather than services, which has dragged down the overall growth rate and prevented living standards in the British economy rising as rapidly as elsewhere. However, there has been a marked change in the trend in recent years, albeit from a low base. Between 1975 and 1980 UK manufactured output declined by 1 per cent per annum compared to growth rates of between 3 per cent and 7 per cent in competitor countries. Performance since then has been much closer to the average of the industrialised countries and above France and Italy. Despite the slight fall in manufacturing output in 1990, growth over the period to 1990 was equal to that of West Germany. There was a sustained increase during the 1980s in real value-added per person employed; UK productivity increased more rapidly than any other country except Japan.

This productivity improvement relative to other European economies has begun to close the 20–30 per cent gap between the UK and continental levels of productivity which had opened up in the 1960s and was already clearly apparent in the early 1970s. The productivity differential with the United States has narrowed and that with Japan has not widened further.

Reflecting this improved productivity performance, the UK share of manufacturing trade stabilised in the mid 1980s and it has since begun to increase. This improvement in export performance sits somewhat strangely alongside the recent deterioration in the current account of the UK balance of payments. However, the main reason for this deterioration in the external balance was not a failure of international competitiveness so much as the rapid growth in UK demand – especially consumer demand – in the late 1980s. If the British economy is unbalanced it is because we spend too much of our national income and save and invest too little. With the UK economy having a particularly high level of import penetration, this led to rapid import growth. Even so, relative to total domestic demand, the last five years also show an improving trend in import penetration: the growth in imports' share of the UK market was the lowest of the major industrialised countries between 1985 and 1990. Manufacturing import penetration in the UK is now broadly in line with West Germany.

These favourable trends in export and import market share, combined with the impact of the recession on levels of domestic demand, have led to an improvement in UK trade performance. For the first half of 1992 the current account deficit amounted to £6.2 billion or 2.1 per cent of GDP, compared with £10.2 billion and 4.3 per cent for the same period two years earlier. In particular the trade gap with the rest of the European Union is closing rapidly. In the first half of 1992 it was running at around £5 billion a year, compared to £16 billion in 1989 and £11 billion in 1990. The continuing strength of manufactured export volumes confirms that this is not just a temporary phenomenon.

Restructuring and inward investment

These improvements in manufacturing performance reflect the large amount of industrial restructuring which has taken place over the past decade. In the early 1980s the effects of this were particularly painful as the decline of traditional industries was compounded by the effect of a worldwide recession. But as economic prospects began to improve in the middle to late 1980s the benefits of restructuring began to emerge. Three particular features stand out from the changes that have taken place over the past decade. First, high technology and high value-added industries have grown more rapidly – relative to low technology and low value-added industries. Many of the industries that have grown most rapidly – electronics, aerospace and chemicals – have a high ratio of exports to sales and appear to have good prospects for the future.

Second, inward investment has played a key role in invigorating key sectors of industry, most notably motor vehicles and consumer electronics. Over 150 Japanese manufacturing companies have a base in Britain, including their ten major consumer electronics firms. The UK now has a trade surplus in colour television sets and video tape recorders, something that was unthinkable ten years ago. The attractiveness of the UK as a preferred location for investment by foreign companies is well-established. Over the past forty years some 40 per cent of all United States and Japanese inward investment into EC countries has come to the United Kingdom. Much of this investment has taken place in recent years: the total stock of overseas direct investment in the UK increased from £18 billion in 1978 to £86 billion in 1989.

Britain is also the most popular destination for German direct investment abroad, attracting 22 per cent of the total in 1989. Altogether three thousand American companies have invested in the UK, including ninety-six of *Fortune* magazine's top hundred. Virtually all European multinationals have subsidiaries in Britain. In 1988 foreign-owned plants accounted for 19 per of total manufacturing output, 21 per cent of capital expenditure and 13 per cent of all manufacturing jobs.

It is sometimes alleged that foreign-owned plants are simply 'screwdriver' operations, which do not enhance the strength of our indigenous manufacturing base. In fact little could be further from the truth:

- productivity and investment levels are, on average, higher in foreign-owned UK manufacturing plants than UK-owned operations
- inward investors are normally world-class players – for example, IBM, Nissan, Toyota, Bosch. By playing host to the best in the world, the UK can expect to reap the benefits of the best practice in manufacturing methods, quality stan-

dards and new product development. The need to satisfy Japanese quality standards is already having a dramatic effect on the UK electronics and motor components supply industries

- many inward investors have shown a strong commitment to developing local supply networks. For example, some 60 per cent of supplies to IBM in Greenock are sourced within the UK
- inward investment has had a crucial role in invigorating regions of the UK adversely affected by declining, traditional industries. While all regions have been the beneficiary to some extent of inward investment, Scotland, Wales, the north-east, the West Midlands and Northern Ireland have attracted the lion's share and inward investment has had a significant impact on employment rates in these regions

Action in hand

A major factor in the improved performance of UK manufacturing has been an increased emphasis on quality, training and innovation. Historically UK manufacturing industry has generally lagged behind its major competitors in these areas. However there are encouraging signs that this is increasingly being recognised and addressed. Companies which concentrate on quality and innovation are much more responsive to customer requirements and hence expand their market share and profitability, adding to the wealth that is generated for employees, shareholders and managers. And, of course, to achieve a high standard of quality and innovation requires skilled and motivated people. A well-educated and highly-trained work-force is of paramount importance in a business environment that is becoming increasingly competitive, where the rate of technological change is increasing and external pressures are intensifying.

The interest in the British Standards Institution (BSI) quality standard BS 5750 is an indication of the growing emphasis on quality in UK manufacturing. BSI has certified some fourteen thousand sites in the UK to BS 5750 – acknowledged internationally as the gold standard of quality assurance – and there are many more registered by other licensing agencies. Many companies are going further than this and applying a total quality management (TQM) approach to their processes. An important catalyst in this process has been the example set by many Japanese companies investing in the UK: a total management commitment to quality; strong emphasis on team work with individual responsibility recognised for resolving problems and cross-functional teams for specific tasks; a high level of education and training so that employees are equipped to recognise and tackle problems before they develop into major defects; and the elimination of inefficiency by applying just-in-time delivery and zero defect policies.

The development of practical and effective approaches to quality management and the drive for total quality in all sectors has rapidly become a management priority. In a recent survey of company responses to the recession, improving customer service and product quality were among the most important factors cited by manufacturers for improving their business prospects over the year ahead. Quality concerns are driving many of the changes in involvement in the workplace – 65 per cent of respondents in a 1991 survey had given individuals more responsibility for quality in the last three years; and of these some two-thirds believed this had made an important contribution to employee involvement. A quarter of respondents reported the operation of quality circles/problem solving groups at their plants – a third of which had been in use for over three years.

To achieve a high level of quality requires a skilled work-force. A measure of the extent to which manufacturers are understanding the benefits to be gained from investment in training can be gauged from the differing responses of employers in the present recession to that in the early 1980s. At that time training budgets were cut heavily and part-time and temporary workers were often the first victims of mass lay-offs. During the recent recession, flexible working patterns have persisted, the use of fixed-term contracts has become more common and employers are making every effort to maintain training programmes. The skills revolution, described earlier, has led to priority being placed on training that leads directly to business objectives and to reaching the standards of competence required for jobs to be done well that underpin the new National Vocational Qualifications. Since the CBI Industrial Trends Survey first asked about manufacturers' training intentions over the year ahead (in 1989) they have reported consistent increases. Indeed training is the only element of manufacturers' investment that has increased through the recession. Surveys of training expenditure in Europe suggest that the amount of resources devoted to training by UK business is now much in line with our main European competitors.

Improvements in quality and training have been matched by a greater emphasis on innovation. Innovation is much broader than just research and development. It covers the whole process of bringing a new or improved product to the markets, involving capital expenditure, market research, Research and Technology, training, marketing and the other services such as those of consultants and research organisations. Nevertheless most of the focus in the discussion of innovation is on R & D expenditure. The latest figures show considerable growth in the UK business contribution to research and development, with expenditure rising 6 per cent a year in real terms between 1981 and 1991, and it has held up well in the last two years despite the recession and the squeeze on investment. While international comparisons suggest that, as a proportion of the added-value, British business spends about the same as the Japanese on research and development, and a greater proportion than the French or the Italians.

A major factor in helping UK manufacturers to increase quality and training and promote new processes and practices has been an improving climate of employee relations. The industrial relations turmoil of the 1960s and 1970s is now a distant, if unpleasant, memory. The number of days lost in industrial disputes in 1992 was equivalent to just three seconds out of the average working day. This was the lowest level since records began well over a century ago.

A number of factors have contributed to this improvement. Changes in the law have redressed the imbalance between management and trade unions. There has been a shift towards company and plant bargaining. National bargaining on terms and conditions of employment has been brought to an end in the engineering industry and wage negotiations have been decentralised to the operating divisions of many organisations. There has also been an increase in employee communication and consultation: managers in the majority of companies are consulting employees upon a wider range of issues than before, including company performance, quality and quality control. Some 58 per cent of companies surveyed recently believed that communications had improved in the past three years and nearly two-thirds (65 per cent) believed their communication to be 'very good', 'good' or 'adequate'. The move towards individual reward systems linked to appraisal schemes and performance pay increased flexibility and focused attention on individual and collective achievement; while the introduction of profit-related pay, Employee Share Option Schemes (ESOPs), profit sharing and share ownership schemes accelerated through-out the decade.

All these changes resulted in a surge in profitability among UK manufacturers during the 1980s, and they allowed continuing gains in productivity right through the trough of the recession, which was a remarkable feat in itself. CBI estimates of the rate of return on investment show that UK manufacturing profitability rose above West German levels in 1987 and 1988 before falling back in response to the recession. In the five years 1986–90, UK manufacturing profitability averaged just 6 per cent below West German levels compared to a differential of 24 per cent a decade earlier.

The fact that Britain's manufacturing weakness is more myth than reality should not blind us to the cost of the years of not-so-benign neglect of the manufacturing sector and of the recent recession. The output of the engineering industry in 1993 is likely to be some £18 billion lower in real terms than in the peak year of 1989. Much of UK industry is still not internationally competitive. We have a growing number of world-class companies but, as yet, these are insufficient to provide the critical mass necessary for a successful manu-facturing economy: we should be seeking to equal the German level in terms of the manufacturing share of GDP, implying an additional £50 billion in manu-facturing value-added. The UK is no better than thir-teenth out of twenty-two countries in the OECD world league of competitiveness, ahead of France, Spain and Italy, but well behind Japan, Germany and the United States; and we rank at or close to the bottom in terms of education and skills. Our productivity remains on average 30–40 per cent below the world's best, and the quality of our national skills base needs to increase. Investment in fixed capital and innovation remains lower than world rivals; and we still fall short of the

best world standards in terms of stock control – closing this gap alone would free some £5 billion for investment annually.

The challenge facing government and industry in the 1990s is to close this overall performance gap to ensure that Britain enters the twenty-first century with an internationally competitive manufacturing base. This will require action by government and regulators as well as those responsible for the direction of individual companies.

Most economists agree that economic growth and new jobs will depend on small businesses growing. But it is far from clear how this growth is going to be financed. The clearing banks are not in a hurry to repeat the experience of the past few years when billions of pounds of loans to small businesses have been written off; while the pension funds, which now own most of British business one way or another, and their advisers see lower-risk ways of earning comparable returns.

Venture capital could be an important part of the solution. But formidable problems need to be tackled first if the venture capital industry is to have the resources that will be needed; it accounts for well under 5 per cent of the external finance raised by smaller businesses at present.

Regular discussions with the CBI's Smaller Firms Council highlighted the problems for me. They came into even sharper focus when I became Chairman of ECI Ventures, one of the longest-established independent venture capital houses in London. And as a Non-Executive Director of the National Westminster Bank, I have had the opportunity to see another side of a problem that we cannot afford not to solve.

13

Risk and Reward

The same opportunities, for high rewards for low risks, will not be available in the new era.

A new era of modest growth and low inflation will challenge investors as well as government and those responsible for the management of Britain's major businesses. Put simply, without a new approach to financing small businesses the chances of sustained economic recovery are poor. And this finance will simply not be made available unless investors are prepared to accept higher risks than they have needed to accept during the 1980s.

The argument is fairly straightforward. Without growth in employment, the overall economic climate in Britain is bound to remain depressed as people fear for their jobs and prefer to save rather than spend. All the experts agree (and they might in this instance be right) that employment growth will come from Britain's three million smaller and medium-size enterprises (SMEs in the jargon). Around 100,000 new businesses start up every quarter: 96 per cent of firms employ fewer than twenty people; but between 1985 and 1989 these smaller firms created over a million new jobs – more than twice the number created by larger firms in this period.

Yet it is far from clear how the growth and expansion of existing small businesses will be financed in the future. When compared with their counterparts in other developed economies, Britain's smaller businesses tend to rely more on their own financial resources (principally retained earnings) rather than borrowings; and when they do raise loans, these tend to be in the form of a bank overdraft or short-term debt. German business, particularly, is more likely to rely on longer-term loans (often subsidised by the government) and trade credit from suppliers; at present only about one in five is seeking a short-term bank overdraft.

Surveys also suggest that the cost of finance is the greatest single constraint to the expansion of smaller UK companies. On average, smaller businesses in Britain raise external finance in the following pattern:

Bank loans	61%
Hire purchase/leasing	16
Partners	8
Factoring	4
Venture capital	3
Other sources	8
	100

The clearing banks are in no position to reduce the cost of finance or meet the funding gap. They already lend around £45 billion to the smaller business sector, and have effectively written off over £10 billion of business loans since 1988; so local managers are not in the mood to take more risks with their small business portfolios. And if they were, Head Office is standing by to set them straight. Venture capital will be hard pressed to fill the gap, particularly with respect to smaller businesses requiring less than £500,000 of capital, very few of which (perhaps 1–2 per cent) have any external investors. It is simply uneconomic to devote the time to sorting out the sound propositions among the flood of ideas from would-be entrepreneurs; the normal ratio is about 10:1. In any case, venture capitalists can only spend around £1 billion a year and are able to back no more than perhaps six hundred companies. Only around £200 million in new venture funds was raised in the UK in 1992, while the Business Expansion Scheme had become little more than a property-based tax-avoidance mechanism.

Of course, an army of wealthy Aunt Agathas might come riding to the rescue. But this seems unlikely, given their understandable worries about the economic future. The government too is in no position to use taxpayers' money to fill the gap left by the market, even if it wanted to – which it probably does not.

So we are seemingly locked into an uninviting economic vicious circle. Unlike Japan or the United States, British industry has little spare capacity after a decade of cost-cutting and a preference for paying dividends rather than investing. Indeed between 1980 and 1990 UK manufacturing capacity grew by just 7 per cent compared with over 30 per cent in the United States and nearly 40 per cent in Japan. Therefore any increase in consumer demand will inevitably result in an ever-widening trade deficit, leading to a weakening of sterling and the risk of importing inflation – thus eroding manufacturing competitiveness further. So domestic demand growth will need to be constrained, and with it the prospects of reducing unemployment and restoring consumer confidence.

Unless, of course, it proves possible to establish a different relationship between the risks that investors run and the rewards they receive. This is urgently needed. Throughout the 1980s investors were spoilt. The economic signals were misleading. It was easy, seemingly, to make useful returns at negligible risk. The new era demands different expectations. Few manufacturing investments will pay for themselves inside four years, as was the target during the so-called feeding frenzy of the mid 1980s.

Meanwhile we are misallocating our most precious resource: skilled people. Much of the City of London remains geared to takeovers or the threat of them. A team advising either side in a major contested takeover could easily be costing £6,000 an hour. Unfortunately for the would-be advisers there has been little to advise about, since few bids have taken place recently. The people who ought to know how to evaluate risk and secure appropriate returns for investors are either preoccupied raising funds to invest or busy as receivers – shutting the stable door after the horse has expired, as it were. A new approach is needed that ignores the misleading signals from the past and recognises the realities of the new era.

Misleading signals

Throughout the 1980s different classes of investor were virtually guaranteed significant returns for very moderate risks. As earlier chapters have observed, almost every one of the fourteen million householders owning their own home at the beginning of the 1980s saw their wealth increase in real terms by the end of the decade. The average new house increased in value in the ten years nearly three times, while the Retail Price Index did not quite double. Similarly the $1\frac{1}{2}$ million people who bought their council house did so at a discount from its market value. So they could expect to realise a worthwhile profit when they came to sell. And of course the risks were perceived to be small, as indeed they were. The taxpayers as a whole met the difference between the purchase price and the open market value – by taking a write-off from the non-existent balance sheets in the public sector.

Others benefited from the free lunch society as well. Indeed we invented a word to describe the beneficiaries. Literally millions of 'SIDS' achieved instant gains if they were successful applicants for shares of newly-privatised companies. Millions of initial shareholders saw a gain on the first day of trading in return for nothing, except the trouble of filling out and sending off an application form. Any idea that these were all longer-term investors is well wide of the mark. In every case the number of individual shareholders fell dramatically as soon as trading in the shares was possible. For example, National Power started off with over 1.7 million individual shareholders and now has only some 650,000.

Those investors backing managers wishing to buy the businesses they were working for could similarly be reasonably confident that the risks involved were modest. After all, the businesses in question invariably had some form of track record and a customer base on which to build; and a competent management would be likely to know more than the board of directors of the company selling the business about its potential and true value. As a result very few of the management buyouts that took place up to 1987 failed. Most were successful for all the stake-holders, some spectacularly so.

Investors in pension funds also found relatively worthwhile returns available at modest risk. Of the hundred largest pension funds on the market in early 1980 not one was showing a loss in money terms at the end of the decade. Under pressure from their institutional shareholders, boards of directors consistently increased dividends faster than earnings or investment; on occasion they were even paid out of reserves. The Exchequer played its part, by allowing all pension fund investment gains to be free of tax. So it is scarcely surprising that pension funds are proportionately much more important in Britain than elsewhere in Europe. In 1991 the market value of private pension funds amounted to over 70 per cent of the nation's GDP. This compared with 7 per cent in West Germany, and 2 per cent in France.

Indeed virtually every investor would have seen worthwhile gains during the 1980s. Savers investing £1 thousand in UK equities at the beginning of the decade would have seen it rise to £8,000 ten years later. Even a deposit of £1 thousand in a building society would have grown to some £3,150, achieving a real risk-free gain above inflation of approximately £1,250 – in other words, investors could expect to double their money after inflation. There is thus a reasonable expectation among investors that there is no need to incur risks since worthwhile returns can be achieved without doing so. This fits very naturally into a national culture which is instinctively risk-averse: we prefer to avoid risks or to insure against them, rather than manage them. Small wonder that in 1992 the property-based Business Expansion Schemes raised more than twice as much new funding as the entire UK venture capital industry. Or that a typical pension fund would have invested considerably less than 5 per cent of its portfolio in unquoted companies or venture capital funds.

Different expectations

But the same opportunities for high rewards with low risks will not be available in the new era of low inflation and modest growth.

Housing and property seem unlikely to return to the heady days of the late 1980s; indeed the present over-supply of office space and industrial property, combined with the demographic outlook, suggests that the sector will do well to hold its present value in real terms. In our twenty largest cities there are some 42 million square feet of empty commercial property, 13 per cent of the total (and 17 per cent in London). A further 10 million square feet is under construction. The high street revolution too may largely have run its course; so the scope for new retailing concepts may be less obvious than in the recent past – even if consumers' confidence in their economic future recovers. While manufacturers will have to invest proportionately more in research and development as well as in up-to-date plant and equipment, thus limiting the scope for the aggressive dividend growth seen in the 1980s.

Moreover the government's cupboard of certain investor profits is somewhat bare. Although there remain around five million council houses in public ownership, the latest drive to sell them to their tenants at discounted prices is bound to come up against the present reality of consumers' new-found reluctance to borrow, for housing in particular. The remaining government holdings in the power-generating companies for example cannot be under-priced, in light of the need to reduce public borrowing; in any event the regulatory risk involved makes these shares less attractive to potential investors than was initially the case.

Furthermore shareholders will not want to leave so much value on the table in future management buyouts; boards of directors are uncomfortably aware that many of the new millionaires of the 1980s owe their wealth to the over-generous terms they agreed when they sold the business in the first place. The Centre for Management Buyout Research estimated in late 1992 that the uninvested pool of capital raised before 1992 and targeted at larger buyouts was not far short of £500 million.

In other words, the days when financial engineering was an acceptable substitute for the real thing may be drawing to a close. And investors will have more reasonable expectations of the rewards they can expect and the risks they must be prepared to accept to achieve them. It could well be that there are lessons to be learned from the United States. There, the 1980s saw large-scale participation by institutional investors in private equity funds. Partnership commitments grew fortyfold, from $2 billion in 1980 to more than $80 billion in 1992. Inevitably, in a period of such heady growth, mistakes were made. But experience of the decade has shown that over the longer term, investments in unquoted companies provided superior returns, but at substantially higher risk – in the sense that the performance varied widely between different fund managers and from year to year. One of the largest US pension funds calculated the expected annual return on different types of investments over the decades as follows:

Government stocks	6.7% p.a.
Fixed interest	8.5
Property	9.9
International equity	10.6
Domestic equity	10.7
Venture capital	15.0

But the same study, and others like it, also showed the volatility of venture capital performance. For example, one study of seventeen funds set up in the 1980s, with a combined capitalisation of over $530 million, showed that by the end of 1991 average annual returns were 15.9 per cent; but the top quartile achieved a return of 18.2 per cent a year, and the best fund over 50 per cent a year.

In some respects the situation in the United Kingdom is not dissimilar. Analysis of the annualised total returns on different investments over the period 1982–92 reveals the following figures:

Property	10.3% p.a.
Fixed interest	11.5
International equity	17.8
UK equity	19.3

The higher returns than in the US on international equity must largely be due to the long-term decline in the value of sterling; while the higher gains on UK equities reflect higher inflation here than in the United States and the institutional pressures for high dividend payments referred to earlier.

As far as small UK companies are concerned, their stock market valuation increased more than twice as fast as that of larger companies during the boom times. But once the recession began to bite in 1989 the position was reversed. Between 1988 and 1992 the smaller companies index rose by under 2 per cent while the total returns of the FTSE 100 companies increased by nearly 50 per cent.

However, the same variation in performance is evident among venture capital funds in the United Kingdom. The industry has been through at least four distinct phases since the early 1980s, when the UK tended to follow the US model of investing in high-technology companies, at an early stage in their development. However there were relatively few players, and entry prices for the venture capitalists were relatively low. Moreover the timing was right, since the UK economy was emerging from recession and the small business was the 'flavour of the year'. So despite problems with high technology and the limited size of the UK market which meant that really massive gains on the American scale were unlikely, the returns for venture capitalists and investors were none the less reasonable.

This early phase was succeeded in the mid 1980s by what might be termed the management buyout bonanza. The concept of management buying the businesses in which they worked was attractive, as the balance of power shifted in favour of management and away from trade unions. Prices were still reasonable, and gearing was modest. The economy was growing strongly, and this was reflected in the stock market. So returns were very attractive to venture capitalists and investors alike. The number of buyouts and buyins in the UK rose steadily from around 250 a year in the period 1982–5, to over 400 in 1987, 500 in 1988 and 600 in 1990.

But by the late 1980s it was clear that the venture capital market was over-heated. There had been a fund-raising boom as institutions scrambled to enter the market; successful fund-raising tends to follow good venture capital (and smaller firms' stock market) performance rather than lead it. Another case of our institutions finding it easier to look at the road through the rear-end mirror, perhaps. Many new entrants meant extravagant promises, high prices for investors and high gearing for companies; this was the era of junk bonds, and very large management buyouts and buyins, all at the peak of the economic cycle.

By the early 1990s the problems with the overall economy had shown up some of the weaknesses in some of the deals done in the late 1980s – particularly the larger buyouts in the retail sectors. A weak stock market meant that it was more difficult to float companies, and managers of venture capital funds became increasingly preoccupied with the problems facing the companies in their portfolios. As a result, returns on venture capital funds raised in the late 1980s had been relatively poor on average and investor interest waned. The book value of quoted venture capital investment trusts moved as follows during this period:

1989	+ 20%
1990	− 18
1991	− 3
1992	+ 3

By the end of 1992 private companies were typically valued at less than ten times their annual earnings, compared with share prices on the London Stock Exchange that valued leading UK companies at around seventeen times their annual earnings. And there is a clear risk that just as the need for new funds to finance the expansion of smaller businesses is greatest at the bottom of the economic cycle, the necessary funds will not be available.

A fresh approach

Plainly a fresh approach is needed. Several initiatives warrant serious consideration.

The clearing banks recognise that they are going to have to play a more constructive role with respect to smaller businesses. It may run counter to the instincts and experience of many of their managers; and arguably counter to their shareholders' interests as well. After all, during the recession the four high street banks have had to provide in their accounts for non-payment of twice as much as was written off in so-called problem-country debt. The Receiver is now the largest owner of hotels in Britain.

Many of these businesses might have survived, and even prospered, given more time and an injection of management expertise and commitment. A nationwide network of enterprise funds, funded by the clearing banks and associated both with the government's Small Business Loan Guarantee Scheme and local Training and Enterprise Councils, could make a world of difference. Already some banks have set up departments to deal with the conversion of debt into equity. In effect the banks and Exchequer between them would be injecting highly-motivated new management and time into businesses that show a realistic prospect of survival. The returns to banks' shareholders from improving the recovery rate on the non-performing loans could make such an initiative very attractive.

But this will essentially amount to an attempt to recover the mistakes of the past. New funds will be required to finance the expansion of medium-size businesses on terms that recognise the higher risks involved. It is unrealistic to expect clearing banks to be willing to lend on equity risks for debt rewards. Nor will the venture capital industry be able to make good the funding gap. Even in 1989, the peak year for raising new venture capital, only some £1.6 billion was raised – far less than will be needed to finance the economic upturn.

There is one obvious source of this finance: pension funds. If each fund invested a minimum of, say, 5 per cent of their portfolio in venture capital funds, at a stroke there would be adequate funding for the missing 'Mittelstand' of British business, an historic source of weakness in the over-concentrated British economy. In any case this would be in pension funds' longer-term interests, given the prospects for lower returns in the future from their traditional investments.

Some analysts suggest that there is little sense in pension funds investing less than 10 per cent of their portfolio in unquoted companies, because the impact on the funds' overall performance of achieving above average returns on venture capital investments would not be great enough to compensate for the extra administrative cost and additional risk. But their mood is not helped by the insistence of the Department of Trade and Industry that all unquoted investments be written down to nil value in the insurance companies' books for the purposes of determining whether the fund is in a position to meet its long-term obligations. This is a hangover from the days when Whitehall failed to recognise either the importance of smaller businesses to the economy or that means were available to realise their value over the medium term.

In addition, informal investors, sometimes known as 'business angels', provide more than twice as much capital for smaller firms as the entire venture capital industry. They should be encouraged. The principles behind the original Business Expansion Scheme (BES) were sound and should not be abandoned simply because the scheme degenerated into a way for the wealthy to avoid paying tax without running any significant business risks with their investment. What is needed is a reformed BES. This could be limited to investments in companies that already exist: it is expansion that needs to be financed, rather than start-ups. Investors would be able to set any investment in a private company against their income tax liabilities, for an initial first period of, say, four years. Such a scheme would obviously limit the scope for tax avoidance as well. The scheme could be run by banks and other financial institutions who would be licensed to ensure that the investments fell within the purpose of any new BES legislation.

The reformed BES should be open to, if not actually limited to, those with a direct connection to the business involved, including directors, management and employees, who have most to lose if things go wrong. Because investment by those closest to the company was explicitly forbidden, Aunt Agatha – not to mention her family, friends, business associates and others who knew something about the potential investment and might be ready to take a greater risk in consequence – was effectively barred from investing in companies enjoying the tax advantages of the original scheme. Predictably, this opened the way to financial middle-men. The results were that investors were detached, risk-shy and more interested in a quick return. Thus of the total of nearly 4,400 companies supported by BES funding in the three years to April 1991, almost 2,900 were in private rented housing, which accounted for some 85 per cent of the total funds raised.

Finally the risks and rewards for smaller businesses themselves need to be rebalanced. Most of those regulating small businesses, or indeed making the lending decisions that make all the difference between prosperity and failure, would not dream of accepting the risks that small businesses are forced to run. Far from assured salaries and inflation-proof pensions, very often all the owner's wealth, including their homes and pensions, are tied up with their business. If it fails, for whatever reason, they are penniless. 'I cannot afford to die', as one failed restaurateur in the West Country put it to the author; and the bankruptcy laws mean that the likelihood of a second chance is negligible. Even if the business succeeds, a goodly proportion of the annual profits will be paid over to the taxman, who will also come to claim his share of the cumulative added-value when the business is sold or the owner dies. Few financial advisers would suggest entering into an arrangement where the risks are so obvious and the financial rewards so constrained. The wonder is that over 400,000 new businesses started up in 1992 alone.

Once again there may be lessons to be learned from across the Atlantic. There, the so-called Chapter Eleven procedure provides companies with temporary protection from their creditors. It can give the necessary breathing space to reorganise the business and introduce new management, and can be a much more productive alternative to receivership. Chapter Eleven has saved many companies which would have failed in the United Kingdom; administrative receivership does not seem to have had the same effect.

There is also a case for improving the tax treatment of those responsible for creating the nation's wealth. Further tax relief could be made available to directors and employees who invest in the companies in which they work. At present there may be little incentive for the owner of a small business to re-invest rather than taking money out to spend on their own lifestyles. Indeed there is a clear tax incentive to invest in a pension rather than the future of the business.

The so-called supply-side revolution of the 1980s was no mirage. The people responsible have not suddenly lost their skill, nerve or commitment. In the main they are working harder now than they ever did. But they have been let down, betrayed even, by the economic policy establishment, Parliament, the Civil Service, and our financial institutions. A nation of speculators and spenders can, and must, again become one of savers and investors. But this will only happen if investors have confidence in the way 'their' companies are managed.

I have long believed that business has a broader role in society than just providing worthwhile returns for shareholders, essential though these are. My experience in north America during the mid 1970s suggested that the frontiers between the public and private sectors in Britain were not necessarily in the right place. And in the early 1980s I had the opportunity to see how they might be moved, in an assignment for the then Scottish Development Agency. At the CBI I was an enthusiast for the work of Business in the Community. However, the politics of envy are seldom absent long from the headlines. There is regular outrage at 'obscene' pay increases for senior executives, especially in newly-privatised concerns. To such an extent that Sir John Hedley Greenborough once suggested that he should discuss the issue of top management pay at the next annual general meeting at which he presided with a guitar around his neck to illustrate the differing standards that people apply. My own salary became a matter of public interest when I was appointed Controller of the Audit Commission. Now, as a Non-Executive Director of several major public companies, I have to consider not the theory of the case but its practical applications in ways which protect shareholders' longer-term interests. The judgements are far from easy.

14
Business and Society

The short-term pressures for results could mortgage the economic future of all the stakeholders in Britain's future.

One of the very few sayings of a senior businessman that might have made it to the *Oxford Dictionary of Quotations* is that of 'Engine Charlie' Wilson, the then Chairman of General Motors, that 'What is good for General Motors is good for the Nation'.

Much has happened since, not least to the once mighty GM, which saw its Chairman replaced in late 1992 in a coup inspired by the independent members of the board. He was replaced by an executive who had made his reputation in Europe, where the turnaround at Vauxhall Motors is one of the success stories of the international motor industry: a case of the old world being called in to redress the balance of the new. But the basic thought remains. Indeed some recent commentators suggested that the new Chairman of General Motors would exert more influence over the prospects for the United States economy than the newly-elected President.

If anything, the prosperity of Britain is even more dependent on the way its major businesses are managed than is the case in the United States. The UK economy is both more exposed to international competition and more concentrated. In addition, during the past decade business has been playing an increasingly prominent role in British society as the frontiers between the public and private sectors have moved. Business must now respond to the needs and aspirations of a wider set of stakeholders – who will demand, among other things, that management pay reflects performance.

Different frontiers

Since the quality of top management is the key to the success of any business, it is especially important that the right people are in place and appropriately motivated at the top of British business. This is not just necessary for the interests of shareholders, but for society at large. In late 1987, speaking in the aftermath of the so-called 'crash' on world stock markets, in his first address to a CBI National Conference the author addressed matters that many at the time must have regarded as marginal from a business standpoint. He set out the following targets for his five-year term:

- every single local secondary school in the country linked effectively with local business
- a doubling in the effectiveness of our training
- management turned into the profession that it must become
- business fully involved in the renewal of the decaying centres of our inner cities
- British business prepared to meet the challenges that the single European market would most assuredly bring.

Since then, there has been remarkable progress in each of these areas, reflecting the efforts of organisations such as Business in the Community, as well as the Training and Enterprise Councils and the Management Charter Initiative, which did not exist in November 1987. In each case, business set out a national strategy and led the way towards goals that commanded broad acceptance.

To take just one example, every secondary school in Great Britain is now twinned effectively with the local business community. Almost all Local Education Authorities have set up education business partnerships. Nearly eight out of ten have reached the level equivalent to a Compact (where local business guarantees to offer school-leavers jobs provided that they meet certain agreed standards of academic attainment, attendance and conduct), compared with less than one in twenty in 1987. Over 130,000 young people a year now have work experience placements under Project Trident, compared with 52,000 in 1987. Secondments of teachers into business arranged by the CBI's Education Foundation have risen from under two thousand in 1987 to approaching twenty-five thousand in 1992.

Similarly, as Chapter 9 shows, it is beyond doubt that British business is taking skills training and management development much more seriously than was the case even a decade ago. Despite an extraordinarily difficult trading climate, expenditure on training is increasingly regarded as an investment in the future, rather than a cost to be minimised. And it is a very substantial investment. Leading companies spend up to 10 per cent of their payroll costs on training. If all training within business ceased immediately, pre-tax profits next year might rise by as much as a quarter. The voluntary commitment of local business leaders to the new Training and Enterprise Councils is impressive testimony to their determination to see the skills revolution through.

It is the same story in many deprived inner city areas as well, as described in Chapter 11. Business leaders are leading local initiatives, in partnership with other stakeholders in local communities. With notable success. Back in 1980 very few people would have given much for the chances of Glasgow becoming the European City of Culture within the decade. Yet it did. Thanks to the combined efforts of a team of local business people, the then Scottish Development Agency, the City Council and over a decade of planning, promotion and investment, Glasgow is indeed 'miles better'. It now rivals Edinburgh in attracting tourists. Similar but unsung successes are in prospect in dozens of towns and cities across Britain. A BBC television series, *It's My City*, attracted around a thousand entrants for a competition in 1989 to show local enterprise in action to improve local communities.

These achievements reflect a change in attitudes. There has been a shift in the border between the public and private sectors. The private sector is now taking on obligations that formerly rested on central and local government. Indeed it is increasingly being recognised that business has a responsibility to a broad range of stakeholders, of whom the shareholders are but one. Apart from customers, the local community, suppliers and employees all have legitimate interests in the success of individual businesses, which boards must increasingly take into account.

In such circumstances it is of paramount importance that an undue proportion of the best people emerging from our education system go into the profession of management, just as in times of war the best officers and troops need to be where the battle is fiercest. However until quite recently this was not the case, as innumerable reports have shown. By international standards, British managers in the late 1970s were poorly qualified, poorly trained, poorly paid and poorly motivated. Not surprisingly, since most of them depended on their pensions for their future financial security, they were usually preoccupied with survival: keeping the business afloat and the bank manager at bay.

The past decade has seen a remarkable change. Today, many more British managers are a match for the best in the world – as our export performance suggests. They are better qualified and better trained: the number of business studies graduates more than doubled during the 1980s; and expenditure on management development has risen dramatically. They are also better paid – although 1992 surveys suggested that Britain's managers rank only in the middle of the OECD league table of the local purchasing power of their net (after tax) salary and benefits. While the spread of performance pay, wider employee share ownership and executive share options mean that they are better motivated as well. For the first time in Britain's recent economic history, the managers of major businesses – as distinct from the owners or their professional advisers – have the opportunity to build their own capital base and with it some measure of the financial independence which is an essential corollary of the willingness to accept risks.

Now, a rather different series of questions is moving up the domestic political agenda. What is the role of business in society? Is it right that the interests of the owners of companies should take precedence over those of the other shareholders? Are senior managers paid too much? Are well-publicised increases in senior executives' pay damaging politically or economically?

More stakeholders

While the directors of Britain's businesses may recognise the need to become involved in the community and the importance of reconciling the sometimes conflicting interests of different groups of stakeholders, the owners of Britain's top companies evidently take a much more short-term view. 'What have you done for me lately?' appears to be the motto of most of the pension funds and financial institutions which, between them, control most of our major companies. The rights of ownership – to sell shares at a time and price of the owner's choice – seem to imply no obligations, let alone duties.

As a result managers feel themselves under very considerable short-term pressure to generate profits and to pay dividends, even if these are at the expense of the long-term competitiveness of the business. Thus over the past few years dividends have grown faster than earnings or investment, and have persistently been higher (as a proportion of post-tax profits) in the United Kingdom than in Japan or Germany. The differential has in fact widened since the recession began to take hold. Even during the years of relative plenty, British industry has been more generous in its dividend policies. In the lean years of the recession the situation became even more serious. In 1992 dividends on industrial and commercial companies shares (£21 billion) accounted for 27 per cent of gross trading profits. In 1988 the figure was 18 per cent. Meanwhile manufacturing investment has fallen at precisely the time when it needs to double, if British industry is to be equipped to compete with the world's best.

As the CBI's National Manufacturing Council has pointed out, manufacturing companies increased their dividends by an average of 12 per cent a year during the 1980s, while profits rose by just 6 per cent and capital investment by only 2 per cent a year. Of the largest six hundred quoted companies reporting in the first half of 1992, well over half increased their dividends while only one in ten reduced them.

The reason for this apparent disregard of the future is straight-forward. Fear of being taken over. Neither directors nor managers wish to lose their independence, let alone their jobs. So they take whatever steps are available to them to ensure that the share price does not fall to levels that might attract a bid – including, on occasion, adoption of some dubious accounting practices to inflate reported earnings, and paying dividends out of reserves.

The fear of being taken over is well-founded. During the late 1980s around 150 public companies a year were being taken over, usually by other UK publicly quoted companies, who saw greater opportunities from buying assets undervalued by the markets than investing in new products, processes or services; and £20 billion to £30 billion a year was being spent by the acquiring companies.

The usual justification for what the economists quaintly call 'an open market in corporate control' is that the mere threat of a takeover keeps managements on their toes and provides the owners of businesses with a relatively painless means of selling out or changing the managements of their companies. The process is not just painless. For most of those involved it is very lucrative. Selling shareholders, merchant bankers, stockbrokers, corporate lawyers, and public relations consultants all benefit directly and considerably from takeover activities. Moreover acquisitions by UK companies overseas have made a notable contribution to the UK economy more generally. In 1991 income from abroad amounted to some £25 billion (in 1981 the figure was just over £9 billion).

The question to be answered is whether what amounts to a corporate casino provides the best environment in which to decide who should manage those businesses which will determine the nation's economic future. The UK is not alone in facing such awkward questions. Takeovers are a characteristic of open financial markets, like those in Australia, Britain and north America – three markets where creative accounting has flourished in recent years, the balance of payments has been negative (to the tune of some $100 billion in total in 1992) and dividend policies have been generous. On the other hand, on the Continent or in Japan contested takeovers, as opposed to agreed mergers, are virtually unheard of. Indeed there is no single word to describe a takeover in the Japanese language.

The research into the economic benefits of takeovers is ambivalent. Although many, if not most, of the takeovers of the past have been shown to be expensive failures, as the current fashion for 'unbundling' and the success of many management buyouts demonstrates.

What is certain is that only the shareholders can play in this particular casino. All the other stakeholders in a business are, in effect, disenfranchised. The shareholders have virtually unfettered right to decide the future of their business. Yet important national issues are often involved which it is obviously unrealistic to expect owners to take into account in their private decision-making. For example:

– Does the ownership of shares in a company confer any obligations, in addition to the right to sell at the moment and price of the owner's choice? Should pension funds and financial institutions take a closer interest in the way the companies they own are run?
– Is there any evidence that the two economies (the United States and the United Kingdom), where the market rules most effectively, have performed better than for example, bank-based systems such as operate in Germany, France and Japan?

- Does it matter if control of British companies is exercised from outside the United Kingdom? Is foreign ownership compatible with corporate social responsibility and a commitment to the local communities where major plants are located?
- Should the market be the sole judge of whether mergers or acquisitions should proceed? Is the 'national interest' a relevant concept in an interdependent world economy? Should the 'playing field' be tilted in favour of defendants?

These questions were raised in a particularly acute form when the Swiss company, Nestlé, launched a takeover bid for Rowntree Mackintosh in the spring of 1988. Speaking at an *Awards for Marketing* dinner in May that year, the author posed the issues in the following terms:

How is it that a Swiss company can value the world-class brands of Rowntree so much higher than our own stock market? We are told on all sides that the offers for Rowntree will simply be too tempting for the City to turn down. I have to tell you, as someone who has a great deal of respect for Swiss businessmen, that they are not given to extravagant offers – quite the reverse, in fact. Switzerland did not achieve its enviable industrial reputation by being careless, nor by taking a short-term view of their strategic situation. Swiss banks do not confuse ownership with speculation.

The City of London has always asserted that it takes the long view; and the analysis supports that position. Now, in the new situation – post-Big Bang and the 'adjustments' of last October – will be the opportunity to see whether the instinct to take the money and run is indeed too powerful for people to resist.

I, for one, find it very difficult to reconcile what I believe about our great institutions and the fact that some 20 per cent of Cadbury shares could have been picked up in the market by a company [General Cinema] with no track record in consumer marketing and no obvious strategic intentions for improving the business. In fact there are very good reasons why companies like Rowntree, in the national interest, should remain in British hands.

In the run-in to 1992 we cannot afford to see major brands sold off; this would amount to selling our seed corn. Rowntrees – and indeed Cadburys – make a huge contribution to the local communities in which they operate . . . Brands have a value – a very considerable value – even if this does not appear in any balance sheet. There is a great danger that we only value things we can measure precisely. Whitehall is not the only place where it is easier to be precisely wrong than roughly right. The kind of exit P/Es* that are widely regarded in the City as being 'too good to resist' would look very modest on the Tokyo Stock Exchange.

These arguments notwithstanding, the pressures on fund managers to improve their quarterly earnings performance proved too irresistible. It is easy to see why. Fees for merger and acquisition activity have played an increasingly important part in the earnings of merchant banks and stockbrokers. In addition the traditional long-standing partnership between client and merchant banker is changing, partly as a result of the amalgamations following Big Bang, and partly because of the readiness of client companies to use a new adviser for a particular deal. This in turn has increased the incentive among corporate finance advisers to generate new business in this way. Companies known to be interested in growth by acquisition can receive as many as six unsolicited proposals from financial middlemen in a single day.

The short-term pressures on fund managers could effectively mortgage our competitive future. It would be very easy to sacrifice the long-run competitiveness of British business to the short-term attractions of bids from the Continent when there is no possibility of UK-based companies acquiring companies in the country concerned. This is one of the principal concerns of the larger ITV companies, who see themselves as vulnerable to overseas bidders but are barred from any pre-emptive action by local laws on media ownership.

The extent of the vulnerability of the UK economy to overseas acquisitions is much greater than is recognised. The London stock market is much more important in determining corporate control than is the case in Paris or Frankfurt, where takeovers are almost unknown because national and regional governments, as well as banks, hold strategic stakes in major companies, and there are more large privately-owned businesses. The UK economy is also highly concentrated. Overall, just a hundred companies account for 45 per cent of our exports (by value). The combined market valuation for companies central to our export performance, such

* The ratio of the stock market valuations of a business to its current annual earnings. The higher the ratio, the longer the markets are looking forward and the greater the perceived growth opportunities. Just before Christmas 1992 Glaxo was selling on a P/E of 23.6 times and British Aerospace 3.6 times, to take two contrasting examples.

as British Aerospace, GEC, GKN, Lucas and Rolls-Royce, was little more than £15 billion in September 1983. This is the same order of magnitude as the combined valuation of leading retail groups such as Argyle, Asda, Dixons, Kingfisher and Tesco. It is substantially less than the annual value of the acquisitions made in the late 1980s.

Despite a debate on the so-called problem of short-termism that lasted throughout the 1980s, the issues have stubbornly refused to go away. A CBI task force reporting in October 1987 concluded that the main problem was a failure of communications between those that owned Britain's businesses and those that manage them. A subsequent report by Professor Paul Marsh of the London Business School and a member of the original CBI Task Force came to substantially the same conclusion. But although improved communication is necessary it will not be sufficient. It remains indisputable that for decades British business has invested less than its principal competitors in up-to-date equipment, innovation, quality and skills. French, German, Japanese and Swiss managers working in Britain are often astounded at the short-term pressures on, and perspective of, British managers. So the problem cannot responsibly be assumed away.

Part of the solution must lie in winning the battle with inflation. Only then will the cost of funds be brought into line and British managers be in a position to take a similarly long-term view of investment. At the same time, if managers of British businesses are not investing to meet the longer-term interests of their owners, there must be something wrong with corporate governance in Britain. During the 1990s further steps will need to be taken to ensure that the boards of public companies are able, and encouraged where appropriate, to take the long view essential to competing successfully in the New Europe. In addition to improving communications between boards and shareholders in general, this could involve ensuring that the UK takeover process is both measured and transparent, so that the owners have the information and time needed to take a considered view of any offer for their business. It should not be possible for UK companies to be acquired by bid-proof competitors against the recommendations of the board of directors without an automatic referral to the Monopolies and Mergers Commission to determine whether the deal is in the overall national interest.

Finally if institutional shareholders are not going to take a direct interest in the running of the businesses they own, they should at least insist on a critical mass of independent directors of good quality and with a personal stake in the longer-term success of the business. It is, after all, the board of a company that needs to reconcile the conflict of interests of the various stakeholders in a business and which should determine how much senior management should be paid.

Pay and performance

Until the late 1970s high marginal rates of personal taxation meant that pay increases were of limited use in motivating middle and senior management in Britain. At one stage in the late 1970s the tax on the investment income of people in the top income tax bracket exceeded their income – that is, there was a penalty for being so foolish as to have savings and invest them. The politics of envy were all too evident: on the shopfloor, in the public services – where NHS consultants found their private practice increasingly constrained – and in the House of Commons, where the then Chancellor of the Exchequer announced to approving cheers from the government benches that it was his intention to make the pips squeak.

In such circumstances, there was a natural tendency among managers and their employers to seek to protect their standard of living from the ravages of inflation in ways that were more tax-efficient than increasing salaries. This was the era of the 'lump', when some builders would only accept jobs if they were paid in cash. Tax avoidance became a growth industry. So-called fringe benefits – notably large cars and drivers, expense accounts, health insurance, first-class air travel – became an increasingly large part of managers' so-called compensation packages. Deferred income in the form of pensions became even more important; to the point where potential new graduate recruits would enquire about the pension arrangements at their initial job interviews.

The situation changed dramatically during the 1980s as marginal rates of income tax fell, first to 60 per cent and then to 40 per cent. For the first time it was reasonable to expect changes in managerial pay to reflect performance in some way or other; and it was equally reasonable for the tax treatment of so-called fringe benefits to be changed. And, in general, managerial pay has reflected the performance of British business over the last decade. Between 1981 and 1991 the profits of Britain's industrial and commercial companies rose by over 60 per cent in real terms (that is, after stripping out the effects of inflation and providing for the depreciation of their assets and the replacement of stocks). Over the same period the average director's salary increased by about 40 per cent, again in real terms.

But this is not how it seemed to the British public. The Top Salary Review Body recommended large increases in the pay of senior public servants in 1990, and aroused considerable public disquiet. Large increases in the pay of senior managers in the newly-privatised industries also caused widespread and unfavourable comment. The situation was not improved by the refusal of one beneficiary to answer a straightforward question on a BBC *Panorama* programme about whether he thought that he had any obligation to set an example to his employees (who were facing a pay freeze) in agreeing his own salary level. Others took up the refrain, comparing changes in the pay of each company's highest paid director with results – usually as reflected in profits or, in some cases (and more reasonably), increases in shareholder value: changes in share price plus dividends.

The analysis was disturbing to say the very least. Any relationship between top management pay and performance seemed purely coincidental. Too often managers' earnings rose while performance apparently declined. Particularly as pay settlements in the economy as a whole fell, top management was exposed to the charge of greed: awarding itself unacceptable salary rises at a time when control of wage inflation was a national priority. The old cry of 'one law for the rich, and another for the poor' acquired new resonance at a particularly unfortunate time.

In fact the evidence presented in support of the case against management was often flawed. The *Sunday Times* was forced to dismiss one of its business news staff and reassign others because an article critical of top management pay included cases of mistaken identity and failed to take account of changes in responsibility or recent appointments to the board. Since annual reports do not name the highest-paid director, it is all too easy to make wrong assumptions about his or her identity. Often the highest-paid directors are employed in the United States; so it is only to be expected that their salaries would be out of line with UK expectations. Few of the critics of the increase in the compensation of the Chief Executive of one of the privatised utilities took account of the fact that, for a large part of the year, he had also served as Chairman and had overseen the particularly successful privatisation (and would be paid substantially less than many of his professional advisers). Particularly when the new executive is appointed in the middle of the year, comparisons of the compensation of the highest-paid director can refer to different people. If the new person does not have a full year's pay in his new post subsequent increases will look more generous than they in fact are.

Moreover, the performance measures against which executive pay is assessed often turn out to be simplistic: the year on year change in pre-tax profits or earnings per share. Leaving aside the ability of companies to manipulate both figures by what some have called 'creative accounting', most business leaders expect to be – and indeed should be – judged on their record over a longer period in generating value for their shareholders in the form of real increases in dividends and share prices. And, in any event, their record will inevitably be influenced by factors such as market conditions, competitive activity and the pace of technical change.

But there remains a problem to be addressed. The recession has found out many of the managerial icons of the mid 1980s, as the subsequent careers of a number of recipients of the *Guardian* Young Businessman of the Year Award demonstrate. Top management pay is generally flexible in one direction only – upwards. Significant pay cuts are rare, even when performance has degenerated substantially. It seems that the annual salary 'fix' remains part of the national business scene. The concept of a 'going rate' for pay increases at all levels may have eroded in recent years; but it has by no means disappeared. The convenient notion of an international market for senior executives has developed, even though very few managers either want to work outside the United Kingdom for extended periods or will have the language skills and local contacts to hold down senior posts overseas. In too many cases, top management pay evidently does not reflect performance, however this might be defined. In such circumstances, either the independent (non-executive) directors were not consulted or they felt unable to insist on changes to their executive colleagues' compensation arrangements. Often this is because of fears that morale will suffer at a difficult time. Frequently too the figures have already been 'justified' by independent consultants who claim to take account of what similar companies are paying their executives.

There is, inevitably, a large element of hypocrisy and envy in the public discussion of executive pay. Those who have voluntarily forgone pay increases to which they are contractually entitled (like the author) rarely notice any positive reaction from those whose attitudes they are seeking to influence. 'He can afford it' is the more usual response. None the less it is not unknown for executives to treat their shareholders' money as though it were their own. Or for pay to be increased substantially while all the fringe benefits are carried forward from the previous era of high taxation. Some of the pay increases that have occasioned most critical comment have been designed to inflate the executives' pensions – granting them large increases in the final year of their employment. Similarly service contracts can insure executives against failure. Indeed one of the quickest ways for managers to accumulate wealth has been to be dismissed and enjoy the balance of a long-term contract.

Top management must accept the obligation of leading by example, if a performance culture is to spread throughout the economy. Every board of directors should inform their shareholders in their annual report how management's performance is assessed and how the assessment relates to their pay. This would be open to challenge by shareholders at the annual general meeting. The independent (non-executive) directors collectively should then ensure that individual senior executives' pay increases only in line with their performance; that the performance-related element in executive compensation is significant; and that there are appropriate penalties for poor performance. Independent directors should approve all long-term service contracts. As far as possible, senior managers should be in exactly the same position as shareholders. There is no known substitute for the 'owner's eye' in ensuring that a business is run with due regard for the owner's interests; and 'real' shares are preferable to options, in that executives invest their own money in the businesses they are managing.

If the politics of greed and envy stage a comeback at Westminster the results could be serious – not least for the public standing of business and the willingness of ordinary people to invest their savings in public com-

panies. So management pay must reflect performance at all levels, and in all sectors of the economy. Then, and only then, is there a reasonable prospect of establishing a performance culture throughout the economy. The regulators' role in creating just such a culture is the subject of the next chapter.

Regulation has become one of the growth industries of the last decade. The privatisation of the electricity, gas, telecommunications and water industries means that companies with a combined stock market value of some £90 billion (as at September 1993), the equivalent of some £4,000 for every UK household, are subject to the decisions of regulators who appear accountable only to themselves.

The question of how the regulators are themselves regulated is therefore important to the future of much of British industry – for which British Gas, BT, and the various water and electricity supply companies are themselves important customers.

As the Controller of the Audit Commission I was in a sense one of the first independent regulators. While at the CBI I was directly concerned to see business protected from the exploitation of the monopoly positions of suppliers of key commodities and services. Now, as the Chairman of Westcountry Television and a Director of National Power, I see the other side of the regulatory process and its interface with the Monopolies and Mergers Commission and the courts.

256

15

Regulating the Regulators

There is no cohesion between regulators ... they could totally screw up the financial future of the company.
[Cedric Brown, Chief Executive of British Gas, 1993]

The future of some of the most important industries in Britain has been determined by regulators rather than the international marketplace. British Airways, British Telecom, British Gas and the electricity, water and television companies are not just important because they meet important everyday needs for almost every household in the country. They can also play a key role in correcting our balance of payments deficit. But they will not be able to do so if they do not retain a strong and profitable position in their home market.

So the various regulators face a difficult balancing act. On the one hand they must prevent abuse of market power and the exploitation of consumers and customers. On the other hand they should be concerned with the long-run international competitiveness of the industries that they are regulating. They certainly have the necessary resources at their disposal for this task, around £60 million a year – although the weight of regulation on the relatively small television industry, with a combined market capitalisation about an eighth of British Telecom's, is somewhat surprising: regulation costs around £1,000 a year for every person employed by the ITV companies.

Unfortunately the evidence to date suggests that the regulators are not remotely concerned with international competitiveness. Rather, they seem preoccupied with domestic considerations: consumer prices and increasing the level of domestic competition by encouraging new entrants into the various markets. Even so, some important questions are now coming to the surface: what is the 'right' level of profitability in a domestic market for a company

257

which enjoys a relatively stable market and little competition; who should pay to meet externally imposed environmental standards that will benefit non-users of the product or service (not to mention future generations); is the achievement of new emissions standards in the water and electricity industries in particular worth the cost that will be involved?

The implications of the regulators' decisions are very considerable. British Gas, with a market capitalisation of £14 billion, risks being broken up. The water industry has been told that its regulator is minded to cut its domestic profitability in half, while it faces the need to spend some £30 billion largely to meet EC quality standards. The electricity generators are threatened, regularly, with an enquiry by the Monopolies and Mergers Commission. At the other end of the industrial spectrum some of the ITV companies argue that the fragmented nature of the industry that resulted from the Broadcasting Act has contributed to its collective failure to make programmes that sell well overseas.

The Monopolies and Mergers Commission's enquiry into the brewing industry repays careful study by those concerned with the way that British industry is regulated. It is a case study in the law of unintended consequences. After the most detailed enquiries, it was clear that British drinkers neither lacked choice nor were paying too much for beer by international standards (which are not difficult to establish). Nor were the major brewers making excessive profits. None the less a 'complex monopoly' was held to exist and the government initiated a comprehensive restructuring of the industry designed to assist smaller regional brewers and limit the size of the pub estates of the major players in the industry. The result has been precisely the opposite of what was intended. Beer prices rose much faster than inflation; closures of smaller local breweries have accelerated; and, overall, the industry has consolidated with less choice available overall to consumers.

The law of unintended consequences has not just applied to the brewing industry. It is to be seen in the electricity industry, as well as in commercial television.

These examples of what economists call 'regulatory arbitrage' come on top of the usual market, technical and management risks that any large business has to cope with. They matter particularly at a time of rapid technical change when British industry ought to be well placed to compete for major contracts in the rapidly growing markets of the Near and Far East: the worldwide demand for energy, clean water supplies, telecommunications and entertainment is certain to grow dramatically in the years ahead. It would be most unfortunate if the opportunities were lost to Britain simply because the regulators were preoccupied with scoring political points at home.

Global opportunities

The best way of illustrating the scale of the opportunities at stake is to take one example known to the author, energy supply. But the scale of the opportunities in water treatment, telecommunications and entertainment is likely to be similarly massive.

Since 1950 the world's consumption of primary energy has increased five times. While consumption in OECD countries has flattened out, at around 6 kW per capita every year, the rate of growth in developing countries – which account for some three-quarters of the world's population – is rising rapidly from 1 kW per capita. Currently, half the world's population is not connected to electricity supply. However the trend to mega-cities is growing in Africa, South America and Asia. In Zambia, for instance, around two-thirds of the population is now living in urban areas compared with less than a quarter in 1965. In Tanzania the urban population has grown over the same period from under 10 per cent to around a third. It is the same story all over the developing world. This trend, combined with the revolution of rising expectations, is certain to result in a doubling of per capita consumption of energy by the year 2050, by which time the world's population could have reached nine billion according to UN forecasts (compared with some five billion today). Since demand for electricity grows faster than total energy demand and twice as fast in developing countries, electricity demand in 2050 is likely to be at least two and possibly three times as great as it was in 1988 – with almost all the growth coming from the developing world. In other words there is a massive global market for energy in which the UK is particularly well placed to compete: we have experience of financing, building and operating power stations all over the world.

All this might seem rather far into the future. However, the Indian government's plans for the five years from 1992 to 1997 called for the addition of 31,000 megawatts of additional generating capacity; this is more than the total generating capacity of National Power (24,000 megawatts), which has a market capitalisation of over £5 billion. If the new electricity generating capacity is not installed, there is no realistic prospect of the progressive degradation of the Indian environment or the drift from the countryside into the cities being halted, let alone reversed. Yet there is no realistic prospect, either, of India being able to borrow the money that will be required to build the needed power stations.

Exactly the same problems confront virtually every other developing economy. For example, the Chinese government has stated that it intends to invest billions before the end of the century in power generation. The scale of the worldwide opportunity in electricity generation is thus vast. The World Bank has forecast that, worldwide, some 800,000 megawatts of new generating plant will be needed over the next decade, costing up to $500 billion.

The key question is how this electricity is to be generated. At current rates of consumption, oil reserves will have been exhausted by around 2020 and gas reserves by 2030. There may be another two hundred years of coal reserves; but India and China may well be increasing their coal burn by over 100 million tonnes a year. Making very ambitious assumptions indeed, renewables (that is, primarily wind and wave power and hydro, which also involve substantial environmental disbenefits) might contribute some 40 per cent towards total world energy demand by 2050. Even this heroic assumption leaves a sizeable gap to be financed.

Imaginative schemes like the swapping of the debt developing countries in return for local investment in conservation projects are simply not equal to the task, however praiseworthy they may be. Since the first debt swap in 1987 the US Nature Conservancy and other environmental groups and official aid agencies between them have only purchased some $100 million of developing country debt (for under $20 million), generating a similar amount of local currency expenditure on conservation schemes of one kind or another.

Most developed countries have looked to nuclear power for the answers. For example, in the USA the President's National Energy Strategy envisaged that nuclear share of electricity generation will double from its current 18 per cent by 2010. Similarly in Japan the nuclear share is expected to increase over the same period from 27 per cent to 43 per cent. France, which exports more nuclear power than is produced in the UK, remains committed to nuclear.

In Sweden the government has introduced legislation to rescind the three-year-old decision to phase out nuclear power by 1995. Russia has announced plans to build at least thirty new nuclear power plants over the next fifteen years or so; while in Switzerland two anti-nuclear initiatives were rejected for the third time in ten years in a national referendum in September 1990.

So the international prospects for the UK electricity supply industry may in turn be bound up with the future of nuclear power, which is due to be reviewed by the government shortly. From the narrow standpoint of domestic demand for electricity, it might not matter if the United Kingdom opts out of the nuclear generating market. After all we can, presumably, always import technology and even electricity to meet our needs. And the Treasury could safely defer a decision, secure in the support of taxpayers generally, the Green movement and the National Union of Mineworkers. In any case this would not be the first time that a British world lead has been frittered away.

In the late 1950s the UK was at the forefront of world nuclear developments and successfully exported Magnox power stations to Japan and Italy. This technical lead was eroded in a series of industrial policy mistakes during the 1960s and 1970s. Today there is only one nuclear power station under construction, Sizewell B, which could all too easily turn out to be an expensive Anglicised prototype; and the mass-producing of prototypes is a long-standing British engineering tradition, of course. The adoption of a foreign reactor system for Sizewell B, with fundamentally different features from the Magnox systems already in operation in Britain, meant that many key parts could not be supplied locally. For example, there are facilities in France, Italy, Spain and Germany capable of manufacturing pressure vessels for pressurised water reactor systems; but there is none in the UK.

None the less the UK electrical engineering and power generation industries are able to compete with the best in the world, as their recent export record demonstrates; in 1992 total electrical engineering exports were worth some £5 billion.

The question which the nuclear review must not be allowed to ignore is whether it makes sense for the UK effectively to abandon its prospects of competing in the world market for nuclear power generation. It is unrealistic to expect to export products which are not apparently thought good (or safe) enough to be built and operated in the UK. Every capital goods manufacturer and defence equipment supplier knows the importance of a domestic flagship customer, and the damage that results if one is not readily identifiable.

But if nuclear power is to have a future the industry must get its act together. There will need to be strategic alliances, perhaps on an EC basis; inter-company rivalry within the UK must be left in the past, where it belongs. There will need to be continued demonstration of safety in operation; public opinion must be convinced that the fuel cycle in its entirety can be handled safely, and that the public is being kept fully informed of any safety concerns. A proactive rather than reactive approach to safety and communications will continue to be of vital importance.

The City of London will also have a critical role to play, structuring deals that provide investors in international power projects with adequate returns for the risks involved while delivering electricity safely and at affordable prices. Perhaps the end of the era of financial engineering will mean that talent and resources are diverted to more productive activities than domestic deal-making. At the same time the world community will need to develop some form of insurance policy against the risk that, by one means or another, a foreign-owned power station is effectively expropriated by the local government. No private company would be able to carry such a risk; one default might well result in bankruptcy. So the international community will need to act in concert, perhaps through the OECD or the World Bank, to put an insurance policy in place. The potential sanctions against any defaulting host country would be serious: no further multi- or bi-lateral aid, soft loans or access to world financial markets.

But none of these possibilities for British industries will materialize unless the framework for regulating the UK energy industry is changed.

Different regulation

As the uncertainties over the future of the nuclear and coal industries demonstrate all too clearly, the framework for regulating the supply of energy and electricity to the UK market is in urgent need of reform. Hidden, as well as overt, subsidies and tax-driven market distortions abound. The different regulators have been sending out contradictory signals. Indeed in the spring of 1993 things had reached a stage more usually associated with the former Soviet Union. In the interests of protecting jobs in the coal mines the board of National Power was being invited by the government to conclude a long-term contract for coal that it did not need to conclude (because there was plenty of coal available in power station stocks and on a spot basis in world markets), for quantities of high-sulphur coal that it did not expect to burn, on terms that were inconsistent with the company's prospectus when it was offered for sale to the public less than three years earlier. Meanwhile the nuclear industry – which was primarily responsible for the decline in domestic demand for coal-fired electricity – continued to be subsidised to the tune of over £1 billion a year. Simultaneously the electricity industry's regulator had ruled that the prices at which the regional electricity distribution companies had contracted for gas were perfectly reasonable, even though these were in general higher than those paid by the generators; while the regulator of the gas industry had announced his intention to retire early, after a series of clashes with British Gas, based on his conviction that industrial gas prices were too high – and following the decision of the Office of Fair Trading to force the company to give up 60 per cent of its industrial gas market within three years.

The present situation is full of strange anomalies. The value of a human life implied by the decisions of the Nuclear Safety Inspectorate is an order of magnitude greater than that for a coal miner or a worker in the offshore oil and gas industry. Yet, despite its environmental and safety disadvantages, the coal industry enjoys more political support than the gas or nuclear industries; while its principal customers are threatened with Monopolies Commission enquiries, and the gas industry benefits from accelerated approvals for projects put forward by electricity distributors. And the unpopular nuclear industry enjoys a large public subsidy.

The anomalies illustrate some endemic weaknesses in the present approach to the regulation of utilities in Britain. For a start, the regulatory process is heavily dependent on the character and competence of the person named to head the regulatory body, and on his or her relationship with the businesses being regulated. Sometimes the 'chemistry' works; but too often it does not. In any case it is not generally clear whom the regulators are accountable to, let alone who is calling them to account. Seemingly, neither ministers nor Parliament has any direct influence over their decisions, while the courts are generally reluctant to intervene, except on procedural grounds; so regulated industries commonly find that their regulators are judges in their own cases, as it were. In addition, decisions of the regulators are often far from transparent, and their timing can be very damaging commercially; Disraeli's maxim of 'never explain' may be good politics but it is not a basis for sound public administration, let alone commercial success.

In addition to these general concerns, examination of the record of the various regulators prompts some fairly basic questions:

- why are all price controls based on the RPI, when there are well-known weaknesses with the Index (not least the fact that it includes mortgage interest payments)? In 1993 the difference between the RPI and underlying inflation was $1\frac{1}{2}$ percentage points
- why are different price rises permitted in apparently similar industries?
- what is the appropriate return on capital for a regulated utility? Each regulator seems to have his own ideas about this but all (perhaps predictably) have lower expectations than for the companies they are regulating
- should profitability be considered in terms of current (replacement) or historic costs? The gas and water regulators think in terms of current costs; the telephone service has been regulated on the basis of historic costs; while the electricity regulator has not yet decided which basis to use, let alone the appropriate level of profitability.

In the particular case of energy supply, the interplay of the decisions of Parliament, the government, the Monopolies and Mergers Commission, the Office of Fair Trading, the various regulators as well as the Nuclear Inspectorate, the Inspectorate of Pollution and those responsible for regulating the safety of the coal mines and offshore oil and gas industry could have been designed to produce the result that is in prospect: an over-regulated, inflexible market with limited competition, less investment in the environment than the situation warrants and higher prices than in competitor countries for the largest industrial users of electricity. Between early 1989 and late 1992 the price of electricity for major users of energy increased by around a quarter. In September 1993 the prices for special contracts for 25 megawatts a year were over 20 per cent higher than in early 1990:

	Pence per kWh (average)
West Germany	4.50
United Kingdom	3.85
Italy	3.60
France	3.15
Belgium	3.10
Netherlands	2.77

For domestic and small users, on the other hand, National Power's supply charge was internationally competitive and some 6 per cent lower in late 1993 than at privatisation; the wholesale charge to the vast majority of users was on average some 10 per cent lower – facts conveniently ignored by the regulator.

As far as the future of nuclear power is concerned, because of the long time-scale involved, as well as the political and regulatory risks, the Exchequer will have to finance the construction and decommissioning costs of nuclear power stations. But the private sector could be expected to become involved as soon as the station is operational and the political, planning and construction risks are clear. The rights to operate all the nuclear power stations now in production (including Sizewell B) should be sold to qualified bidders for the balance of their useful lives, with the government retaining the responsibility for decommissioning. The nuclear subsidy could then be eliminated, since the government will meet the costs of decommissioning from the sale proceeds and subsequent corporation tax receipts. Construction of Hinckley C should now go ahead, funded by the Exchequer, on condition that a European consortium evolves to build it able to compete in world markets. The station would be offered for sale as soon as it is commissioned. There will need to be effective international surveillance of the whole nuclear fuel cycle for civil and military purposes; nuclear energy is tarred with the brush of public horror of nuclear weapons. The public enquiry and licensing process will need to be well-defined and consistent in terms of time and cost. There will need to be agreed design and operational standards, at least on a European basis. Nuclear power would then be seen to represent an environmental improvement, as well as a national 'hedge' against the time when oil and gas prices rise and against future disruption to coal supplies.

These requirements are the British entry ticket to an important world market. It would be all too convenient for the 1994 Nuclear Review to conclude that Britain had no need for additional electricity generating capacity at present – and thus no need to order further nuclear power plants. As a consequence we would be surrendering any prospect of a significant presence in one of the highest potential world markets for manufacturing in the next century.

More to the point, perhaps, very much the same story could be told with respect to the potential opportunities in meeting the water supply, telecommunications and indeed entertainment needs of the developing world. So it is worth drawing some general lessons for regulatory policy.

At present, regulators have been given wide general duties such as 'to promote competition'. But these are usually so broad as to be of limited value to consumers and suppliers alike. After all, competition is not an end in itself but a means to achieving lower costs and better service. It does not follow, particularly where public utilities are concerned, that more competition automatically produces the looked-for benefits. For instance, if every old and inefficient power station were to be sold to new entrants to the market, this would almost certainly result in more efficient and environmentally-friendly generating capacity lying idle, and higher cost, dirtier plants coming back on stream. In the long term the result would be higher rather than lower costs, quite apart from the impact on the environment and the heavy electrical engineering industry.

Rather, it would be better if the regulators' duties were defined more precisely, and in terms such that their effectiveness could be independently assessed. In the case of the electricity supply industry the regulators' duties might be to ensure that prices for all classes of domestic customer are no higher than those available elsewhere in the European Community and increase by at least one point less than the underlying rate of inflation every year. The regulator might also be required to have regard both to the industry's need to earn returns for shareholders which exceed those available on index-linked gilt-edged securities by, say, five points, and to the balance of payments on heavy electrical machinery.

Once the necessary legislation is in place the regulators could be completely independent of government; their decisions should be subject to appeal first to the Monopolies and Mergers Commission and then to the High Court. But, like district auditors, the regulators should be required to hold public hearings before giving reasons for their decisions. It is yet another anomaly of the present regulatory scene that the process for ensuring that local government spends money in accordance with the law is far more open and subject to legal challenge than the fragmented process for regulating the oil, gas, nuclear and electricity supply industries. For some reason Parliament is determined that shareholders in newly-privatised companies should not have rights that have been available to local electors for over a century.

It would also be sensible to take any personal animus out of the regulatory process. The future of major industries and companies is too important to be left to the vagaries of personal ambition and political and media pressure for conflict simply to show that a regulator is being effective. We could learn from the judicial system, at least in the sense that appeals in the High Court are heard by three judges and in the House of Lords by five. Each regulatory body could consist of a three-person tribunal, with unanimity required for all decisions and each member serving for a fixed (and non-renewable) five-year term. The regulatory tribunals should be seen as separate from their executive arm – just as the District Audit Service is statutorily independent of the Audit Commission, although district auditors are the commission's employees. The members of the tribunal would then sit in judgement on the cases put to them by their staff, consumer groups or indeed the regulated companies themselves. Where necessary the regulators' decisions could be appealed to a panel of the Monopolies and Mergers Commission without the need for a full-scale independent enquiry.

From time to time there would be advantage in independent reviews of the results of regulators' decisions and recommendations. It would be particularly timely, for instance, to review the present situation in the beer industry against the Monopolies and Mergers Commission's initial objectives. Just as boards of directors should review the returns from their major investment decisions, so also should the results of public policy decisions be subjected to detailed audit to make sure that the hoped-for benefits have been realised.

There is a more important general lesson to be drawn from the British approach to regulating utilities. We tend to be preoccupied with short-term domestic pressures at the expense of the longer-run ability of British industry to compete internationally. A recent study of water, gas, electricity and telephone regulation by the Consumers' Association failed even to mention the prices paid for the same services elsewhere in Europe as a benchmark for determining whether British households were getting a reasonable deal. The study was more concerned with the distribution of wealth than its creation; and so, too often, are the regulators. But only government can correct the situation. Its role in helping to restore Britain's position as a workshop for the world is taken up in Chapter 16.

Long acquaintance with Whitehall and its ways convinces me that government should stay out of the business of picking winners or telling managers how to manage. But French experience, particularly, suggests that there are ways in which government can promote the long-run competitiveness of local businesses without resorting to protectionism or exploiting domestic consumers.

I learned the first lesson myself at McKinsey, working with companies that were (then) in public ownership. The dead hand of Whitehall and the Treasury in particular is no myth; nor is its combined ability to take a short-term view at the expense of longer-term competitiveness. The second lesson emerged from my time at the CBI, listening to the experience of British companies doing business on the Continent and to senior French officials involved with the nuclear power and railway industries. During five years as a member of the British Overseas Trade Board and from visits to export markets in North Africa, the Middle East and India, in particular, I saw both how effective Britain's export promotion effort can be – and the difficulties faced by British exporters up against competitors better supported by their governments.

16

Government – Referee or Player?

Government want to be a catalyst for change. [Michael Heseltine, President of the Board of Trade, 1993]

'We make it, New York adds 10 per cent and Washington spends it.' So runs a description of the American economy beloved of managers in the rust belt of the United States. Typically they see the Federal government as part of their problems, an overhead burden to be paid for, rather than as a contributor to meeting international competition. Henry Ford II was wont to say, for instance, that the Ford Motor Company spent more money on health care than it did on steel.

By contrast, managers in Britain have always looked to the Department of Trade and Industry (DTI) in hope and expectation. As one of only two central departments concerned primarily and directly with the creation of wealth, as opposed to raising tax revenues or spending them, it was reasonable to anticipate that the DTI would be accorded some special status within Whitehall. Even though few public servants (and fewer ministers) liked to be reminded that governments create no wealth, and have no resources other than the power to tax.

These hopes have generally been disappointed. Turnover among Secretaries of State at the department has been so rapid, at roughly one every eighteen months during the 1980s, as to defy any expectation that individual ministers can make a material difference. To ambitious politicians the department must seem like an accident waiting to happen from which few are likely to emerge with their political reputations unscathed. Since 1987 the DTI budget has been reduced by around two-thirds in real terms to some £1.3 billion. Even including the former Department of Energy, its budget is smaller than that of the Ministry for Agriculture,

Fisheries and Food, even though manufacturing plays a more important role in the economy than agriculture.

Meanwhile banana skins have been in plentiful supply. The débâcle over energy policy and the future of the mining industry is but the latest in a long line of fiascos. These stretch back to the lame duck era of the 1970s, when ministers were unwilling to visit the night shift of car plants in which substantial public funds had been invested for fear of how many people they would find asleep. Westland, the Monopolies and Mergers Commission-inspired 'reforms' of the brewing industry, the House of Fraser, Barlow Clowes, the Maxwell affair, the hidden inducements to persuade British Aerospace to take over Rover, the Iraqi super-gun and Matrix Churchill affairs have combined to undermine the department's position.

Behind the scenes business has been concerned that its case was going by default in Whitehall and at Westminster, as well as in Brussels. The department seemed ineffective in preventing inflationary own goals being scored by players elsewhere in Whitehall and lacked the detailed understanding of how key sectors of the economy would be affected by particular measures. A survey in September 1990 of some 700 companies, accounting between them for over three million employees, revealed the depth of the dissatisfaction: on a scale of 0 to 5, the average effectiveness rating for the department's seven priority programmes was 1.3. A senior official, now retired from the DTI, commented at around this time:

I fear that we are too naïve, too theoretical, too parochial, too slow to respond to the real world and too conditioned by the institutional infrastructure and idiom of our colonial past to have the flair of the French approach. Sadly, at the same time we lack the sheer delight in chaos to achieve success the Italian way. Nor can we afford the huge subsidies of the US and lack their captive market.

One lesson from French common sense should, however, be clear: where government deploys resources, these should be focused on competitiveness in the international market, on enterprises that can measure up to the competition and be pursued from a continuous inception to marketing. That simple lesson could apply to all levels of public purchasing and involvement. But maybe our system just obstructs common sense.

Government has a critical role to play in restoring our position as a workshop for the world. First, in Michael Heseltine's phrase, it must create a benign climate, for manufacturing particularly. It must act more as a player supporting British business internationally rather than as a referee or regulator. A Department for Commerce should take the lead in Whitehall in ensuring that the entire government machine is alert to the opportunities to promote the long-run international competitiveness of Britain's manufacturing base.

A benign climate

One of the best-loved analogies of British public life has the Chancellor of the Exchequer at the controls of an aircraft. Whatever the conditions, he is expected to achieve a smooth take-off for the economy with steady and sustainable non-inflationary growth, as well as a soft landing if the weather turns nasty.

Of course it is not quite like that, as the last few years have demonstrated. For a start, the more appropriate analogy would come from biology, rather than aeronautical engineering. Any developed economy is characterised by complex and difficult to measure feedback mechanisms which can, and do, affect economic behaviour far more than marginal changes in public spending or even interest rates. In any case the controls available to Chancellors are relatively limited in their direct impact. For example, in his autumn statement in 1992 the Chancellor introduced a package of measures costing some £4 billion designed to affect the long-term prospects for a total economy of more than £500 billion.

Nevertheless the illusion persists, through good times and bad, that governments (and Chancellors in particular) are somehow managing our economy. Notwithstanding the reality that the prosperity of any developed economy is determined by the competitiveness of its businesses and its manufacturing base in particular. So every year the Treasury produces its own economic forecasts, uncomfortably aware of the dangers of self-fulfilling prophecies of doom, while one of the tired Rites of Spring in London has been the annual spasm of national economic policy-making culminating in the Budget – which almost invariably results in a redistribution of less than 2 per cent of the GDP. It is hardly surprising that only India and Ireland follow a practice that would be inconceivable in Washington, Tokyo, Bonn or Paris, where politicians and Civil Servants have long since recognised the futility of trying to 'fine-tune' a developed western economy.

But although any Chancellor has only limited direct influence on the state of the economy, his indirect influence can be very great indeed. Following the 1988 Budget, the 'feel good' factor resulted in a surge in consumer spending that far exceeded the reductions in personal taxation. Four years later the situation was reversed. In 1992, because of lack of consumer confidence, retail sales volumes were almost exactly the same as they had been in 1989 – notwithstanding a reduction of eight points in interest rates between January 1990 and December 1992.

The charge against the economic policy establishment during the late 1980s was that it failed to recognise that the economy was entering a recession until it was all too apparent, even to the casual observer. For nearly three years, from late 1989 to mid 1992, the focus of public policy was on containing inflation through high interest rates, which simply made the recession steeper and longer than it would otherwise have been. It was a classic instance of solving yesterday's problem at the expense of making tomorrow's worse.

The failure to recognise what was happening in the real economy reflected a combination of poor information and institutional arrogance: a refusal to believe that business, in particular, might have a more accurate understanding of the situation than the economic policy establishment, as well as appropriate prescriptions for action. And, naturally, it caused great concern among those who were in a position to determine investment and spending patterns in the economy. Senior business people simply lost confidence in the ability of the Treasury and Bank of England; and major investment decisions were put on hold. Both the information shortfall and the lack of communication with business were of long standing. The wish to 'shoot the messenger' bearing unwelcome news has always been strong. So when the CBI's Manufacturing Trends Survey turned negative in mid 1989 the reaction from Downing Street was more critical of the CBI than concerned about the problems ahead.

Rather than seeking to fine-tune the economy in the short term, government should focus on the requirements that must be satisfied if the UK is to be a world-class provider of high-quality and cost-competitive products by the end of the century. The CBI's Manufacturing Advisory Group considered that this vision of the future could become a reality: an expanding and increasingly profitable manufacturing base, productivity levels which match or exceed those in other major economies, a UK share of main manufacturing countries' exports in excess of 10 per cent and a trade surplus in manufactured goods. At the same time outstanding and well-qualified people would be making their careers in manufacturing, because it was professionally and personally fulfilling – and fun. But this vision could only become reality if government creates the right climate:

- low inflation and steady demand growth at home, so that the damaging 'boom and bust' cycle is a relic of the past
- a thriving research community operating at the leading edge of technology. There must be close links between manufacturers and the academic and other establishments carrying out basic research
- continuous innovation – to meet the requirements of world markets – in terms of technology, design and product development. UK manufacturers must have earned a universally respected reputation for responsiveness to customer needs
- commitment to sustained investment in world-class equipment and processes, fully supported by banks and shareholders
- highly-motivated, skilled and flexible people – at all levels – educated and trained to above-average standards in relevant disciplines and committed to continuous learning
- an internationally competitive manufacturing support infrastructure, including access to business information, a network of suppliers closely tied into their key customers, and a superlative transport infrastructure
- energy prices and support for exporters which at least match those available to our principal OECD competitors.

As previous chapters have made plain, these conditions require action from a number of different Whitehall departments. Someone needs to be in charge to make things happen.

Player-coach wanted

An important part of the reason for lack of business confidence in government has been the failure to define a worthwhile role for the Department of Trade and Industry. At least two Conservative Secretaries of State had appeared to think that the department should be wound up; and this strategy (or lack of it) was rapidly communicated to industry as well as to the officials involved, with entirely predictable consequences. Indeed, for most of the 1980s, the prevailing orthodoxy was that competent businesses did not need government help, and that helping the incompetent was an expensive waste of public funds – especially since Civil Servants lack the skills, experience or motivation to render worthwhile assistance. Better by far to trim the handouts and subsidies as far and fast as was politically possible, and to concentrate on allowing the unseen hand of the markets to work their will. Meanwhile programmes like the Enterprise Initiative could always be presented as the positive face of government in industry.

The strategy worked rather well, until the catalogue of inflationary own goals and other policy errors in the late 1980s caused business to question the department's effectiveness. By September 1990 only 5 per cent of companies rated the DTI 'good' or 'very good' at explaining the business case in Whitehall which was seen as the department's primary function. Changes in the department's organisation structure, moving from a sector to a topic-oriented approach, were felt to have weakened the links between government and business. This was particularly damaging since the two-way flow of secondees between business and government was still very limited, particularly at senior level. Things had reached the point when, in some instances, government officials and ministers did not even seek information from individual UK companies before undertaking negotiations on major international collaborative projects which would affect them. There were occasions when British Aerospace was not consulted before negotiations over the future of Airbus (it even proved difficult to persuade ministers to arrive for the discussions in a British executive jet).

Perhaps most importantly, the department was not clear whether it was primarily supposed to be a referee of the business scene or a player seeking to promote the long-run competitiveness of British business. For most of the 1980s the balance was towards regulation, as major industries were privatised and the economic and political dangers of government intervention in industry became ever more apparent. The failed Labour experiment with the Department of Economic Affairs twenty years earlier continued to throw a long shadow, as did the mixed record of people moving from board-rooms to the higher reaches of Whitehall. Business leaders despaired of a British government being able and willing to rep-licate the easy and close consultation with business and the indus-trial policy machinery that existed in France, Germany and Japan.

By the end of the decade it was evident to the CBI President's Committee that:

> The importance of manufacturing within the economy is not sufficiently well-recognised within Whitehall or at Westminster. As a result, too often, political decisions result in an erosion of the com-petitive position of UK manufacturing simply because this is not seen to be an especially important priority from a national point of view. Furthermore the general standing of the engineering profession within UK society is not as high as it needs to be.

It was also clear that it would be unwise to rely on a continued surplus in invisibles, as international and European competition in banking, insurance and tourism intensified. Competition would be fiercer as trade barriers within Europe were progressively dis-mantled, and new suppliers with lower labour costs entered the market from eastern Europe and South East Asia. British industry would no longer be able to rely on a ready local market in previously nationalised industries or in defence equipment – historically very important customers of the electronics, electrical engineering, construction and aerospace industries.

The lack of an effective voice for manufacturing in Whitehall was particularly damaging because the government had opted to seek to control inflation in ways which bore disproportionately on manufacturing and capital intensive businesses: a policy of high interest rates which (properly) eschewed devaluation as a short-term remedy inevitably impacted businesses exposed to inter-national competition and those needing to invest more than other sectors of the economy. Manufacturing also suffered particularly from the national bias against scientific and technical subjects and in favour of the arts. There was a clear risk too that improvements in the environment would be at the expense of the ability of

Britain's manufacturers (or at least important sectors of manufacturing) to compete internationally. Environmental legislation would almost certainly entail massive investment by manufacturers to reduce emissions. The uneven relationship between business and the financial markets was particularly difficult for manufacturers who needed to invest heavily, not just in long lead-time product development but in innovation and capital projects: confusing financial engineering with the real thing is particularly damaging in a manufacturing context.

In addition, manufacturing sectors such as aerospace, automotive engineering, defence, information technology, machine tools and telecommunications are of such importance that their prosperity has major regional, if not national, implications. For instance, the United Kingdom has a world-class complex of defence industries, second only to the United States within the OECD in terms of exports. The problems of adjustment to the new international realities will bear particularly heavily on British industry and on the south-west especially. Any peace dividend will, in effect, be paid by manufacturing to the rest of the economy in one way or another. Similarly the state of the world market for civil aircraft and domestic demand for cars and lorries has important implications for the steel, machine tools, electronics and controls industries.

Also, by the late 1980s it was becoming apparent how unwise it had been for the British government simply to opt out of activities where our European competitors were not nearly so fastidious. In the cliché of countless speeches by the author during this period: 'We are unlikely to win at cricket if the other side is playing karate.' In particular, manufacturers pointed to a number of ways in which they were at a serious competitive disadvantage compared to their continental or Japanese rivals:

- more creative use of public purchasing. This is particularly relevant in high-technology industries where manufacturing overheads and research and development costs are important: aerospace, defence equipment, information technology, medical and office equipment, power regeneration and telecommunications. In all these sectors government was a very important purchaser; and there was considerable scope to use this purchasing power to enhance the long-run competitiveness of domestic industry

- more state aid for manufacturers. Governments can help industry in a wide variety of ways, including subsidising research and development costs (for example, 'hiding' them in higher education budgets or subsidising independent research institutes), providing regional investment incentives and training grants, subsidising rents for factories, taxing holidays to attract inward investment. OECD figures have indicated that at the end of the 1980s state aids to manufacturing were lower in the United Kingdom than in any other major EC economy. The difference represented some £1 billion a year to British industry, compared with France; and there was a shortfall of £4 billion compared with the situation then enjoyed by Italian industrialists
- more generous support for exporters. Because of past mistakes, compared with some of our principal competitors, UK exporters have often found that export credit insurance in non-OECD markets is both more limited and more expensive. This has been a particular handicap in winning orders for major capital projects, where the UK is well below its potential as indicated by our share of world manufactured exports. The difference is probably worth some £5 billion a year in annual exports
- lower energy prices for intensive users of electricity such as the chemicals, steel, paper and plastics industries which account for some £30 billion of sales and a million jobs. The British economy is significantly more energy-intensive than that of any other EC country in the sense that commerce consumes around a third more energy for every dollar of GDP than is the case in Germany and 40 per cent more than Italy and Spain. It is not a question of UK industry being wasteful of energy; if anything, the reverse is the case in that intensive users particularly have invested heavily in energy efficiency.
- hidden barriers to trade, or illegal and covert support to local manufacturers. The ingenuity of officials south of the olive-tree line in Europe in protecting their own local industries is legendary: uneven enforcement of environmental, customs, health and safety laws; failure to collect taxes; particularly stringent or awkward testing requirements on imported products; turning a blind eye to the smuggling of imported raw materials. All these practices can make a material difference to British exporters' prospects in continental markets.

279

Astonishing as it might seem, throughout most of the 1980s the Trade and Industry ministers responsible either denied that these problems even existed (in the case of electricity prices and export support) or did nothing material to tackle them. Only since the General Election in 1992 have ministers turned their attention to the possibilities of evolving a partnership between government and industry to promote the long-run international competitiveness of British business. As Michael Heseltine put it, in a lecture at the Royal Society of Arts on the future of Britain's manufacturing industry:

> The key word here is partnership. We in Government want to be a catalyst for change. We want to start focusing together on competitiveness ... we all need to have a clear picture of strengths to build on, weaknesses to work on, opportunities to seize, threats to watch out for. We need to think about what must be done to bring companies nearer and nearer to the world-class standard. [*RSA Journal*, August 1993]

The Department of Trade and Industry must be a player/coach working with companies in international markets rather than a referee of domestic competition. Indeed there must be some doubt as to whether it is sensible to seek to combine these two roles in one department. Regulatory matters will inevitably crowd out efforts to promote Britain's industrial competitiveness: they attract more press and parliamentary interest, and thus ministerial attention. What is needed is a new Department for Commerce.

A Department for Commerce

Abolition of the Treasury and strengthening the Cabinet Office (see Chapter 1) would create a power vacuum within Whitehall which a new Department for Commerce would be well placed to fill. It would have no shortage of allies as it sought to acquire new standing in Whitehall and at Westminster. The National Manufacturing Council has made good progress in drawing together the leaders of Britain's manufacturers; the views of those who have been competing successfully with the very best in the world at last command attention and respect, as they should.

Ministers could invite the executive of the Manufacturing Council to regular and formal meetings, using the council itself as a channel for funds to support the spread of good management practice more widely within British industry. Once a year the President of the Board of Trade could give a public account of the state of the manufacturing nation, which might be published every autumn, following an annual Mansion House speech on the subject. At minimum, such an account would have more substance than the coded messages which have comprised too many recent Mansion House speeches by Chancellors of the Exchequer.

The new Department for Commerce would also have a key role in monitoring the inflationary impact of policy proposals in other government departments, so that inflationary own-goals are not scored inadvertently in the future. A counter-inflation unit, focused on other Whitehall departments and charged with the responsibility for ensuring that no government measures add to domestic inflation, will deliver far more than any number of de-regulation initiatives – desirable though these are, as anyone setting up a business will attest.

The regulators of the various newly-privatised utilities could all be sponsored by the new department. This would underline the need pointed out in Chapter 15 for all regulators to have regard both to the economic health of the industry they are regulating and its impact on consumers. It might even be possible to ensure that the national approach to industrial regulation is consistent. There is no reason, either, why the independence of the regulators should be compromised by such an arrangement. The Audit Commission is sponsored by the Department of the Environment; but the district auditor is clearly seen as an independent person, whose decisions can be appealed to the courts by local authorities. Indeed there must be a case for establishing the Monopolies and Mergers Commission as an entirely independent and free-standing body, albeit sponsored by the department, to interpret competition legislation and to work with the competition authorities in Brussels. The commission's decisions should no longer require ministerial endorsement, but should have the force of law, with businesses having the right to appeal to the courts from its decisions if they believe they are justified in doing so. Apart from anything else, such an approach would reduce the scope for ministerial embarrassment and the banana skins that have proved so damaging in the past.

It also makes sense to restructure our export promotion efforts, focusing on major capital projects and supporting successful exporters in those markets (and only those markets) where the government can add real value. In addition to direct promotion of exports via the British Overseas Trade Board, the new Department for Commerce should be responsible for removing barriers to UK trade with OECD countries. It should also take the lead in bringing to the attention of the European Commission cases where EC law has been flouted to advantage local industries against their UK competitors. There is much to be said too for establishing a single European Export Credit Insurance Scheme, perhaps administered by the European Development Bank, based in London. At least this would make it more difficult for overseas customers to play the credit arrangements of one EC supplier against another. At minimum, the Department for Commerce should have full managerial responsibility for the Export Credit Guarantee Department which now falls under the control of the Treasury.

At the same time the new department should build on the excellent work of the Invest in Britain Bureau, encouraging internationally mobile investment projects into the United Kingdom. Given the effectiveness of Scottish Enterprise and the Welsh Development Agency, there is much to be said for similar publicly-funded regional agencies being set up to promote investment into those UK regions where unemployment rates are higher than in either Scotland or Wales. Regional Development Agencies, which might secure some funding from the European Commission, would be much more cost-effective than the disparate and under-funded initiatives of local authorities.

Finally a Department for Commerce could act as a catalyst for improving management performance in Britain's manufacturing companies. There is no problem in defining good management practice. The bookshelves are full of publications on the subject and the conference circuit has no shortage of excellent presentations and case examples. The Management Charter Initiative is bringing some order into management education and development, as well as to the array of managerial qualifications from the shopfloor to the boardroom. The Partnership Sourcing philosophy pioneered by Japanese industry and leading retailers in the UK is gathering pace. More recently, the National Manufacturing Council has established a steering group to define manufacturing best practice in practical detail. As its most recent report makes clear, the council's initial task was to identify those other organisations with an interest in the promotion of UK manufacturing industry, both to avoid duplication of effort and to structure its own activities. In late 1992 a hundred different organisations were offering such initiatives (with the DTI classified as one). While each scheme or programme is undoubtedly worthy, there is considerable potential for overlap and dilution of impact. As the National Manufacturing Council's initial report makes clear:

> Manufacturers clearly recognise that a significant part of the responsibility for improving international competitiveness rests with industry itself in terms of the identification and adoption of world-class best practice. This does not necessarily involve major capital investment or state of the art technology. In many cases it is more about a commitment to organisational change, the adoption of best practice processes and a belief and drive for the most effective development of people at all levels.

The Council has established steering groups looking at various aspects of best practice, including the manufacturing process, benchmarking (to identify world-class performance standards), innovation, marketing and investor relations. It is also working closely with the joint CBI-DTI Partnership Sourcing initiative. A considerable amount of case-study material is available from a variety of published sources, award schemes and existing initiatives, both about successes and failures and benchmarks of world-class performance.

Once good management practice has been defined – and it is always worth remembering that in this, as in so many other aspects of life, the best can be the enemy of the good – it will need to be communicated throughout the length and breadth of British industry. The stakes are very high. Overall, manufacturing productivity in Britain is some 30–40 per cent below world class. Yet the Census of Production in 1989 revealed that value-added per employee in manufacturing in Britain varied from under £10,000 a year to over £60,000; the productivity average of the top 25 per cent of Britain's manufacturers was over *five times* that of the average of the bottom 25 per cent. If the performance of the average manufacturing company in terms of export marketing, quality, relationships with suppliers, stock turn, people management and overall productivity were closer to the level of the best in their industry, there would be no balance of payments problems, the investment gap would be halved and there would be faster economic growth with all the benefits that would produce.

A Department for Commerce could indeed act as a catalyst to spread this good management practice, working closely with the National Manufacturing Council, as well as the high street banks, Training and Enterprise Councils, Trade Associations and revitalised Chambers of Commerce. If the department were able to draw all these strands together, using their considerable commitment, knowledge and resources effectively, something akin to the very useful advisory services of the Ministry of Agriculture might evolve, focused on the smaller firms which are bound to provide the bulk of any increases in manufacturing employment. The network of One-Stop Shops that is now being developed could provide exactly the impetus for change that Michael Heseltine envisages.

However, much will depend on the way the department approaches this opportunity. Preaching at business seldom works, especially if the preacher has a Whitehall address. 'I'm from the government and I'm here to help' is a claim greeted with scepticism by managers the world over. But it is a different matter if major customers lay down conditions that they expect to see met by their local suppliers, or if local bank managers make clear that further loans will be conditional on specific management actions.

If shareholders and boards of directors are incapable of ensuring that their management is up to standard, others will have to fill the gap. Therefore, once the National Manufacturing Council has completed its work, each Trade Association, Training and Enterprise Council and Chamber of Commerce could be invited to bid for public funds to help spread the word. These organisations could distribute the National Manufacturing Council's conclusions and recommendations through video-based distance learning packages, workshops or seminars, local information centres, and a consultancy based on local business schools. Major local companies and banks could act as hosts or indeed provide expert advisers on issues of particular concern to local businesses. Such an effort, along the lines of the Department of the Environment's successful City Challenge initiative, would pay handsome dividends for a modest investment of no more than £100 million a year.

In summary, the government is not faced with a choice between 'picking winners' on the one hand or a *laissez-faire* regulatory approach on the other. For a minimal investment in the overall context of a public expenditure budget of some £280 billion a year, it could help British business generally build on the success and experience of those world-class companies that have emerged from the turmoil of the 1970s and one of the most severe recessions in recent memory. The economy as a whole stands to reap substantial benefits from the creation of a new Department for Commerce to promote the long-run international competitiveness of Britain's business in general and manufacturing in particular. Such a department, at the heart of Whitehall, could play a central role in ensuring that we manage the demands of the new era successfully and that Britain is once again a workshop for the world.

Postscript

There are obvious hazards in writing a book such as *The Anatomy of Change*. As Chairman of the Local Government Commission for England, I could be seen as part of the system for which I have prescribed radical change. Surely it would be better to follow tradition and wait until my career as a public servant is safely over before proposing any reforms. Alternatively, if the charge of disloyalty is not to be pursued, there is always that of 'trimming': why has it taken so long for these ideas to see the light of day? If the prospect is so dire, surely those with solutions to offer have a duty to put their ideas forward – to 'run their flag up the flagpole and see who salutes', to borrow yet another cliche from the management textbooks.

As it happens, *The Anatomy of Change* contains no ideas that are not already on the public record in one form or another. This book in a sense represents a consolidated and public accounting of views that I have formed over the last twenty-five years and which have been reflected in my conduct of the various public positions that I have held.

The charge of disloyalty to present and former colleagues – and indeed to the Government, which now employs me for part of the time – is more difficult. Probably the lookout on the Titanic felt pangs of remorse as he tried to interrupt the celebrations below deck; he may even have felt it his duty to allow passengers to enjoy themselves and to go on spending money for as long as possible before sounding the alarm. The role of Cassandra – like that of the Chorus in a Greek tragedy – is not always a particularly appealing one. But few people have had the breadth of experience in the public or private sectors, which has been my privilege. And such privileges bring with them obligations which cannot responsibly be ignored in present circumstances.

A second hazard inherent in writing about ideas and the future is to be overtaken by events. *The Anatomy of Change* went to press before Lady Thatcher's revelations about her Downing Street years, Lord Justice Scott's Enquiry into arms sales to Iraq, Kenneth Clarke's first unified Budget and the public and political reaction to the expenditure reductions he rejected and the resulting tax increases, and before the hesitant nature of the long-heralded economic recovery became clear.

If anything, recent events have reinforced the central message of *The Anatomy of Change*. A new era of low growth, low inflation and intensified competition from the Far East in particular, demands a new blueprint for action which our existing system of Government is poorly equipped to devise, let alone deliver.

To be sure, some of the ideas set out earlier appear to be gaining currency. Public concern about the urban underclass is rising, fuelled by the cost of Social Security support for single parent families and horrific examples of cruelty to very young children. The Department of Trade and Industry is considering new ways to finance smaller growing businesses, as well as alternatives to the present Dickensian bankruptcy procedures. The Department of Transport is taking road pricing seriously; and the Treasury has set up a working party to overcome the barriers to attracting private finance into infrastructure investments. There is even some longer-term thinking about the nation's finances and public debt, and our ability to afford the Welfare State in its present form.

But progress has been limited in scope, very painful for all involved and slow. The 'system' is simply not up to the challenges of the new era. The law of unintended consequences of recent legislation receives daily reinforcement, as anyone involved with the television and power generation industries can attest. The sight of the House of Commons playing politics with the nation's European future was as unedifying as it was disturbing. So was the willingness of Parliament to vote for railway privatisation when many of the Government's supporters had profound misgivings about the whole concept.

The review of the structure of local government in Shire England is as good an illustration as any of the urgent need for change. The Government has taken a different approach in England to the one it has adopted in Scotland and Wales. It has established an independent Commission to recommend in each County area in Shire England whether local interests would be better served by one purpose authorities in place of the existing two-tier system of county and district councils and, if so, to recommend particular structures to the Government which can then present them to Parliament.

As the Chairman of the Local Government Commission, I have had many of my concerns about our system of government confirmed:

– apart from the Commission's work, strategic thinking about the future role of local government has been largely absent. All the pressures have been to placate the various interested lobbies

– three Secretaries of State for the Environment, each with different ideas about the review process as well as the desirable outcome, have been involved with the Commission's work since I was invited to chair it in early 1992

– detailed policy and procedure guidance to the Commission (which ran to well over forty pages) was designed to circumscribe the Commission's independence of action; and it had to be revised, and the approach and timetable changed less than a year into what was a four-year programme

– the Treasury demonstrated its obsession with minutiae. Despite an agreed overall budget for the Commission (of some £5 million a year), the details of the time each *individual* Commission member would be allowed to devote to its work had to be agreed both by the Department of the Environment and HM Treasury, as did the details of the performance pay arrangements of the Commission's long-suffering staff. These had still not been agreed a year after proposals were submitted

– the Government, the Audit Commission, many business leaders and most professional groups oppose the only change likely to appeal to most Members of Parliament; unitary authorities based on existing district boundaries. More to the point, a Balkanised local government seems to hold very little appeal for the general public in rural areas

– consequently, recommendation reflecting the Commission's strategic framework have resulted in instant criticism, usually before the critic has read the report and the evidence on which it is based. Soundbite politics cannot be a sound basis for determining the future structure of local government in Shire England

– meanwhile, nearly all the special interests involved seem to have no advice to offer beyond the wish to see the Commission start from somewhere else. There has been virtually no public discussion of the desirable pace of structural change or the importance (or lack of it) of local support for any reforms. The media, with some honourable exceptions, have not addressed the strategic and constitutional issues involved, preferring to focus on a seemingly relentless pursuit of the trivial

– individual members of the Commission, and its Chairman, have been subjected to pressures with which very few Royal Commissions have had to contend in the past: personal abuse, 'off-the-record' briefings, leaks of correspondence, continual threats of appeals to the Courts (of Justice, rather than local opinion), as well as regular calls for resignations

Despite all this, the reform of local government is not a solution looking for problems. To the contrary, it is difficult to see how juvenile crime, the ill-treatment of elderly people living in the community and the economic problems facing many rural areas can be tackled successfully so long as the existing two-tier system of local government remains in place. Moreover, there is considerable public support for the changes that the Commission is proposing; and administrative cost savings worth in excess of £500 million a year are quite possible – investment required would pay for itself in under three years.

But these longer-term objectives, which require a comprehensive 're-engineering' of the way local government in Shire England works, risks being lost in a welter of political intrigue and rhetoric. The Commission's recommendations have been greeted with entirely predictable howls of outrage from those whose existing positions are threatened. Ministers face pressure in Parliament to overturn the Commission's recommendations, notwithstanding the local support for them and the attendant risk of committing exactly the same kind of mistakes that were made in 1974 – when Avon, Cleveland and Humberside were created.

There *is* a better way to sort out the future structure of local government in Shire England, as the Commission has suggested in its progress report, *Renewing Local Government in Shire England.*

But, the odds against a satisfactory outcome are long indeed. The priority should be to fix only those problems that local people consider need fixing, and to put in place a *process* to facilitate a gradual transition to unitary structures, as and when local people are ready. Meanwhile, the political barometer is falling, the flood-waters are rising and the storm cones remain very much in evidence. In short, I am living through yet another example of 'business as usual' within our system of public administration.

But the New Era will ensure that change cannot be long delayed. If it is, voters and taxpayers are likely to exact the kind of penalties that the people of Canada, France, Italy and the United States have recently levied on their political establishments. Revolutions may not be our style, as Baroness Thatcher discovered. But neither is continued and unnecessary relative economic and social decline.

Acknowledgements

In a sense, *The Anatomy of Change* brings together the lessons that I have learned and the views that I have formed since I joined the Foreign Office in Downing Street in the Autumn of 1962, as a (very) Temporary Assistant Principal on the Libya and Sudan desk of what was then quaintly known as the Levant Department.

Over the succeeding thirty-one years I have been especially fortunate in the people I have worked with and for. So my greatest debt is to all those with whom I have worked as colleagues, clients or customers in the Foreign Office, J. Walter Thompson, The Wallpaper Manufacturers Limited, McKinsey & Co, the Audit Commission and the Confederation of British Industry.

Invidious though it is, I would like to take this opportunity to acknowledge the help and encouragement that I have received at every stage of my professional life from particular people, in addition to those identified at the beginning of individual chapters. In the Foreign Office, the late Robert John showed me what the words 'on the job training' can and should mean in practice. At J. Walter Thompson, Dr John Treasure taught me a respect for consumers and the folly of giving them what they ought to want without finding out whether they really did. Ronnie Taylor and remarkable people managing Crown wallpaper mills in the mid 1960s instilled in me a fascination with manufacturing and an understanding of the crucial importance of middle-management, as well as that best of Lancastrian traits of saying what you mean and meaning what you say. At McKinsey, Marvin Bower, Hugh Parker, Roger Morrison, Henry Strage and many others around the world (literally) taught me the meaning of the word 'professional' and the importance of sound analysis in approaching business problems and public policy issues alike.

To Michael Heseltine, I owe the opportunity of public service. An independent local government Audit Commission was his idea, and one which he hung on to while the Conservatives were in opposition and pushed through a recalcitrant Whitehall and an indifferent Parliament in the *Local Government Finance Act* of 1982. He invited me to be its first Controller, knowing full well that I was not 'one of us'. A decade later he invited me to chair the Local Government Commission for England which might be thought of as somewhat careless if the objective was to install someone reasonably 'biddable' by the special interests involved.

At the Audit Commission, successive Chairmen (John Read and Sir David Cooksey) and the members of the Commission gave me more support than I had any right to expect. While Cliff Nicholson, Peter Brokenshire, Ross Tristem, David Henderson-Stewart and too many members of the District Audit Service kept the enthusiasms of their Controller under some semblance of control. This role was fulfilled with equal skill and effectiveness by the members and staff of the Local Government Commission a decade later.

To successive Presidents of the Confederation of British Industry during my time at Centre Point I owe an immense debt: Sir David Nickson, Sir Trevor Holdsworth, Sir Brian Corby and Sir Michael Angus each brought their own particular brand of commitment and style as well as competence to one of the most difficult and undervalued roles in British public life. The long-suffering members of the CBI President's Committee and Council restrained me when I needed restraining and encouraged me when I needed encouragement.

Responsibility for the views expressed in *The Anatomy of Change* rest with me. But I owe especial thanks to my present colleagues at ECI Ventures, the Local Government Commission, National Power, the National Westminster Bank, Tarmac and Westcountry Television, for allowing me to try my ideas out on them, and for being willing to risk guilt (or at least criticism) by association.

Françoise Bryan has not only read the manuscript far too many times for comfort; on occasion she has rejected chapters and insisted that they were re-written until they met her exacting standards. She has kept my professional life going for the last seven years, enabling me to keep the myriad commitments which I have entered into often against her advice and better judgement.

Kenneth Mahood produced more brilliant ideas for the illustrations for each chapter than I could have imagined possible, in an impossibly short time.

Dr Mike Staunton of the London Business School cross-checked, painstakingly, the many facts and figures cited in the book, against publicly available information.

Ion Trewin and Catherine Lightfoot at Weidenfeld & Nicolson were at once firm, efficient and sensitive to the constraints on an author who is simultaneously a public servant.

Finally, I must thank my family. Having a son, brother, father and husband on the fringes of public life must surely be an embarrassment waiting to happen, with the perpetual risk that his mind will be somewhere else when it is needed. Yet they all urged me to 'go for it' when the possibility of writing *The Anatomy of Change* was first mooted.

*   *   *

I hope that the help of all these people is repaid in the only way that they would hope for: beneficial change in the way we manage our affairs.

Bibliography

There are three main sources of material in *The Anatomy of Change*: official statistics, generally published by the United Kingdom Government's Central Statistics Office; reports by the Audit Commission for Local Authorities published while I was the Controller of Audit between 1983 and 1987; and publications of Task Forces established by the Confederation of British Industry while I was Director-General for five years ending in June 1992.

Official Statistics

The following HMSO publications were the principal sources of information on the British economy, patterns and trends in public spending and social conditions:

- UK National Accounts
- UK Balance of Payments
- Financial Statistics
- Economic Statistics
- Public Expenditure Analysis for 1995–1996
- UK Balance of Payments
- Monthly Digest of Statistics
- Social Trends

In addition, for the Chapter on health care, I drew on OECD Health Systems: *Facts and Trends 1960–1991*. While the material on the urban underclass includes analysis and information presented in the 1992 Policy Studies Institute publication *Urban Trends*.

The Audit Commission

The first duty of any military commander is said to be to choose the ground on which to fight. As the first Controller of the Audit Commission I selected the areas on which the Commission staff and its auditors

293

should focus. In each case, I followed a practice familiar to every partner of McKinsey & Co: exercising detailed oversight over the special studies into different local government services and government policies, and editing the resulting reports. These were modelled in presentation and tone on the earlier reports of the Central Policy Review Staff, with which I worked on a study of *The Future of the British Car Industry*, published in 1975.

I am grateful for the permission of the Chairman of the Audit Commission to quote from the following publications, all of which have been published by HMSO:

- Reducing the Cost of Local Government Purchase, July 1984

- Securing Further Improvements in Refuse Collection, August 1984

- The Impact of the Bloc Grant Distribution System, August 1984

- Improving Vehicle Fleet Management, December 1984

- Obtaining Better value in Secondary Education, December 1984

- Managing Social Services for the Elderly, February 1985

- Obtaining Better Value from Further Education, June 1985

- Saving Energy in Local Government Buildings, November 1985

- Managing the Crisis in Council Housing, March 1986

- Towards Better Management of Secondary Education, May 1986

- Improving Cash Flow Management, October 1986

- Improving Council House Maintenance, November 1986

- Making a Reality of Community Care, December 1986

- Preventing the Breakdown of [London's] Services, January 1987

In addition, the Commission has published a number of reports on aspects of the management of the National Health Service, also available from HMSO.

The Confederation of British Industry

It has always been my view that there is a buoyant market for solutions to difficult problems – and a notably thin one for ritual whinges that come too late to influence events. In the period that I was Director-General, a series of Task Forces of Members produced recommendations for action by business and Government on a wide range of problems of national concern. I am grateful to my successor, Howard Davies, for permission to quote from the following reports:

- Investing for Britain's Future, October 1987

- Rates Reform, November 1987

- Initiatives Beyond Charity, September 1988

- Building a Stronger Partnership Between Business and Secondary Education, September 1988

- The Competitive Advantage, October 1988

- Trade Routes to the Future, November 1989

- Towards a Skills Revolution, November 1989

- A Nation of Shareholders, October 1990

- Business Agenda for the 1990s, April 1991

- Competing with the World's Best, October 1991

- Shaping the Nation, November 1992

Index